Explorations in World Literature

Readings to Enhance Academic Skills

Explorations in World Literature

Readings to Enhance Academic Skills

Carole M. Shaffer-Koros
Kean College of New Jersey

Jessie M. Reppy
Kean College of New Jersey

Editor: Naomi Silverman
Managing editor: Patricia Mansfield-Phelan
Project editor: Talvi Laev/Amy Horowitz
Production supervisor: Alan Fischer
Art director: Sheree Goodman
Text design: Howard Petlack, A. D., A Good Thing Inc.
Photo research: Elsa Peterson
Line Art: Silvia Koros
Maps: Maryland CartoGraphics
Cover design and art: Hothouse Designs, Inc.

8 7 6 5 4
f   e   d c b a

For information, write:
St. Martin's Press, Inc.
175 Fifth Avenue
New York, NY 10010

ISBN: 0-312-08119-7

Acknowledgments

Wolkstein, Diane and Samuel Noah Kramer. "The Huluppu-Tree" from *Inanna, Queen of Heaven and Earth: Her Stories and Hymns from Sumer* by Diane Wolkstein and Samuel Noah Kramer, published by Harper Perennial 1983.

Erodes, Richard and Alfonso Ortiz, ed. "The Well-Baked Man." From *American Indian Myths and Legends* by Richard Erodes and Alfonso Ortiz. Copyright © 1984 by Richard Erodes and Alfonso Ortiz. Reprinted by permission of Pantheon Books, a division of Random House, Inc.

Cook, Albert. Excerpt from *The Odyssey*. Reprinted from *The Odyssey*, Homer, A Norton Critical Edition, translated by Albert Cook, by permission of W. W. Norton & Company, Inc. Copyright © 1974, 1967 by Albert Cook.

Fitts, Dudley and Robert Fitzgerald. Excerpts from *The Antigone of Sophocles: An English Version* by Dudley Fitts and Robert Fitzgerald, copyright 1939 by Harcourt Brace Jovanovich, Inc. and renewed 1967 by Dudley Fitts and Robert Fitzgerald, reprinted by permission of the publisher. Caution: All rights including professional, amateur, motion picture, recitation, lecturing, performance, public reading, radio broadcasting, and television are strictly reserved. Inquiries on all should be addressed to Harcourt Brace Jovanovich, Inc. Permissions Department, Orlando, Florida 32887.

Acknowledgments and copyrights are continued at the back of the book on page 215, which constitutes an extension of the copyright page.

Preface

Explorations in World Literature is an introductory world literature text for all students, whether they are advanced speakers of English as a second language or foreign language, or native speakers of English. This anthology presents complete and excerpted authentic literary selections and is intended to stimulate student interest in multiculturalism. The selections are from diverse cultures and periods of history and provide a balanced racial, ethnic, and gender perspective. Authors from both the traditional English canon and the "new canon" are included.

While learning about literature and world cultures, students will have the opportunity to improve their critical-thinking skills in all four language areas: reading, writing, speaking, and listening. *Explorations in World Literature* is a flexible introductory literature text and is intended to be used with supplementary grammar and/or writing text(s).

The book is informed by several teaching approaches, including (1) **reader-response theory,** which encourages the student to be an active reader and helps him/her to recognize the ambiguity of literary texts, and (2) **content-based language instruction,** which teaches language through academic subject matter. Thus, students using the book improve their English language skills through the study of world literature.

Flexibility

Explorations in World Literature is designed for flexible use in the classroom. The readings are arranged chronologically, from ancient to modern times, in the book and in the table of contents, and may be taught in this order. However, the instructor may choose to group them by themes as suggested in Table 1 (on p. xviii), by genre as shown in Table 2 (on p. xix), or by geographical area as listed in Table 3 (on p. xx). In addition, instructors may choose the number and variety of reading selections and activities they wish to cover with a particular class.

Contents

The book contains 32 literary selections in 26 chapters. Selections include both traditional works of Western literature such as those of Sophocles, Shakespeare, and Chekhov, and culturally diverse pieces by authors such as Naguib Mahfouz, Claribel Alegría, and Paule Marshall, representing many parts of the world and including complete or excerpted works from most major literary forms.

Each selection is representative of the literary tradition of its native culture. To expand students' understanding of the work, each selection is set in an appropriate historico-cultural context.

Explorations in World Literature includes the following features:

- **Peer work in collaborative study groups** is emphasized throughout the text. Study groups can be used to discuss pre-reading questions, to compare notes after mini-lectures, and to work on activities at the end of each chapter. The peer interaction maximizes student learning.

- **World and regional maps** help to orient students geographically; locating works on a **time line** helps them to understand chronological relationships.

- **Pre-reading questions** determine students' prior knowledge about the selection and its content. These questions focus students' attention on the selection. There are no "correct" answers, and not all students will be able to discuss every question.

- The **key terms** listed are important for understanding the cultural background and the literary selections. They are used in the mini-lectures and class discussions.

- The **mini-lectures** provided in the Instructor's Manual further expand the historico-cultural background given in each chapter and introduce the students to the selection. While the instructor is giving the mini-lecture, students have the opportunity to practice their note-taking skills. Additional historico-cultural information is also included in the Instructor's Manual.

- A **list of selected vocabulary** from the reading is included in each chapter. This list is meant to be an aid to the student and is not exhaustive. The entry for a given word indicates how that word functions in its context (what part of speech it is) and provides a brief definition, again based on the context. The first occurrence of a listed vocabulary word is boldfaced in the text. Furthermore, where a new literary genre is introduced, a brief explanation of it is provided at the beginning of the chapter. Additionally, at the end of the book there is a **literary glossary** for student reference.

- **Activities** at the end of each chapter include reading, writing, and sometimes speaking and listening tasks. Instructors have the flexibility to choose appropriate activities for their classes. The activities are followed by suggested additional readings.

- While it is not necessary to do every activity in a chapter, **reading journal assignments** are recommended to help the students to interact with the reading selection. Sample reading journal entries are provided in the manual.

- Periodic **quizzes** in the form of short essay questions are recommended. A sample quiz is included in the manual.

Acknowledgments

We wish to extend special thanks to Kean College faculty who have piloted chapters of *Explorations in World Literature*. These colleagues include Sylvia Mulling, Linnea Tornqvist, and the many adjunct faculty in the English as a Second Language Program. Our thanks also to Barbara Wheeler, director of the Africana Studies Program, for her advice and to Gerald Hillenbrand for his technical assistance. We are especially grateful to the Kean College students from many countries around the world who have used the materials and helped in their development. Moreover, we are indebted to the New Jersey Department of Higher Education for the Humanities grants that helped to initiate this project and to Mark Lender, director of advanced study and research at Kean College, for his assistance in securing the grants.

Also, we would like to thank the following reviewers for providing thoughtful critiques and suggestions: Leslie Freeman, Teachers College, Columbia University; Christine Holten, UCLA; Marianne Phinney, University of Texas at El Paso; Howard Sage, New York University–American Language Institute; Meritt Stark, Henderson State University; Nancy Strickland, New Mexico State University–Dona Ana; and Paul Tucci, University of Maryland at University College and Anne Arundel Community College.

A special thank-you to Stacia and Stanley V. Reppy for the academic foundation they gave their daughter.

We dedicate this book to our husbands: to Robert M. Koros for his unfailing moral and technical support, and to John P. Keker, without whose help and encouragement this book would not have been completed.

Carole M. Shaffer-Koros
Jessie M. Reppy

Contents

Alternate Table of Contents 1:
Thematic Groupings

Alternate Table of Contents 2: Genre Groupings

Alternate Table of Contents 3: Geographical Groupings

Introduction:
To the Student

Explorations in World Literature will introduce you to literature from many different cultures and times. It will also help you to understand and use important literary terms and concepts. Selections include examples from various literary forms, or genres, such as poetry, drama, and fiction. These selections represent the contemporary global village and will help you to appreciate its multicultural nature.

As you read the selections, you will be observing and discussing what is revealed about culture and cultural values in the literary pieces. Culture is the way in which groups of people organize their lives. It includes their political system, their language, their gender roles, their leisure time, and their social relations.

For each literary selection, your instructor may have you work in study groups of three or four students. You may discuss the pre-reading questions, check one another's notes after the mini-lecture presented by the instructor, provide input for one another's reader-response journals, and work on various activities in study groups.

While working with *Explorations in World Literature*, you will have opportunities to improve your critical-thinking skills as well as your academic skills in all four language areas: reading, writing, speaking, and listening.

The mini-lecture preceding each reading will help to expand your knowledge and give you added practice in a very important academic skill, note-taking during a lecture. The key terms before each lecture will help you to focus your attention on important ideas and information in the mini-lecture. To check the accuracy of your notes, you may compare them with those of other members of your study group.

You may also keep a journal in which you record your reactions, questions, observations, ideas about connections between selections, and, in some cases, assignments. Your instructor can help you to set up this journal. Also, a time line is included in the text to help you understand the chronological relationships among the literary selections. Maps will help to orient you geographically.

We hope that you will enjoy your *Explorations in World Literature* and will find using the text an enriching experience.

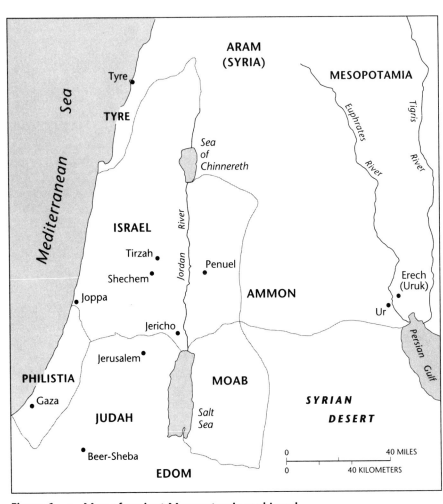

Figure 1 • Map of ancient Mesopotamia and Israel

1

"The Huluppu-Tree" from *Inanna, Queen of Heaven and Earth*

Anonymous (ca. 2000 B.C.E.)
Oral Tradition and Poetry: Epic or Heroic Poem

Background

"The Huluppu-Tree" is from the beginning of the anonymous Sumerian epic cycle *Inanna, Queen of Heaven and Earth*. The epic dates to about 2000 B.C.E. (before the common era, a nonreligious system of dating) and concerns an important figure in Sumerian mythology. Sumer was the earliest civilization in Mesopotamia, the area between the Tigris and Euphrates rivers in the Middle East and the site of present-day Iraq. New technology enabled the Sumerians to support large numbers of people in urban areas, and, as a result, many city-states were established, connected by a common religion and language. The network of city-states was politically organized as Sumeria.

The Sumerians invented a system of writing, *cuneiform*, that was first used to keep business accounts. The scribe used a stick, or stylus, to press characters into wet clay. The tablets were then baked to preserve them. This ancient poem, lost for many centuries, is taken from clay tablets excavated from the *tell*, or mound, of the city of Nippur. The tablets were discovered and translated by scholars in the twentieth century.

Pre-Reading Activities

1. With your study group, discuss how you think a culture that has no writing transmits important values to future generations.
2. What do you think the earliest forms of writing might have looked like? What materials might have been used? Why might people want to write?

Key Terms

These terms and concepts are important for understanding the culture that created "The Huluppu-Tree." They will be used in the mini-lecture and in class discussion.

B.C.E. (before the common era)	oral tradition
carpentry	polytheistic
city-states	prehistorical
clay	quest
cuneiform	Sumer/Sumerian
domesticate	technology
epic	Tigris and Euphrates rivers
leather-working	weaving
Mesopotamia	ziggurat
myth/mythology	

"The Huluppu-Tree"
Anonymous

In the first days, in the very first days,
In the first nights, in the very first nights,
In the first years, in the very first years,

In the first days when everything needed was brought into being,
In the first days when everything needed was properly **nourished**,   5
When bread was baked in the **shrines** of the land,
And bread was tasted in the homes of the land,
When heaven had moved away from earth,
And earth had separated from heaven,
And the name of man was fixed;   10
When the Sky God, An, had carried off the heavens,

Figure 2 • **Cylinder-seal impression of Inanna (right center) surrounded by seven stars** *(Walters Art Gallery, Baltimore)*

And the Air God, Enlil, had carried off the earth,
When the Queen of the Great Below, Ereshkigal, was given the
    underworld for her **domain**,

He **set sail**; the Father set sail,   15
Enki, the God of Wisdom, set sail for the underworld.
Small windstones were tossed up against him;
Large hailstones were hurled up against him;
Like onrushing turtles,
They charged the **keel** of Enki's boat.   20
The waters of the sea **devoured** the bow of his boat like wolves;
The waters of the sea struck the **stern** of his boat like lions.
At that time, a tree, a single tree, a *huluppu*-tree
Was planted by the banks of the Euphrates.
The tree was **nurtured** by the waters of the Euphrates.   25
The whirling South Wind arose, pulling at its roots
And ripping at its branches
Until the waters of the Euphrates carried it away.

A woman who walked in fear of the word of the Sky God, An,
Who walked in fear of the word of the Air God, Enlil,   30
Plucked the tree from the river and spoke:

"I shall bring this tree to Uruk.
I shall plant this tree in my holy garden."
Inanna cared for the tree with her hand.
She settled the earth around the tree with her foot.   35
She wondered:
"How long will it be until I have a shining **throne** to sit upon?
How long will it be until I have a shining bed to lie upon?"

The years passed; five years, then ten years.
The tree grew thick,   40
But its bark did not **split**.
Then a **serpent** who could not be charmed
Made its nest in the roots of the *huluppu*-tree.
The *Anzu*-bird set his young in the branches of the tree.
And the dark maid Lileth built her home in the trunk.   45
The young woman who loved to laugh **wept**.
How Inanna wept!
(Yet they would not leave her tree.)

As the birds began to sing at the coming of the dawn,
The Sun God, Utu, left his royal bedchamber.   50
Inanna called to her brother Utu, saying:
"O Utu, in the days when the fates were **decreed**,
When abundance overflowed in the land,
When the Sky God took the heavens and the Air God the earth,
When Ereshkigal was given the Great Below for her domain,   55
The God of Wisdom, Father Enki, set sail for the underworld,
And the underworld rose up and attacked him . . .
At that time, a tree, a single tree, a *huluppu*-tree
Was planted by the banks of the Euphrates.
The South Wind pulled at its roots and ripped at its branches   60
Until the waters of the Euphrates carried it away.
I plucked the tree from the river,
I brought it to my holy garden.
I **tended** the tree, waiting for my shining throne and bed.

Then a serpent who could not be charmed   65
Made its nest in the roots of the tree.
The *Anzu*-bird set his young in the branches of the tree,
And the dark maid Lileth built her home in the trunk.
I wept.
How I wept!   70
(Yet they would not leave my tree.)"

Utu, the **valiant** warrior, Utu,
Would not help his sister, Inanna.

As the birds began to sing at the coming of the second dawn,
Inanna called to her brother Gilgamesh, saying: 75
"O Gilgamesh, in the days when the fates were decreed,
When abundance overflowed in Sumer,
When the Sky God had taken the heavens and the Air God the earth,
When Ereshkigal was given the Great Below for her domain,
The God of Wisdom, Father Enki, set sail for the underworld,   80
And the underworld rose up and attacked him.
At that time, a tree, a single tree, a *huluppu*-tree
Was planted by the banks of the Euphrates.
The South Wind pulled at its roots and ripped at its branches
Until the waters of the Euphrates carried it away.   85
I plucked the tree from the river,
I brought it to my holy garden.
I tended the tree, waiting for my shining throne and bed.

Then a serpent who could not be charmed
Made its nest in the roots of the tree,   90
The *Anzu*-bird set his young in the branches of the tree,
And the dark maid Lileth built her home in the trunk.
I wept.
How I wept!
(Yet they would not leave my tree.)"   95

Gilgamesh the valiant warrior, Gilgamesh,
The hero of Uruk, stood by Inanna.
Gilgamesh **fastened** his armor of fifty **minas** around his chest.
The fifty minas weighed as little to him as fifty feathers.
He lifted his bronze ax, the ax of the road,   100
Weighing seven **talents** and seven minas, to his shoulder.
He entered Inanna's holy garden.

Gilgamesh struck the serpent who could not be charmed.
The *Anzu*-bird flew with his young to the mountains;
And Lileth smashed her home and fled to the wild, uninhabited   105
    places.
Gilgamesh then loosened the roots of the *huluppu*-tree;
And the sons of the city, who accompanied him, cut off the branches.
From the trunk of the tree he carved a throne for his holy sister.
From the trunk of the tree Gilgamesh carved a bed for Inanna.

From the roots of the tree she fashioned a *pukku* for her brother.   110
From the crown of the tree Inanna fashioned a *mikku* for Gilgamesh,
  the hero of Uruk.

Vocabulary

decree *(v.)*   to decide
devour *(v.)*   to eat up hungrily or greedily
domain *(n.)*   territory or land under one government or ruler
fasten *(v.)*   to join, connect
keel *(n.)*   main wooden piece extending along the entire length of the
  bottom of a boat
*mina *(n.)*   varying unit of weight and money used in ancient Greece,
  Egypt, and Sumeria, generally equal to 1/60 talent or one pound
nourish *(v.)*   to feed a plant or animal
nurture *(v.)*   to feed; to nourish
pluck *(v.)*   to pull out
*pukku and **mikku** *(n.)*   untranslated Sumerian words for a boy's toy
  hoop and stick, symbols of the gods' power
serpent *(n.)*   snake
set sail *(v.)*   to begin a voyage
shrine *(n.)*   sacred or holy place
split (split, split) *(v.)*   to break apart
stern *(n.)*   rear end of a boat or ship
*talent *(n.)*   ancient unit of weight equal to about 58 pounds
tend *(v.)*   to take care of
throne *(n.)*   chair on which a ruler sits
*underworld *(n.)*   land of the dead
valiant *(adj.)*   brave; courageous
weep (wept, wept) *(v.)*   to cry

Activities

1. With a partner, read lines 1–10 of the poem "The Huluppu-Tree"
   aloud to each other. What do you notice about the language in these
   lines that indicates they were once part of oral tradition? Can you see
   any similar pattern elsewhere in the poem?
2. Lines 1–28 summarize the beginning of time according to the
   Sumerian myth of creation. What are important events in this creation
   story? List them in your journal. Discuss your ideas with your class.

*Denotes low-frequency word.

Figure 3 • Sumerian cuneiform tablet (ca. 9th–8th century B.C.E.) describing the separation of heaven and earth *(University Museum, University of Pennsylvania, Philadelphia)*

3. What specific characteristics of an epic do you see in the poem "The Huluppu-Tree"? (Notice that an important male Sumerian epic hero, Gilgamesh, is included in the poem.) Make notes in your journal.

4. How does Inanna change from the beginning of the poem to the end?

5. In your study group or alone, make a list in your journal of items that are important to Sumerian culture as shown in the poem "The Huluppu-Tree." For example, what does the poem tell us about Sumerian religion? Compare your list with those of other students.

6. Based on your notes and the discussion, write a summary of important cultural information about the Sumerians. If you cite the exact wording of the text, be sure to use quotation marks (". . .") around what you are quoting and give the line number in parentheses. For example:

The poet tells us about an important early Sumerian food by stating that at the beginning of time, "bread was baked in the shrines of the land / And bread was tasted in the homes of the land"(6–7).

7. Based on your notes and the discussion, write an essay on Sumerian oral tradition.

For Further Reading

Kramer, Samuel Noah. *History Begins at Sumer*. Philadelphia: U of Pennsylvania P, 1981.

———. *The Sumerians: Their History, Culture and Character*. Chicago: U of Chicago P, 1963.

Wolkstein, Diane, and Samuel Noah Kramer. *Inanna, Queen of Heaven and Earth*: *Her Stories and Hymns from Sumer*. New York: Harper, 1983.

Woolley, C. Leonard. *The Sumerians*. New York: Norton, n.d.

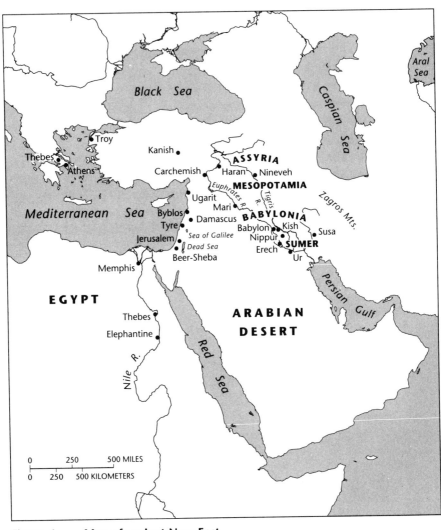

Black Sea

Aral Sea

Caspian Sea

Troy

Thebes
Athens

Kanish

ASSYRIA

Carchemish   Haran   Nineveh

Euphrates R.   MESOPOTAMIA

Ugarit

Tigris R.

Zagros Mts.

Mari

Mediterranean   Sea   Byblos

BABYLONIA

Tyre   Damascus   Babylon   Kish

Sea of Galilee   Nippur   Susa

Jerusalem   Dead Sea   Erech   SUMER

Beer-Sheba   Ur

Memphis

Persian Gulf

EGYPT

ARABIAN
DESERT

Thebes

Elephantine

Red Sea

Nile R.

0   250   500 MILES

0   250   500 KILOMETERS

Figure 4 • Map of ancient Near East

2

Genesis (Chapters 1 and 2) from the Old Testament

Anonymous (first century B.C.E.)
Oral Tradition and Poetry: Sacred Text

Background

Genesis is the first book of the Bible and the Old Testament. Based on several oral traditions, the Old Testament was assembled by Hebrew scholars in the first century B.C.E. (before the common era). This sacred text is important for a number of major religions and has had an important cultural and literary impact worldwide.

The Old Testament was originally written in Hebrew on a continuous papyrus scroll. Papyrus, made from beaten reeds, was prepared in large quantities in the city of Byblos on the eastern Mediterranean. The word *Bible* originates from *Byblos*. The Greeks divided the text of the Bible into chapters and verses and named the first book Genesis because of its opening line, "In the beginning. . . ." *Genesis* means "beginning" in Greek.

The following selection, from the English version authorized by King James of England in 1611, has been chosen for the beauty of its language. Since this translation of Genesis was written in the seventeenth century, the language is somewhat different from modern English. English is a living, changing language, and therefore it has varied through time. For example, in this selection, notice the forms *hath* instead of *has* and *creepeth* instead of *creeps*. Also notice that because the language is poetic, some of the word order is inverted.

Two Important Sources of the Old Testament

Source	Date	Information about the Text
J (Yahweh)	950 B.C.E.	The deity is called Yahweh (translated as Lord God). Style is vivid, lively, imaginative, and picturesque. Answers most important human questions: Why do we die? Why does evil exist? Originated in the south in Judah, around King Solomon's time. (Solomon dies ca. 930 B.C.E.)
	597 B.C.E.	Nebuchadnezzar, King of Babylon, conquers Jerusalem and exiles the Hebrews to Babylon.
	586 B.C.E.	Nebuchadnezzar again conquers Jerusalem, burns the Temple, destroys the city, and exiles the Hebrews to Babylon.
P (Priestly)	539 B.C.E.	The deity is called God in English translation. Originated from priests at Jerusalem Temple; took shape during Hebrew exile in Babylon in sixth century B.C.E. Concerned with the law, interest in genealogies and precise dates of events. Persian King Cyrus conquers Babylon and allows exiled Hebrews to return to Jerusalem, where they are free to practice Judaism.

Pre-Reading Activities

1. With your study group, discuss what you know about the Bible, the Old Testament, and the New Testament. In what language do you believe the Old Testament was written?

2. With your study group, discuss what important questions about human life you think might be answered in a sacred text such as the Old Testament. Why was it necessary to write these ideas down?

Key Terms

These terms and concepts are important for understanding the cultural background of the Old Testament. These key terms will be used in the mini-lecture and in class discussion.

Abraham
Babylon/Babylonian
Bible
Byblos
Canaan/Canaanite
Cyrus the Great (600?–529 B.C.E)

Jew/Judaism
Judah
King Solomon (960–925 B.C.E.)
monotheistic
Nebuchadnezzar II (605–562 B.C.E.)
New Testament

Genesis   Old Testament (OT)
Hebrew *(h'apiru)*   P (Priestly) Source
Israel   papyrus
J (Yahweh) Source   patriarch
Jacob   Torah
Jerusalem

Genesis (Chapters 1 and 2)
Anonymous

Chapter 1

In the beginning God created the heaven and the earth.

And the earth was without form, and **void**; and darkness was   2
upon the face of the deep. And the Spirit of God moved upon the
face of the waters.

And God said, Let there be light: and there was light.   3

And God saw the light, that it was good: and God divided the   4
light from the darkness.

And God called the light Day, and the darkness he called Night.   5
And the evening and the morning were the first day.

Figure 5 • Re-creation of King Solomon's Temple in Jerusalem (ca. 10th century B.C.E.)

And God said, Let there be a **firmament** in the midst of the   6
waters, and let it divide the waters from the waters.

And God made the firmament, and divided the waters which   7
were under the firmament from the waters which were above the
firmament: and it was so.

And God called the firmament Heaven. And the evening and   8
the morning were the second day.

And God said, Let the waters under the heaven be gathered   9
together unto one place, and let the dry land appear: and it was so.

And God called the dry land Earth; and the gathering together   10
of the waters called he Seas: and God saw that it was good.

And God said, Let the earth bring forth grass, the herb **yield-**   11
ing seed, and the fruit tree yielding fruit after [its] kind, whose seed
is in itself, upon the earth: and it was so.

And the earth brought forth grass, and herb yielding seed after   12
[its] kind, and the tree yielding fruit, whose seed was in itself, after
[its] kind: and God saw that it was good.

And the evening and the morning were the third day.   13

And God said, Let there be lights in the firmament of the   14
heaven to divide the day from the night; and let them be for signs,
and for seasons, and for days, and for years.

And let them be for lights in the firmament of the heaven to   15
give light upon the earth: and it was so.

And God made two great lights; the greater light to rule the   16
day, and the lesser light to rule the night: he made the stars also.

And God set them in the firmament of the heaven to give light   17
upon the earth.

And to rule over the day and over the night, and to divide the   18
light from the darkness: and God saw that it was good.

And the evening and the morning were the fourth day.   19

And God said, Let the waters bring forth abundantly the mov-   20
ing creature that hath life, and **fowl** that may fly above the earth in
the open firmament of heaven.

And God created great whales, and every living creature that   21
moveth, which the waters brought forth abundantly, after their kind,
and every winged fowl after [its] kind: and God saw that it was good.

And God blessed them, saying, Be fruitful, and multiply, and   22
fill the waters in the seas, and let fowl multiply in the earth.

And the evening and the morning were the fifth day.   23

And God said, Let the earth bring forth the living creature after   24
[its] kind, cattle, and creeping thing, and beast of the earth after [its]
kind: and it was so.

And God made the beast of the earth after [its] kind, and cattle 25
after their kind, and every thing that **creepeth** upon the earth after
[its] kind: and God saw that it was good.

And God said, Let us make man in our image, after our like- 26
ness: and let them have **dominion** over the fish of the sea, and over
the fowl of the air, and over the cattle, and over all the earth, and
over every creeping thing that creepeth upon the earth.

So God created man in his own image, in the image of God he 27
created him; male and female created he them.

And God blessed them, and God said unto them, Be fruitful, 28
and multiply, and **replenish** the earth, and **subdue** it: and have dominion over the fish of the sea, and over the fowl of the air, and over
every living thing that moveth upon the earth.

And God said, Behold, I have given you every herb bearing 29
seed, which is upon the face of all the earth, and every tree, in which
is the fruit of a tree yielding seed; to you it shall be for meat.

And to every beast of the earth, and to every fowl of the air, 30
and to every thing that creepeth upon the earth, wherein there is life,
I have given every green herb for meat: and it was so.

And God saw every thing that he had made, and, behold, it was 31
very good. And the evening and the morning were the sixth day.

Chapter 2

Thus the heavens and the earth were finished, and all the
host of them.

And on the seventh day God ended his work which he had 2
made; and he rested on the seventh day from all his work which he
had made.

And God blessed the seventh day, and **sanctified** it: because 3
that in it he had rested from all his work which God created and
made.

These are the generations of the heavens and of the earth when 4
they were created, in the day that the Lord God made the earth and
the heavens,

And every plant of the field before it was in the earth, and 5
every herb of the field before it grew: for the Lord God had not
caused it to rain upon the earth, and there was not a man to **till** the
ground.

But there went up a **mist** from the earth, and watered the 6
whole face of the ground.

And the Lord God formed man of the dust of the ground, and 7 breathed into his **nostrils** the breath of life; and man became a living soul.

And the Lord God planted a garden eastward in Eden; and there he put the man whom he had formed.   8

And out of the ground made the Lord God to grow every tree that is pleasant to the sight, and good for food; the tree of life also in the midst of the garden, and the tree of knowledge of good and evil.   9

And a river went out of Eden to water the garden; and from there it was parted, and became four heads.   10

The name of the first is Pisan: that is it which compasseth the whole land of Havilah, where there is gold;   11

And the gold of that land is good: there is **bdellium** and the **onyx** stone.   12

And the name of the second river is Gihon: the same that **compasseth** the whole land of Ethiopia.   13

And the name of the third river is Tigris: that is it which goeth toward the east of Assyria. And the fourth river is Euphrates.   14

And the Lord God took the man, and put him into the garden of Eden to dress it and to keep it.   15

And the Lord God commanded the man, saying, Of every tree of the garden thou mayest freely eat: 16

But of the tree of the knowledge of good and evil, thou shalt not eat of it: for in the day that thou eatest thereof thou shalt surely die.   17

And the Lord God said, It is not good that the man should be alone; I will make him a help meet for him.   18

And out of the ground the Lord God formed every beast of the field, and every fowl of the air; and brought them unto Adam to see what he would call them: and whatsoever Adam called every living creature, that was the name thereof.   19

And Adam gave names to all cattle, and to the fowl of the air, and to every beast of the field; but for Adam there was not found a help meet for him.   20

And the Lord God caused a deep sleep to fall upon Adam, and he slept: and he took one of his **ribs**, and closed up the flesh instead thereof;   21

And the rib, which the Lord God had taken from man, made he a woman, and brought her unto the man.   22

And Adam said, This is now bone of my bones, and flesh of my flesh: and she shall be called Woman, because she was taken out of Man.   23

Therefore shall a man leave his father and his mother, and   24
shall **cleave** unto his wife: and they shall be one flesh.

And they were both naked, the man and his wife, and were   25
not ashamed.

Vocabulary

*bdellium *(n.)*   myrrhlike substance (myrrh—ingredient used in making
    incense, perfume, and medicines; obtained from bushes in Arabia and
    eastern Africa)
*cleave *(v.)*   to be faithful to
compass *(v.)*   to go around
creep *(v.)*   to move slowly
*dominion *(n.)*   power to rule
*firmament *(n.)*   sky
fowl *(n.)*   bird
mist *(n.)*   water particles in the air (similar to fog but less dense)
nostril *(n.)*   either of the external openings of the nose
onyx *(n.)*   semiprecious black stone
replenish *(v.)*   to make full again
rib *(n.)*   any of the arched bones enclosing the chest cavity
sanctify *(v.)*   to make holy
subdue *(v.)*   to conquer
till *(v.)*   to prepare land for raising crops
void *(adj.)*   empty
yield *(v.)*   to produce; to give up

Activities

1. With a partner, read Chapter 1, verses 1 through 13, of Genesis out
    loud to each other. What do you notice about the verses that indicates
    they were once part of oral tradition?
2. What important human questions are answered in these portions of
    the Old Testament?
3. Genesis contains two versions of the Hebrew creation story. In your
    study group, try to identify where the first version ends and the sec-
    ond one begins. Justify your answer.

---

* Denotes low-frequency word.

4. In your journal, make a list of the important events and the order in which they occur in each version of the creation. Compare your list with those of other class members. How do the events in the two versions of the creation differ?

5. Look at the way language is used in the two creation stories. In your journal note differences and similarities in the tone and images used in the two versions. Now refer to the table on p. 14 comparing the sources of the Old Testament. On which source do you think the first version of the creation is based? On which source do you think the second version is based? Justify your answers.

6. Using your journal and notes to develop supporting details, write an essay comparing and contrasting the two versions of the creation story in Genesis.

7. Based on your notes and class discussion, write an essay on oral tradition in Genesis.

For Further Reading

Alter, Robert, and Frank Kermode, eds. *The Literary Guide to the Bible.* Cambridge, MA: Havard UP, 1987.
Friedman, Richard Elliot. *Who Wrote the Bible?* New York: Summit, 1987.
The Holy Bible, Containing the Old and the New Testaments. New York: New York Bible Society, n.d.

Additional Reading

"The Well-Baked Man"

Anonymous (recorded in the nineteenth century)
Oral Tradition and Poetry: Sacred Text

Background

This creation story is drawn from the Pima-Papago Indians in the southwestern United States. The tribe lives in adobe pueblos—that is, villages built mainly from clay. Originating in oral tradition, the story was recorded and translated in the 1880s. Coyote, a trickster, is a traditional Native American story figure, sometimes represented as an animal, sometimes as a human.

"The Well-Baked Man"
Anonymous

The Magician had made the world but felt that something was missing. "What could it be?" he thought. "What could be missing?" Then it came to him that what he wanted on this earth was some beings like himself, not just animals. "How will I make them?" he thought. First he built himself an *horno*, an oven. Then he took some clay and formed it into a shape like himself. 5

Now Coyote was hanging around the way he usually does, and when Magician, who was Man Maker, was off gathering firewood, Coyote quickly changed the shape of that clay image. Man Maker built a fire inside the *horno*, then put the image in without 10 looking at it closely.

After a while the Magician said, "He must be ready now." He took the image and breathed on it, whereupon it came to life. "Why don't you stand up?" said Man Maker. "What's wrong with you?" The creature barked and wagged its tail. "Ah, oh my, Coyote has 15 tricked me," he said. "Coyote changed my being into an animal like himself."

Coyote said, "Well, what's wrong with it? Why can't I have a pretty creature that pleases me?"

"Oh my, well, all right, but don't interfere again." That's why 20 we have the dog; it was Coyote's doing.

So Man Maker tried again. "They should be companions to each other," he thought. "I shouldn't make just one." He shaped some humans who were rather like himself and identical with each other in every part. 25

"What's wrong here?" Man Maker was thinking. Then he saw."Oh my, that won't do. How can they increase?" So he pulled a little between the legs of one image, saying, "Ah, that's much better." With his fingernail he made a crack in the other image. He put some pleasant feeling in there somewhere. "Ah, now it's good. Now 30 they'll be able to do all the necessary things." He put them in the *horno* to bake.

"They're done now," Coyote told him. So Man Maker took them out and made them come to life.

"Oh my, what's wrong?" he said. "They're underdone; they're 35 not brown enough. They don't belong here—they belong across the water someplace." He scowled at Coyote. "Why did you tell me they were done? I can't use them here."

So the Magician tried again, making a pair like the last one
and placing them in the oven. After a while he said, "I think they're   40
ready now."

"No, they aren't done yet," said Coyote. "You don't want
them to come out too light again; leave them in a little longer."

"Well, all right," replied Man Maker. They waited, and then
he took them out. "Oh my. What's wrong? These are overdone.   45
They're burned too dark." He put them aside. "Maybe I can use them
some other place across the water. They don't belong here."

For the fourth time Man Maker placed his images inside the
oven. "Now don't interfere," he said to Coyote, "you give me bad
advice. Leave me alone."   50

This time the Magician did not listen to Coyote but took them
out when he himself thought they were done. He made them come
to life, and the two beings walked around, talked, laughed, and be-
haved in a seemly fashion. They were neither underdone nor overdone.   55

"These are exactly right," said Man Maker. "These really
belong here; these I will use. They are beautiful." So that's why we
have the Pueblo Indians.

Activities

1. What are the important events in this story? What does the story explain?
2. You have now read several creation stories. Using your imagination,
   write your own creation story, including the making of the first human beings.
3. Write an essay comparing and contrasting the creation of human beings in "The Well-Baked Man" with the version in Chapter 2 of
   Genesis.

For Further Reading

Erdoes, Richard, and Alfonso Ortiz, eds. *American Indian Myths and Legends*.
   New York: Pantheon, 1984.
Mails, Thomas E. *Plains Indians: Dog Soldiers, Bear Men, and Buffalo Women*.
   New York: Prentice-Hall, 1985.
Radin, Paul. *The Trickster: A Study in American Indian Mythology*. New York:
   Schocken, 1972.

CHAPTER 3

From *The Odyssey*

Homer (eighth century B.C.E.)
Oral Tradition and Poetry: Epic or Heroic Poem

Background

Who was the Greek poet Homer? Was the author one poet or many? Was the poet perhaps not a man but a woman? The answers to these questions about Homer's identity have long been debated by scholars. The most commonly accepted view at present is that Homer was a blind poet who lived between 700 and 850 B.C.E. and came from a Greek colony on the eastern Mediterranean Sea.

Homer's two epics, *The Iliad* and *The Odyssey*, are based on heroic events from Bronze Age Greece (about 1200 B.C.E.). *The Odyssey* consists of 24 books. In the beginning of Book I the poet summarizes the 20-year-long struggle of the hero Odysseus to return home to the island of Ithaca after the Greeks have defeated Troy. The selection also draws a parallel with the return of another Greek hero, Agamemnon, to his home, where a tragic end awaits him. The story of Agamemnon tells Odysseus what he must avoid doing in order to reach home safely.

Pre-Reading Activities

1. With your study group, review what you know about the epic as a literary form.
2. Discuss with your group what you know about the religion of the ancient Greeks. Who were some of the important gods? What were they like?
3. Look at a map of the Mediterranean region, especially Greece and the

surrounding area. How would geography affect the daily life of the ancient
Greeks?

Key Terms

Agamemnon, son of Atreus

Aigisthos, lover of Clytemnestra

archaeological investigations

Bronze Age Greece

Clytemnestra, wife of Agamemnon

epic hero

epithet

invocation

Ithaca

Menelaos, brother of Agamemnon

Mount Olympus

muse

Mycenae

Odysseus/odyssey

Orestes, son of Agamemnon and
        Clytemnestra

Penelope, wife of Odysseus

Troy/Trojan War

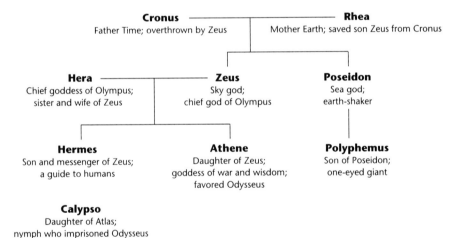

Figure 6 • Gods, goddesses, and supernatural beings in *The Odyssey*

From *The Odyssey*
Homer

Tell me, **Muse**, about the man of many turns, who many
Ways wandered when he had **sacked** Troy's holy **citadel**;
He saw the cities of many men, and he knew their thought;
On the ocean he suffered many pains within his heart,
Striving for his life and his companions' return.   5

But he did not save his companions, though he wanted to:
They lost their lives because of their **recklessness**.
The fools, they devoured the cattle of Hyperion,
The Sun, and he took away the day of their return.
Begin the tale somewhere for us also, goddess, daughter of Zeus.   10
Then all the others, as many as escaped **sheer** destruction,
Were at home, having fled both the war and the sea.
Yet he alone, longing for his wife and for a return,
Was held back in a **hollowed** cave by the queenly **nymph** Calypso,
The divine goddess, who was eager for him to be her husband.   15
But when in the circling seasons the year came around,
The gods **spun** the thread for him to return to his home,
To Ithaca; and he did not escape struggle there either,
Even among his dear ones. All the gods **pitied** him,
Except Poseidon, who **contended unremittingly**   20
With godlike Odysseus, till the man reached his own land.
But the god had gone to the far-off Ethiopians—
The Ethiopians, **remotest** of men, divided **asunder**,
Some where Hyperion sets, and some where he rises.
He was taking part in the sacrifice of bulls and rams,   25
And enjoyed being present at a feast there. The others
Were gathered together in the halls of Olympian Zeus.
The father of men and gods began to speak among them.
In his heart he was remembering excellent Aigisthos
Whom Agamemnon's son, far-famed Orestes, had **slain**.   30
Thinking of that man, he made his speech to the immortals:
"Well now, how indeed mortal men do blame the gods!
They say it is from us evils come, yet they themselves
By their own recklessness have pains beyond their **lot**.
So this Aigisthos married beyond his lot the lawful   35
Wife of the son of Atreus, and killed him on his return;
Knowing he would be destroyed, since we told him beforehand:
We had sent sharp-eyed Hermes, the slayer of Argos,
To tell him not to kill the man and not to **woo** his wife,
Or payment would come through Orestes, descendant of Atreus,   40
As soon as he came of age and **longed for** his own land.
So Hermes told him; but, though of good mind himself, he did not
Change Aigisthos's mind. And now he has paid for it all."
Then the bright-eyed goddess Athene answered:
"Our father, son of Cronus, highest of all rulers,   45
As for that man, he surely lies in a fitting death.
May anyone else also **perish** who would do such deeds.

But the heart within me is torn over skillful Odysseus,
The hard-fated man, who long suffers griefs far from his **dear** ones
On a flood-circled island where the **navel** of the sea is.   50
The island is wooded, a goddess there has her dwelling,
The daughter of destruction-minded Atlas, who knows
The depths of the whole sea, and holds apart earth and heaven.
His daughter has kept back the **wretched** and grieving man,
And perpetually, with tender and **wheedling** speeches,   55
She charms him to forget Ithaca. Odysseus, however,
Wanting to catch sight even of smoke leaping up
From his own land, is longing to die. But your own heart
Does not turn toward it, Olympian one. Did Odysseus
Not please you in broad Troy by the ships of the [Greeks]   60
When he made sacrifice? Why, then, are you so angry at him, Zeus?"
In answer to her, cloud-gathering Zeus spoke out:
"My child, what sort of word has gotten past the bar of your teeth?
How could I at any time forget godlike Odysseus,
Who stands out among mortals for thought, and for the sacrifices   65
He has given the immortal gods who possess broad heaven?
But Poseidon, who holds up the earth, remains **obstinately**
Enraged about the Cyclops whom he blinded in the eye,
Godlike Polyphemus, [his son of great] strength. . . .
For that, to be sure, earth-shaking Poseidon has not   70
Killed Odysseus but makes him wander far from his homeland.
Well, come now, let all of us here carefully **devise**
His return, so he may arrive; and Poseidon will **slacken**
His rage, for **counter** to all the immortals he cannot
Carry on the **strife** alone against the will of the gods."   75

Vocabulary

*asunder *(adv.)*   into parts; apart
citadel *(n.)*   fortress
contend *(v.)*   to struggle
counter *(adv.)*   opposite
dear *(adj.)*   loved
devise *(v.)*   to plan to bring about
enraged *(adj.)*   filled with rage or extreme anger
hollowed *(adj.)*   concave; sunken
long for *(v.)*   to feel a strong desire for
lot *(n.)*   share

* Denotes low-frequency word.

*Muse (*n.*)   any of the nine sister goddesses in Greek mythology presiding over the arts and sciences, especially song and poetry
*navel (*n.*)   central point; middle
*nymph (*n.*)   any of the minor divinities of nature in classical mythology, represented as beautiful maidens living in mountains, forests, trees, and waters
obstinately (*adv.*)   stubbornly
perish (*v.*)   to die
pity (*v.*)   to feel sympathetic sorrow for
recklessness (*n.*)   disregard for the possible consequences (of an action)
remote (*adj.*)   distant
sack (*v.*)   to strip of valuables; to loot, especially a defeated city
sheer (*adj.*)   total; absolute
slacken (*v.*)   to lessen
slay (slew, slain) (*v.*)   to kill
spin (spun, spun) (*v.*)   to draw out and twist fiber into yarn or thread
strife (*n.*)   fight; struggle
strive (strove, striven) (*v.*)   to struggle for
*unremittingly (*adv.*)   constantly
*wheedle (*v.*)   to influence by soft words
woo (*v.*)   to court a woman
wretched (*adj.*)   distressed in body or mind

Activities

1. Because he is an epic hero, Odysseus must have qualities that were admired by the ancient Greeks. For example, what epithet does Homer use to describe Odysseus? With your study group, read the poem closely and make a list in your journal of these good qualities. Compare your list with the lists made by the rest of the class.

2. Why is Poseidon, the god of the sea, angry at Odysseus? How does he show his anger? Why would Poseidon be important to the Greeks?

3. In his epic poem, Homer shows the importance of narration by telling a story within a story. For example, within the main story about Odysseus, the god Zeus tells us the story of Aigisthos. In your study group, look at the details of the story about Aigisthos and those of the story about Odysseus. How are they similiar? How are they different? What moral lesson do you think the story of Aigisthos teaches?

4. In your study group, look at the details of the poem again. Make a list in your journal of ideas you believe were important to the Greeks of Homer's time. Compare your list with the lists made by the rest of the class.

5. An epic poem combines realistic details with the fantastic. Look again at the text, and make notes in your journal about which events in the

poem seem to be realistic and which are fantastic (not real). Discuss your findings with the class.

6. Using your notes and details from discussion, write a summary of the events Homer describes in this portion of Book I of *The Odyssey*.

7. Using your notes and your journal, write an essay on Odysseus as an epic hero.

8. Write an essay comparing the Greek gods with the Sumerian gods or with God in Genesis.

For Further Reading

Bowra, C. M. *Heroic Poetry*. London: Macmillan, 1964.

Burkert, Walter. *Structure and History in Greek Mythology and Ritual*. Berkeley: U of California P, 1979.

Dimock, George E. *The Unity of The Odyssey*. Boston: U of Massachusetts P, 1989.

Murray, Gilbert. *The Rise of the Greek Epic*. London: Oxford UP, 1967.

Parry, Adam, ed. *The Making of Homeric Verse: The Collected Papers of Milman Parry*. London: Oxford UP, 1971.

CHAPTER **4**

From *Antigone* from *The Theban Plays*

Sophocles (496?–406 B.C.E.)
Drama: Tragedy

Background

Tragedy is one of the most important contributions of the ancient Greeks to civilization. The origins of the Greek tragedy have been traced back to the prehistorical worship of Dionysus, a Greek god associated with wine and spring fertility. Female worshippers of the god drank wine and, in a drunken state, sang and danced to honor him.

By the end of the sixth century B.C.E., worship of Dionysus had become civilized. The god was honored in large open-air theaters at annual spring competitions in which prizes were given to the best plays. The religious significance of the performances meant that business was suspended, and every Greek, regardless of class or gender, was expected to attend.

Antigone is a Greek tragedy written by Sophocles. A major competitor and winner in the dramatic contests of the fifth century B.C.E., Sophocles was one of the three most famous tragedians of his time. Based on myths known to the ancient Greek audience, the play concerns the struggle of the young Antigone to bury her brother against the wishes of her uncle, Creon, king of Thebes. Creon makes the gods angry by refusing to allow the burial, and therefore he must be punished for his religious sin.

The Prologue is the opening scene of the tragedy, in which the sisters, Antigone and Ismene, introduce the conflict. The second passage, "Ode to Man," is sung by the Greek chorus and explores the potential and the limits of human beings.

Pre-Reading Activities

1. With your study group, discuss why a culture would want to dramatize certain events in its history. What kinds of events would they probably act out?
2. Using a good reference work, research the differences between mythology and religion. You should also consider what you have learned so far in your reading. You may also view "The Power of Myth," a videotaped interview with Joseph Campbell. Discuss your ideas with your group.

Key Terms

Learn these important terms and concepts to better understand the importance of drama and tragedy to the ancient Greek and modern Western cultures. They will be used in the mini-lecture and in discussion.

Aeschylus (525–456 B.C.E.)	ode
Antigone	Oedipus, former king of Thebes
Aristotle (384–322 B.C.E.)	orchestra
chorus	Pericles/Periclean Athens
conflict	Polyneices
Creon, king of Thebes	protagonist
Dionysus/Dionysia	scene
Eteocles	Thespis/thespian
Euripides (480?–406 B.C.E.)	tragedy
Iocaste	tragic flaw
Ismene	tragic hero
Legend of Thebes	

From *Antigone*
Sophocles

Prologue

SCENE: Before the palace of Creon, king of Thebes. A central double door, and two lateral doors. A platform extends the length of the facade, and from this platform three steps lead down into the "orchestra," or chorus-ground.

TIME: Dawn of the day after the defeat of the **Argive** army in their assault on Thebes.

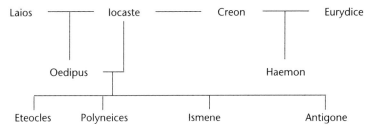

Figure 7 • Royal House of Thebes

Antigone and Ismene enter from the central door of the palace.

ANTIGONE: Ismene, **dear** sister,
    You would think that we had already suffered enough
    For the curse on Oedipus:
    I cannot imagine any **grief**
    That you and I have not gone through. And now—   5
    Have they told you of the new **decree** of our King Creon?

ISMENE: I have heard nothing: I know
    That two sisters lost two brothers, a double death
    In a single hour; and I know that the Argive army
    Fled in the night; but beyond this, nothing.   10

ANTIGONE: I thought so. And that is why I wanted you
    To come out here with me. There is something we must do.

ISMENE: Why do you speak so strangely?

ANTIGONE: Listen, Ismene:
    Creon **buried** our brother Eteocles   15
    With military honors, gave him a soldier's funeral,
    And it was right that he should; but Polyneices,
    Who fought as bravely and died as miserably,—
    They say that Creon has sworn
    No one shall bury him, no one **mourn** for him,   20
    But his body must lie in the fields, a sweet treasure
    For **carrion birds** to find as they search for food.
    That is what they say, and our good Creon is coming here
    To announce it publicly; and the penalty—
    Stoning to death in the public square!   25
                         There it is,
    And now you can prove what you are:
    A true sister, or a traitor to your family.

ISMENE: Antigone, you are mad! What could I possibly do?

ANTIGONE: You must decide whether you will help me or not.   30

ISMENE: I do not understand you. Help you in what?

ANTIGONE: Ismene, I am going to bury him. Will you come?

ISMENE: Bury him! You have just said the new law forbids it.

ANTIGONE: He is my brother. And he is your brother, too.

ISMENE: But think of the danger! Think what Creon will do!   35

ANTIGONE: Creon is not strong enough to stand in my way.

ISMENE: Ah sister!
   Oedipus died, everyone hating him
   For what his own search brought to light, his eyes
   Ripped out by his own hand; and Iocaste died,   40
   His mother and wife at once: she twisted the **cords**
   That **strangled** her life; and our two brothers died,
   Each killed by the other's sword. And we are left:
   But oh, Antigone,
   Think how much more terrible than these   45
   Our own death would be if we should go against Creon
   And do what he has **forbidden!** We are only women,
   We cannot fight with men, Antigone!
   The law is strong, we must give in to the law
   In this thing, and in worse. I beg the Dead   50
   To forgive me, but I am helpless: I must yield
   To those in authority. And I think it is dangerous business
   To be always **meddling.**

ANTIGONE: If that is what you think,
   I should not want you, even if you asked to come.   55
   You have made your choice, you can be what you want to be.
   But I will bury him; and if I must die,
   I say that this crime is holy: I shall lie down
   With him in death, and I shall be as dear
   To him as he to me.   60
             It is the dead,
   Not the living, who make the longest demands:
   We die forever. . . .
            You may do as you like,
   Since apparently the laws of the gods mean nothing to you.   65

ISMENE: They mean a great deal to me; but I have no strength
   To break laws that were made for the public good.

ANTIGONE: That must be your excuse, I suppose. But as for me,
   I will bury the brother I love.

IsMENE: Antigone,   70
  I am so afraid for you!

ANTIGONE: You need not be:
  You have yourself to consider, after all.

IsMENE: But no one must hear of this, you must tell no one!
  I will keep it a secret, I promise!   75

ANTIGONE: O tell it! Tell everyone!
  Think how they'll hate you when it all comes out
  If they learn that you knew about it all the time!

IsMENE: So **fiery**! You should be cold with fear.

ANTIGONE: Perhaps. But I am doing only what I must.   80

IsMENE: But can you do it? I say you cannot.

ANTIGONE: Very well, when my strength gives out,
  I shall do no more.

IsMENE: Impossible things should not be tried at all.

ANTIGONE: Go away, Ismene: 85
  I shall be hating you soon, and the dead will too,
  For your words are hateful. Leave me my foolish plan:
  I am not afraid of the danger; if it means death,
  It will not be the worst of deaths—death without honor.

IsMENE: Go then, if you feel you must.   90
  You are unwise,
  But a loyal friend indeed to those who love you.

"Ode to Man"

CHORUS: Numberless are the world's wonders, but none   Strophe 1
  More wonderful than man; the stormgray sea
  Yields to his **prows**, the huge **crests** bear him high;
  Earth, holy and inexhaustible, is **graven**
  With the shining **furrows** where his **plows** have gone
  Year after year, the timeless labor of **stallions**.
  The lightboned birds and beasts that **cling** to cover,   Antistrophe 1
  The **lithe** fish lighting their **reaches** of dim water,
  All are taken, tamed in the net of his mind;
  The lion on the hill, the wild horse windy-maned,
  Resign to him; and his **blunt** yoke has broken
  The sultry shoulders of the mountain bull.

  Words also, and thought as rapid as air,   Strophe 2
  He fashions to his good use; **statecraft** is his,

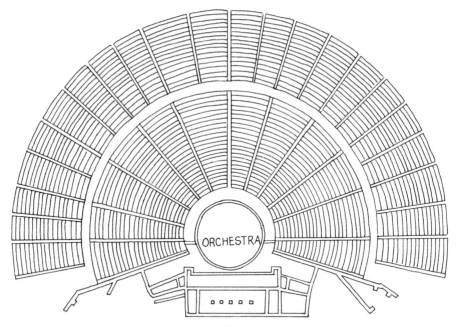

Figure 8 • Plan of an ancient Greek theater

And his the skill that **deflects** the arrows of snow,
The spears of winter rain: from every wind
He has made himself secure—from all but one:
In the late wind of death he cannot stand.
O clear intelligence, force beyond all measure!   Antistrophe 2
O fate of man, working both good and evil!
When the laws are kept, how proudly his city stands!
When the laws are broken, what of his city then?
Never may the **anarchic** man find rest at my **hearth**,
Never be it said that my thoughts are his thoughts.

Vocabulary

PROLOGUE

*Argive *(adj.)*   from the Greek city of Argos
bury *(v.)*   to put into the earth
*carrion birds *(n.)*   birds that eat dead flesh
cord *(n.)*   rope

*Denotes low-frequency word.

dear *(adj.)* precious; loved
decree *(n.)* formal decision made by an authority
fiery *(adj.)* full of emotion
flee (fled, fled) *(v.)* to run away
forbid (forbade, forbidden) *(v.)* to command against
grief *(n.)* deep feeling caused by loss; sorrow
meddle *(v.)* to be interested in something that is not one's concern
mourn *(v.)* to feel or express grief or sorrow
rip out *(v.)* to tear out
strangle *(v.)* to choke

"ODE TO MAN"

*anarchic *(adj.)* causing political disorder
blunt *(adj.)* not sharp
cling *(v.)* to hold on tightly to
crest *(n.)* top of a wave
deflect *(v.)* to turn from course
furrow *(n.)* line in the earth made by a plow
*graven *(adj.)* cut; carved
hearth *(n.)* floor of a fireplace; home
lithe *(adj.)* very flexible and graceful
plow *(n.)* agricultural tool used to turn over the earth
prow *(n.)* front part of a ship
reach *(n.)* expanse; stretch
resign *(v.)* to submit
stallion *(n.)* male horse
statecraft *(n.)* art of conducting state affairs

Activities

1. Looking at the Prologue, make notes in your journal about the characters or personalities of the two sisters, Ismene and Antigone. How are they different?

2. With your study group, discuss the meaning of each stanza (group of lines) in "Ode to Man." What kind of imagery does Sophocles use? Write a brief summary of the entire ode in your journal.

3. An ode is a poem that praises a person or an object. What qualities about human beings does Sophocles admire in "Ode to Man"? What are human beings capable of controlling? What can they not control?

4. How is "Ode to Man," especially the last stanza, connected to the conflict presented in the Prologue? What kind of law is Antigone breaking? What kind of law is Creon breaking? With your study group, discuss the importance of each of the two kinds of law. Organize and record your ideas in your journal.

5. What is the role of religion in this drama? What is the role of myth? Why would the Greeks act these elements out?

6. Write an essay comparing and contrasting Antigone and Ismene.

7. Based on the discussion and your journal notes, write your own essay comparing and contrasting the law that Antigone believes in and the kind of law that Creon makes. In your essay, evaluate the importance of each.

For Further Reading

Burkert, Walter. *Greek Religion*. Cambridge, MA: Harvard UP, 1985.

Grant, Michael. *The Classical Greeks*. New York: Scribner's, 1989.

Hogan, James C. *A Commentary on the Plays of Sophocles*. Carbondale: Southern Illinois UP, 1991.

Ley, Graham. *A Short Introduction to the Ancient Greek Theater*. Chicago: U of Chicago P, 1991.

Figure 9 • Map of East Asia

5

From "Red Thread Maiden"

Yuan Chiao (late ninth century)
Fiction: Short Story

Background

Elizabeth Te-Chen Wang, translator and editor of *Ladies of the T'ang*, took this story from a collection of short stories by Yuan Chiao. Not much is known about the author, but she seems to have been an educated lady of the court in northern China. Unlike most popular storytellers of her day, Yuan Chiao was able to write down her stories as well as recite them. "Red Thread Maiden" reflects the civil strife during the T'ang dynasty (618–906). The story is strongly influenced by the religious and ethical concerns of Buddhism, the religion brought from India, and of the native Chinese Confucianism.

The T'ang dynasty was the golden age of Chinese poetry. A well-known collection of the best poets, *Poems from the T'ang Dynasty*, became a school literary text and has been translated several times into English.

During the T'ang dynasty, foreign trade increased and new ideas were brought to China. In particular, monks from India and Central Asia strengthened the influence of Buddhism. Buddhist religious relics appeared, and soon Chinese men and women were retiring to live in monasteries apart from the strife of the courts. Although efforts were made to control Buddhism, its effects on Chinese life were permanent.

The T'ang dynasty was weakened by a rebellion led by the Empress Wu in 683. However, the T'ang were restored to power in 705. A second major rebellion occurred in 755 when the northern Chinese general An Lu-Shan fought against the emperor. Although An Lu-Shan was defeated in 763, the T'ang dynasty was undermined and later lost most of its control over northeast China. The political difficulties of the T'ang are depicted in the story of "Red Thread Maiden."

Pre-Reading Activities

1. Civil war or other serious conflict may occur anywhere, at any time. Discuss with your group or class how people might try to resolve such conflict. What role might women play in solving the conflict?
2. With your group or class, discuss what you know about reincarnation. Which religions do you think might consider it an important concept?

Key Terms

These terms are important for the mini-lecture and class discussion.

An Lu-Shan Rebellion (755–763 C.E.)	dynasty
	humanism
Buddhism/Buddhist	monastery
civil service	Second Imperial Period
Confucian Five Classics	T'ang dynasty (618–906 C.E.)
Confucius (551–479 B.C.E.)/ Confucianism	warlord

From "Red Thread Maiden"
Yuan Chiao

In the household of General Hsueh Sung, the military governor of Luchow, lived the maid Red Thread. Because Red Thread was **well grounded** in the classics as well as in letter writing, Hsueh appointed her as his personal secretary. . . . But he was particularly fond of her for another reason. She was good at music and could tell the emotional state of the player by listening to the tune of a musical instrument.   1

One day General Hsueh gave a feast for his staff members and the soldiers under his command. Red Thread was ordered to be present. While she was enjoying the musical performance, she noticed something wrong with the drummer.   2

"Something sad is on the drummer's mind," she remarked, "for the tune of the drum is sorrowful." 3

Hsueh Sung also understood music; he agreed with Red Thread and said, "I think so." He then summoned the drummer and questioned him. 4

The drummer was frightened. "My wife died last night," he **murmured**, with tears in his eyes. "Since I dare not ask for **leave**, I cannot control my **grief** when I beat the drum. Please forgive me if I have offended Your Excellency." Hsueh immediately gave him leave to go to the funeral. 5

It was during the period of Chih Teh, right after the rebellion led by An Lu-Shan, and everything was not yet restored to order. Along the **Yangtze** and **Yellow rivers** there still existed unrest and fighting, for the warlords did not trust one another and constantly made trouble. In addition to General Hsueh Sung, the most powerful and notable military governors were General Tien Cheng-tze of Weipo and General Ling-Hu Chang of Huachow. 6

Although the Emperor had put Hsueh Sung in charge of the newly organized Chaoyi Regiment with orders to set up his headquarters in Fuyang in order to control the whole of Shantung province, it was still doubtful whether there could be peaceful coexistence between the three **rampant** warlords. To **pacify** them the Emperor had arranged for the daughter of Hsueh Sung to wed the son of Tien Cheng-tze, and for Hsueh's son to marry the daughter of Ling-Hu Chang. Messengers and presents were sent back and forth, and there was **superficial** harmony among the three states. 7

Then Tien Cheng-tze fell ill with a kind of sickness caused by the bad weather. He felt worse during the summertime. "If I can change my office with Hsueh Sung and move to Shantung, where the weather is much cooler," he thought to himself, "I probably can cure my disease and live a few years longer." With this in mind, he **conscripted** three thousand soldiers, ten times braver than the ones he already had, and gave them special training. He paid them well and called them Outside Guards. Each night he ordered three hundred of them to take turns guarding his residence. A lucky date was chosen; he intended to move to Luchow by any means. This meant that an open conflict would occur between Weipo and Luchow. 8

When Hsueh Sung heard of the intention of General Tien, he was surprised and worried, not because he did not want to have a fight with his **kinsman**, but because the troops he had were getting old and could not compete with the fresh soldiers of the Outside Guards. He did not know what to do except to worry all day long. 9

It was midnight. The gates of the headquarters were **bolted**.   10
Hseuh Sung, cane in hand, was **pacing agitatedly** along the **corridors** of the courtyard. He had no other attendant besides Red
Thread. "Why is it that Your Lordship has not slept or eaten well for
the entire past month?" asked Red Thread. "Is it due to something
from the neighboring state?"

"A big affair that concerns the safety of the whole country is   11
something you cannot understand," answered Hsueh Sung.

"Though I am a **bondmaid**, perhaps I know how to lift the   12
burden from the mind of Your Lordship."

Hsueh Sung confided the whole story to her. "I inherited this   13
command from my father and would like to keep it till the end of my
life and bestow it on my son. If I lose this, I will lose everything."

"It is a simple matter and should not worry Your Lordship,"   14
said Red Thread. "Just let me go to Weipo to make a **reconnaissance**.
I shall leave here at the first **watch** and come back by the third.
Please prepare a good horse and a friendly letter and wait till my return."

. . . Red Thread then went back to her own chamber and   15
changed her costume. She wound her long hair into a knot and
pinned it up with a golden hairpin made into the shape of a **phoenix**
and covered her head with a red scarf. **Donning** an embroidered
purple robe and a pair of black shoes, she hung around her waist a
dagger that bore the sign of a dragon. On her forehead she wrote
the name of the god Tai Yi to guard her from evil spirits. She saluted
Hsueh Sung and at once disappeared.

Hsueh Sung walked into his room and, closing the door, sat   16
down in tense silence, with his back to the candlelight. He drank a
dozen cups of wine, but felt neither drunk nor sleepy. As he was
waiting in suspense, he heard the distant sound of the morning horn.
A sudden breeze rustled by and a leaf fell from a dewy tree. Before
he had time to wonder what it was, Red Thread was already standing
in front of him. Hsueh Sung was in **rapture**.

"Was everything all right?" asked he.   17

"How dare I fail to carry out a mission for Your Lordship?"   18

"Did you do any killing?"   19

"No, I only took a golden box from beneath General Tien's   20
pillow."

She gave the golden box to Hsueh Sung and then described   21
her trip.

"About three-quarters of an hour before midnight I arrived at   22
General Tien's residence. I passed through several courtyards and fi-

nally reached his bedroom. His Outside Guards were sleeping in the corridors, snoring like thunder. Other soldiers were pacing in the courtyard so vigilant that a wisp of breeze would start them shooting. But I made no noise as I opened the door and approached General Tien's bed. When I lifted the bed curtains, I saw old General Tien sound asleep on a rhinoceros-horn pillow, with his chest uncovered. His hair was bound up in a piece of yellow silk. Beside his pillow there lay a sword with seven stars carved upon it, and in front of the sword there lay a golden box containing the eight characters of his horoscope and the name of the god of the North Pole.

". . . All of General Tien's bodyguards and servants were   23
getting drowsy. Some rested their heads against the screens. Others leaned on their weapons and covered themselves with hand towels. I pulled the hairpin from one and touched the clothes of another, but they all slept like sick men or drunkards. Finally, I took the golden box from beside General Tien's pillow and left the city of Wei by the west gate. After I had walked two hundred **li** away, I looked back and saw the bronze casement towering among the clouds above the Chang River, which runs eastward. It was beautiful to see the morning breeze beginning to stir the grass and flowers of the wild meadows and the declining moon half hidden by the tall trees.

"I was so glad to be back that I entirely forgot my worries   24
and the fatigue of the **strenuous** trip. It makes me feel happy to be of a little service to you to repay some of your kindness. To show my gratitude to you is the main reason that I ran the risk of entering an enemy state, passing five or six cities, and completing a trip of about seven hundred li in three watches' time. I did this to lessen your grief, so I have no complaint."

Hsueh Sung hurriedly **dispatched** a messenger on the horse   25
that he had prepared, giving him the letter that he had written. The letter was for Governor Tien, and it read:

"Last night a guest came from Your Lordship's headquarters   26
and presented me with a golden box which he said he took from beneath your pillow. As your humble relative, how can I accept such a gift which is so precious and important to you? Therefore, I am sending it back with my best regards."

The messenger galloped as fast as he could. When he reached   27
Weipo at daybreak, he found General Tien's headquarters in great confusion searching for the missing golden box. Everyone was under suspicion. The messenger hammered on the gate with his horsewhip and asked for the governor. Tien Cheng-tze immediately came out and, upon receiving the box, was terrified to think that someone

could steal anything from beneath his pillow. The man who dared to do this must be of **unsurpassable** courage and skill, and could easily have cut his head off. He decided that he had better be loyal to General Hsueh from that time on, since the latter possessed such a magically **endowed** knight.

Governor Tien therefore invited the messenger to stay in his   28
residence, treating him to a big feast and giving him many gifts. Next day, upon sending the messenger back, he presented to Governor Hsueh thirty thousand pieces of fine silk, two hundred good horses, and many other presents. He also wrote an exceeding polite letter to Governor Hsueh:

"My life was at the mercy of a man from your state last night.   29
As a relative, you have been very kind to me. How can I do anything that might cause you great concern? Please suspect me no more. The so-called Outside Guards were trained to deal with robbers and bandits only. Now I have discharged them and sent them back to their farms in order to show you my cooperation. From now on I shall be at your service. If you care to give any orders, I shall follow your carriage to carry them out; and if you ever come to my **humble** state, I shall stand by to watch your horse for you."

Thus the two governors were **reconciled**. Greetings were ex-   30
changed frequently, and the tension eased between the south and north sides of the Yellow River.

A month or so later Red Thread asked for **leave**. "You were   31
reared in my house," exclaimed Hsueh Sung. "Where can you go? Moreover, you have done me a great favor and I depend on you for my safety. How can I let you go?"

But Red Thread told him: "I was a man in my previous life, an   32
herb doctor who wandered from village to village to cure people with prescriptions from the book of Shen Lung. One day I ran across a pregnant woman suffering from a kind of **dropsy**. I gave her some wine made of a certain kind of flower that caused her death and the death of her unborn twins. My mistake in killing three persons with one dose was reported to the king of the underworld, and as punishment I was reincarnated as a woman in this life. I was moreover punished by being born a lowbred maid with an ill star of ability to act like a burglar. It was fortunate that I was sold to your house. For nineteen years I have been so well treated that I have even tired of the soft dresses that you give me and the delicious food I have eaten day after day. You have been exceedingly kind to me. I was even honored by being appointed your personal secretary.

"Because our country had just survived the **calamity** of re-   33 bellion, I hated to see the warlords make trouble again and endanger the peace and safety of the whole nation. So I went to Weipo to give General Tien a warning. I did that to repay your kindness and to avoid a civil war which would no doubt destroy thousands of lives. My little deed of saving two states from destruction and warning the warlords of the cost of an open conflict has made it possible for the military strategists to set their minds at ease. As a woman, I feel that I have done enough to **redeem** the crime I committed in my previous life, and now it is time for me to **retreat** from this world. I hope to become a man again and live an immortal life."

. . . Seeing it was **futile** to persuade her to stay, Hsueh Sung 34 gave her a big farewell party, with all the high officers invited. In the midst of the elaborate food and toasts, Hsueh Sung asked Lung Chao-yang, a guest and also a poet, to compose a poem for him to sing to Red Thread. The poem became very famous. It runs as follows:

> From the orchid boat comes the sad
>   water-chestnut song—
> Standing on the tall tower, everyone
>   grieves over the parting.
> Like Fairy Lo flying to the clouds, you
>   now leave,
> Boundless is the blue sky and the water
>   runs on forever.

Hsueh Sung felt the weight of great sadness after he had sung 35 the song. Red Thread wept. Because she did not want to **tarry** any longer, she made an excuse that she was drunk and must retire. She saluted the general and the guests and left. No one ever saw her again.

Vocabulary

agitatedly *(adv.)*   with rapid or violent action
bolt *(v.)*   to close with locks
*bondmaid *(n.)*   woman bound to service without wages; slave
calamity *(n.)*   disaster
conscript *(v.)*   to force into military service
corridor *(n.)*   passageway into which rooms open
dagger *(n.)*   sharp-pointed knife for stabbing

*Denotes low-frequency word.

dispatch *(v.)*   to send off with speed, especially on official business

*don *(v.)*   to put on

*dropsy *(n.)*   abnormal fluid in body tissues; edema

endowed *(adj.)*   gifted

futile *(adj.)*   serving no useful purpose

grief *(n.)*   sorrow

humble *(adj.)*   low-ranking

*kinsman *(n.)*   male relative (in this case by marriage)

*leave *(n.)*   permission to leave

*li *(n.)*   Chinese measure of distance, about one-third of a mile

murmur *(v.)*   to speak in a low voice or unclearly

pace *(v.)*   to walk with a measured step

pacify *(v.)*   to settle; to restore to a peaceful state

*phoenix *(n.)*   mythological Chinese bird of good fortune

rampant *(adj.)*   wild; without restraint

rapture *(n.)*   state of overwhelming emotion

rear *(v.)*   to raise; bring up

reconcile *(v.)*   to restore to harmony

*reconnaissance *(n.)*   preliminary inspection

redeem *(v.)*   to make amends for; to atone for

retreat *(v.)*   to withdraw

strenuous *(adj.)*   calling for energy or stamina

superficial *(adj.)*   on the surface; without substance

*tarry *(v.)*   to delay

unsurpassable *(adj.)*   not to be exceeded

watch *(n.)*   period of guard duty

well grounded *(adj.)*   having a firm foundation

Yangtze River *(prop. n.)*   the longest and largest river in China; begins in Tsinghai province and runs to the East China Sea north of the city of Shanghai

Yellow River *(prop. n.)*   the second-longest river in China, nicknamed "China's Sorrow" because of its periodic and devastating floods. The lower part of the Yellow River was the site of China's earliest civilization. Loyang, capital of the T'ang dynasty, is located on its banks.

Activities

1. Why was Red Thread born? How does she pay her debt?

2. With your study group or class, find evidence that magic or the supernatural is important in the story. Make notes in your journal and compare your answers with the answers of other members of your class.

*Denotes low-frequency word.

3. Look at the details of the story and make notes in your journal about the cultural values or beliefs that are important to the Chinese of the T'ang dynasty. For example, how is the role of women viewed? Discuss these beliefs with your class.

4. Based on your notes and class discussion, write an essay on the importance of the balance of physical strength with emotional sensitivity in "Red Thread Maiden."

5. Based on your notes and discussion, write an essay on the cultural values of the T'ang Chinese court.

For Further Reading

Bary, William de, et al, eds. *Sources of Chinese Tradition*. New York: Columbia UP, 1960.

Grousset, René. *The Rise and Splendour of the Chinese Empire*. Berkeley: U of California P, 1953.

Meskill, John, ed. *An Introduction to Chinese Civilization*. New York: Columbia UP, 1960.

Moore, Charles A. *The Chinese Mind: Essentials of Chinese Philosophy and Culture*. Honolulu: U of Hawaii P, 1986.

Shimer, Dorothy Blair, ed. *Rice Bowl Women*. New York: Meridian, 1982.

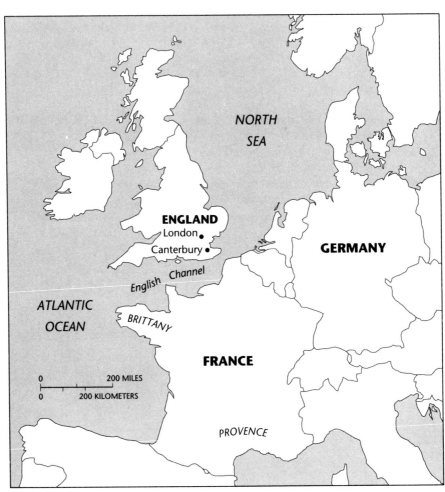

NORTH SEA

ENGLAND
London
Canterbury

English Channel

ATLANTIC OCEAN

BRITTANY

GERMANY

FRANCE

PROVENCE

0   200 MILES
0   200 KILOMETERS

Figure 10 • Map of England, France, Germany, and the English Channel

6

"Bisclavret" from *The Lais of Marie de France*

Marie de France (late twelfth century)
Fiction: Short Story

Background

Little is known about the life of the medieval author called Marie de France. Immensely popular in French and English aristocratic courts during her lifetime, Marie de France composed religious pieces in Latin but is most remembered for her secular literature. Marie wrote these pieces in Old French, the language spoken from the ninth century C.E. until Modern French evolved in the sixteenth century. Old French was also the language of high culture in the English court after the French Norman Conquest of England in 1066.

The Lais, a collection of 12 short poems, tells of the adventures of noblemen and noblewomen as they follow or disobey the principles of courtly love. Marie herself says that as her source material she used lais from Brittany, an area in northwestern France where a Celtic language is spoken. These Breton lais were traditionally adventures of ancient origin told in verse and set to music. Whether Marie heard these lais in Old French or in Celtic is not clear.

The subject of the lai "Bisclavret" is one that fascinated medieval Europeans: the power to transform oneself or another into a wolf by the use of magic. In the tale, this strange phenomenon tests the courtly conventions of the relationship between husband and wife and between noble and feudal lord.

Pre-Reading Activities

1. With your study group, discuss what you think is the purpose of litera-
    ture. Should it merely entertain, or should it teach a moral lesson?
2. Imagine what life was like in Europe 800 years ago. In your journal
    list your ideas about why storytelling would be important for people
    living at that time. Discuss your ideas with your group.

Key Terms

Breton/Brittany   Middle Ages/medieval
chivalry   Old French
courtly love   piety
feudal system   Provence/Provençal
folklore   secular
knights and ladies   vernacular
lai (lay)   werewolf
loyalty

"Bisclavret"
Marie de France

In my effort to compose lais I do not wish to omit "Bisclavret". . . . In days gone by . . . many men turned into werewolves
and went to live in the woods. A werewolf is a **ferocious** beast
which, when possessed by this madness, devours men, causes great
damage and **dwells** in vast forests. I leave such matters for the moment, for I wish to tell you about Bisclavret. [1–14]*

In Brittany there lived a **baron** whom I have heard greatly   2
praised. He was a good and handsome knight who conducted himself
nobly. He was one of his lord's closest advisers and was well loved by
all his neighbors. As his wedded wife he had a woman who was wor-
thy and attractive in appearance. He loved her and she returned his
love. But one thing caused her great worry: Each week he was absent
for three full days without her knowing what became of him or
where he went. . . .

*Line numbers refer to original French text.

Figure 11 • Medieval werewolf, an imaginary wolf-man

One day, when he had returned home in high spirits, she   3
questioned him: "Lord," she said, "my dear, sweet love, I would
gladly ask you something, if only I dared; but there is nothing I fear
more than your anger." [15–35]

When he heard this, he embraced her, drew her towards him   4
and kissed her. "Lady," he said, "come, ask your question! There is
nothing you can ask which I shall not tell you, if I know the answer." "In faith," she said, "I am relieved to hear this. Lord, I am so
fraught with anxiety the days you are apart from me, my heart is
so heavy and I have such a fear of losing you that I shall surely die
shortly from this unless I soon get help. Please tell me where you go,
[and] what becomes of you. . . . I think you must have a lover
and, if this is so, you are doing wrong." "Lady," he said, "in God's
name, have mercy on me! If I tell you this, great harm will come

to me, for as a result, I shall lose your love and destroy myself."
[36–56]

    When the lady heard what he said, she thought it was no   5
laughing matter. She questioned him repeatedly and **coaxed** him so
persuasively that he told her his story, keeping nothing secret. "Lady,
I become a werewolf: I enter the **vast** forest and live in the deepest
part of the wood where I feed off the **prey** I can capture." When he
had related everything to her, she asked him whether he undressed
or remained clothed. "Lady," he said, "I go about completely naked."
"Tell me, in the name of God, where do you leave your clothes?"
"That I will not tell you, for if I lost them and were discovered in that
state, I should remain a werewolf forever. No one would be able to
help me until they were returned to me. That is why I do not wish
this to be known." [57–79]

    "Lord," the lady replied to him, "I love you more than the   6
whole world. You must not hide anything from me. . . . That would
not seem like true love. What have I done wrong? What sin have I
committed that you should doubt me in any way? Do tell me—you
will be acting wisely." She **tormented** . . . him so much that he
could not do otherwise but tell her.

    "Lady," he said, "beside the wood, near the path I follow,   7
stands an old chapel. . . . There beneath a bush is a broad stone,
hollowed out in the center, in which I put my clothes until I return
home." The lady heard this remarkable revelation and her face became flushed with fear. She was greatly alarmed by the story, and began to consider various means of parting from him, as she no longer
wished to lie with him. [80–102]

    She sent a messenger to **summon** a knight who lived in the   8
region and who had loved her for a long time, wooed her **ardently**
and served her generously. She had never loved him or promised
him her affection but now she told him what was on her mind.
"Friend," she said, "rejoice; without further delay I grant you that
which has tormented you; never again will you encounter any refusal. I offer you my love and my body; make me your mistress."

    He thanked her warmly and accepted her pledge, whereupon   9
she received his oath and told him of her husband and what became
of him. She described the path he took to the forest and sent him for
her husband's clothes. Thus was Bisclavret betrayed and wronged by
his wife. Because he was often missing, everyone thought that this
time he had gone away for good. They searched . . . for him a long
while but no trace of him was found. . . . Then the knight married
the lady he had loved for so long. [103–34]

A whole year passed by until one day the king went hunting   10
and headed straight for the forest in which Bisclavret was living.
When the hounds were unleashed they came upon Bisclavret and
the dogs and hunters spent the whole day in pursuit until they were
just about to capture him, tear him to pieces and destroy him. As
soon as he saw the king he ran up to him and begged for mercy. He
took hold of his **stirrup** and kissed his foot and his leg. The king saw
him and was filled with dread. He summoned all his companions.
"Lords," he said, "come forward! See the marvellous way this beast
humbles itself before me! It has the intelligence of a human and is
pleading for mercy. Drive back all the dogs and see that no one
strikes it! The beast possesses understanding and intelligence. Hurry!
Let us depart. I shall place the creature under my protection, for I
shall hunt no more today." [135–60]

The king then left with Bisclavret following him. He kept very   11
close to the king, as he did not want to be separated from him. . . .
The king, who took him straight to his castle, was delighted and
overjoyed. . . . He considered the wolf to be a great wonder and
loved it dearly, commanding all his people to guard it well for love of
him and not to do it any harm. None of them was to strike it and
plenty of food and water must be provided each day for it. His men
were happy to look after the creature and each day it would sleep
amongst the knights, just by the king. It was loved by everyone and
so noble and gentle a beast was it that it never attempted to cause
any harm. Wherever the king might go, it never wanted to be left behind. . . . It showed clearly that it loved him. [161–84]

Now hear what happened next. The king held court and all   12
his barons and those who held **fiefs** from him were summoned so
that they could help him celebrate the festival. . . . Amongst them,
richly and elegantly attired, was the knight who had married
Bisclavret's wife. He did not realize and would never have suspected
that Bisclavret was so close by. As soon as he arrived at the palace,
Bisclavret caught sight of the knight and **sped** towards him, sinking
his teeth into him and dragging him down. . . . He would soon
have done the knight serious harm if the king had not called him and
threatened him with a stick. On two occasions that day he attempted to bite him. Many people were greatly astonished at this for
never before had he shown signs of such behavior towards anyone
he had seen. Throughout the household it was remarked that he
would not have done it without good reason. The knight had
wronged him somehow or other, for he **was bent on** revenge. . . .
[185–218]

Not long afterwards, as I understand it, the king, who was   13
wise and courtly, went into the forest where Bisclavret had been discovered. Bisclavret accompanied him and on the way home that
night the king took **lodging** in that region. Bisclavret's wife learnt of
this and, dressing herself elegantly, went next day to speak to the
king, taking an expensive present for him. When Bisclavret saw her
approach, no one could restrain him. He dashed towards her like a
madman. Just hear how successfully he took his revenge. He tore the
nose right off her face. What worse punishment could he have
inflicted on her?

From all sides he was threatened and was on the point of being   14
torn to pieces, when a wise man said to the king: "Lord, listen to me.
This beast has lived with . . . us over a long period. . . . Never before has he touched a soul or committed a hostile act, except against
this lady here. By the faith I owe you, he has some **grudge** against
her and also her husband. She is the wife of the knight you used to
love so dearly and who has been missing for a long time without our
knowing what became of him. Question the lady to see if she will tell
you why the beast hates her. Make her tell you, if she knows! We
have witnessed many marvels happening in Brittany." [219–60]

The king accepted his advice. Holding the knight, he took the   15
lady away and **subjected** her to torture. Pain and fear combined
made her **reveal** everything about her husband; how she had betrayed him and taken his clothes, about his account of what happened, what became of him and where he went. Since his clothes
had been taken he had not been seen in the region. She was quite
convinced that the beast was Bisclavret. The king asked her for the
clothes and . . . made her bring them and return them to
Bisclavret. When they were placed before him, Bisclavret took no notice of them. The man who gave the advice earlier called to the king:
"Lord, you are not acting properly: Nothing would **induce** him to
put on his clothing in front of you or change his animal form. You do
not realize the importance of this; it is most **humiliating** for him.
Take him into your bedchamber and bring him the clothes. Let us
leave him there for a while and we shall soon see if he turns into a
man." [261–92]

The king himself led the way and closed all the doors on the wolf.   16
After a while he returned, taking two barons with him. All three entered the room. They found the knight sleeping on the king's own
bed. The king ran forward to embrace him, and kissed him many
times. It was not long before he restored his land to him; he gave him
more than I can tell and banished the woman from the country, exil-

ing her from the region. The man for whom she betrayed her husband went with her. She had a good many children who were thereafter recognizable by their appearance. Many of the women in the family, I tell you truly, were born without noses and lived noseless. [293–314]

The adventure you have heard actually took place, do not doubt   17
it. The lai was **composed** about Bisclavret to be remembered for ever more. [315-18]

Vocabulary

ardently *(adv.)*   with intense feeling
*baron *(n.)*   nobleman
*be bent on *(v.)*   to be determined or strongly inclined [to have]
coax *(v.)*   to urge gently
compose *(v.)*   to create by mental or artistic labor
dwell *(v.)*   to live as a resident
ferocious *(adj.)*   given to extreme fierceness and unrestrained violence
*fief *(n.)*   feudal estate
*fraught [with] *(adj.)*   full [of]
grudge *(n.)*   feeling of deep resentment or ill will
humiliating *(adj.)*   extremely destructive to one's self-respect
induce *(v.)*   to persuade; to influence
inflict *(v.)*   to carry out by physical assault; to impose
lodging *(n.)*   temporary place to stay for the night
prey *(n.)*   any animal hunted or killed for food
reveal *(v.)*   to make publicly known something that was secret or hidden
speed (sped, sped) *(v.)*   to move quickly
*stirrup *(n.)*   part of a saddle for the rider's foot
subject *(v.)*   to force someone to endure something unpleasant
summon *(v.)*   to call forth; to demand the presence of
threaten *(v.)*   to express one's intention of hurting or punishing
torment *(v.)*   to cause severe distress of body or mind
vast *(adj.)*   very great in size

Activities

1. As a character, Bisclavret is presented as a model of chivalry. Make notes in your journal of his courtly behavior. How is he rewarded? Discuss your ideas with your class.

*Denotes low-frequency word.

2. The story "Bisclavret" focuses on fidelity, or faithfulness, an important concept in the feudal system. What kinds of fidelity play a role in the story? What happens to those who are unfaithful?

3. Based on your notes and class discussion, write a description of courtly life in the Middle Ages.

4. With a partner or alone, note the portions of the story where Marie de France uses her imagination to entertain her audience. Write a summary of the use of the fantastic (the not-real) in "Bisclavret."

5. Based on your notes and discussion, write an essay on "Bisclavret" as a fictional story that both entertains and teaches a moral lesson.

For Further Reading

Clifford, Paula. *Marie de France*. London: Grant and Culter, 1982.

Marie de France. *The Lais of Marie de France*. Trans. and intro. by Glynn S. Burgess and Keith Busby. London: Penguin, 1986.

Morewedge, Rosmarie Thee, ed. *The Role of Woman in the Middle Ages*. Albany: State U of New York P, 1975.

Rose, Mary Beth, ed. *Women in the Middle Ages and the Renaissance: Literary and Historical Perspectives*. Syracuse: Syracuse UP, 1986.

Wilson, Katherina M., ed. *Medieval Women Writers*. Athens: U of Georgia P, 1984.

7

From "The Miller's Tale" from *The Canterbury Tales*

Geoffrey Chaucer (1340?–1400)
Oral Tradition and Poetry: Verse Narrative

Background

The most important author writing in English in the European Middle Ages was Geoffrey Chaucer. The son of a London merchant, Chaucer was sent to the house of a noble family where he received a classical education including the study of French, Italian, and Latin. Chaucer's educational experiences served as major sources for his writing. His travel to the European continent also provided material for his work. The influence of these sources can be seen in his most famous effort, *The Canterbury Tales*.

Chaucer frames his tales in verse as a story of 29 men and women making a religious pilgrimage to the tomb of St. Thomas à Becket at Canterbury Cathedral in England. The pilgrims represent the upper middle class of medieval society. The travelers compete in telling stories to entertain their companions during the trip. In his tale, the Miller parodies, or makes fun of, the previous story of courtly love told by a knight.

Pre-Reading Activities

1. With your study group, discuss why religious pilgrims might tell funny stories to pass the time. What does this say about the character of the pilgrims?
2. What kinds of things make people laugh?

Key Terms

These terms and concepts are important for understanding *The Canterbury Tales*. They will be used in the mini-lecture and in class discussion.

Absalon

bawdy

biblical

Boccaccio, Giovanni (1313–1375)

Canterbury Cathedral

Cato

comedy

couplet

Decameron

fabliau/fabliaux

framed narrative

Greek and Roman classics

King Henry II (ruled 1154–1189)

Middle English

moral

parody

pilgrim/pilgrimage

ribald

St. Thomas à Becket (1118–1170)

satire

slapstick

From "The Miller's Tale"
Geoffrey Chaucer

Some time ago there was a rich old **codger**
Who lived in Oxford and who took a **lodger**.
The fellow was a carpenter by trade,
His lodger a poor student who had made
Some studies in the arts, but all his fancy   5
Turned to astrology and **geomancy**,
And he could deal with certain propositions
And make a forecast under some conditions
About the likelihood of drought or showers
For those who asked at favorable hours. . . .   10
This lad was known as Nicholas the **Gallant**,

Figure 12 • Pilgrims on the road to Canterbury *(The Granger Collection)*

And making love in secret was his talent. . . .
He rented a small chamber in the **kip**
All by himself without companionship. . . .
He had an **astrolabe** to match his art   15
And calculating counters laid apart. . . .
This carpenter had married a new wife
Not long before, and loved her more than life.
She was a girl of eighteen years of age.
Jealous he was and kept her in the cage,   20
For he was old and she was wild and young;
He thought himself quite likely to be **stung**.
He might have known, were Cato on his shelf,
A man should marry someone like himself;

A man should pick an equal for his mate.   25
Youth and old age are often in debate. . . .
She was a fair young wife, her body as slender
As any weasel's, and as soft and tender. . . .
She wore a broad silk **fillet**, rather high,
And certainly she had a **lecherous** eye. . . .   30
The wisest man you met would have to wrench
His fancy to imagine such a wench. . . .
Her mouth was sweet as **mead** or honey—say
A hoard of apples lying in the hay. . . .
Now, gentlemen, this Gallant Nicholas   35
Began to romp about and **make a pass**
At this young woman, happening on her one day,
Her husband being out, down Osney way.
Students are sly, and giving way to whim,
He made a grab and caught her by the limb   40
And said, "O God, I love you! Can't you see
If I don't have you it's the end of me?" . . .
She gave a spring, just like a **skittish** colt
Boxed in a frame for shoeing, and with a jolt
Managed in time to wrench her head away,   45
And said, "Give over, Nicholas, I say!
No, I won't kiss you! Stop it! Let me go
Or I shall scream! I'll let the neighbors know!
Where are your manners? Take away your paws!"
Then Nicholas began to plead his cause   50
And spoke so fair in **proffering** what he could
That in the end she promised him she would,
When she had an opportunity.
"My husband is so full of jealousy,
Unless you watch your step and hold your breath   55
I know for certain it will be my death. . . ."
Said he, "A scholar doesn't have to stir
His wits so much to trick a carpenter."
. . . There was a parish clerk
Serving the church, whose name was Absalon.   60
His hair was all in golden curls and shone;
Just like a fan it strutted outwards, starting
To left and right from an accomplished parting.
Ruddy his face, his eyes as grey as goose,
His shoes cut out in **tracery**, as in use   65
In old St. Paul's. The **hose** upon his feet

Showed scarlet through, and all his clothes were neat
And proper. In a jacket of light blue,
Flounced at the waist and tagged with laces too. . . .
There was no public-house in town or bar   70
He didn't visit with his merry face
If there were **saucy** barmaids round the place.
He was a little **squeamish** in the matter
Of **farting**, and satirical in chatter.
This Absalon, so jolly in his ways,   75
Would bear the censer round on holy days
And **cense** the parish women. He would cast
Many a love-lorn look before he passed,
Especially at this carpenter's young wife;
Looking at her would make a happy life,   80
He thought, so neat, so sweet, so lecherous.
And I daresay if she had been a mouse
And he a cat, she'd have been pounced upon. . . .
What was the good? Were he as bold as brass,
She was in love with gallant Nicholas;   85
However Absalon might blow his horn
His labor won him nothing but her scorn. . . .
Now, show your paces, Nicholas you Spark!
And leave lamenting to the parish clerk.
. . . Nicholas and Alison   90
Agreed at last in what was to be done.
Nicholas was to exercise his wits
On her suspicious husband's foolish fits,
And, if so be the trick worked out all right,
She then would sleep with Nicholas all night. . . .   95
"Now, John," said Nicholas, "believe you me,
I have found out by my astrology,
And looking at the moon when it was bright,
That Monday next, a quarter way through night,
Rain is to fall in torrents, such a **scud**   100
It will be twice as bad as Noah's Flood.
This world," he said, "in just about an hour,
Shall be all drowned, it's such a hideous shower,
And all mankind, with total loss of life."
The carpenter exclaimed, "Alas, my wife! . . .   105
Is there no remedy," he said, "for this?"
"Thanks be to God," said Nicholas, "there is,
If you will do exactly what I say

And don't start thinking up some other way. . . .
I want you, now, at once, to hurry off   110
And fetch a shallow tub or **kneading-trough**
For each of us, but see that they are large
And such as we can float in, like a barge.
And have them loaded with sufficient **victual**
To last a day—we only need a little. . . .   115
And I shall save your wife, you needn't doubt it,
Now off you go, and hurry up about it.
And when the tubs have been collected, three,
That's one for her and for yourself and me,
Then hang them in the roof below the **thatching**   120
That no one may discover what we're **hatching**.
When you have finished doing what I said
And stowed the victuals in them overhead,
Also, an axe to **hack** the ropes apart
So, when the water rises, we can start. . . .   125
Your wife and you must hang some way apart,
For there must be no sin before we start,
No more in longing looks than in the deed.
Those are your orders. Off with you! God speed!" . . .
And on the Monday when it drew to night   130
[John] shut his door and doused the candle-light
And made quite sure all was as it should be.
And shortly, up they **clambered**, all the three. . . .
The carpenter, with all the work he'd seen,
Fell dead asleep—round curfew, must have been . . .   135
And snored because his head was turned **awry**.
Down by their ladders, stalking from on high
Came Nicholas and Alison, and sped
Softly downstairs, without a word, to bed. . . .
And thus lay Nicholas and Alison   140
At busy play in eager quest of fun. . . .
The first cock crew at last, and thereupon
Up rode this jolly lover Absalon . . .
And by the casement window took his stand
Breast-high it stood, no higher than his hand.   145
He gave a cough, no more than half a sound;
"Alison, honeycomb, are you around?" . . .
"You go away," she answered, "you Tom-fool!
There's no come-up-and-kiss-me here for you.
I love another and why shouldn't I too?   150

I want to get some sleep. You go to Hell!"
"Alas!" said Absalon. "I knew it well;
True love is always mocked and girded at;
So kiss me, if you can't do more than that,
For Jesu's love and for the love of me!"   155
"And if I do, will you be off?" said she.
"Promise you darling," answered Absalon.
"Get ready then; wait, I'll put something on. . . ."
She flung the window open then in haste
And said, "Have done, come on, no time to waste,   160
The neighbors here are always on the spy."
Absalon started wiping his mouth dry.
Dark was the night as pitch, as black as coal,
And at the window out she put her hole
And Absalon, so fortune framed the farce,   165
Put up his mouth and kissed her naked **arse**
Most savorously before he knew of this.
And back he started. Something was amiss;
He knew quite well a woman has no beard,
Yet something quite rough and hairy had appeared.   170
"What have I done?" he said. "Can that be you?"
"Teehee!" she cried and **clapped** the window to.
Off went poor Absalon sadly through the dark.
"A beard! a beard!" cried Nicholas the Spark.
Who's busy rubbing, scraping at his lips   175
With dust, with sand, with straw, with cloth, with chips
But Absalon? He thought, "I'll bring him down!
I wouldn't let this go for all the town.
I'd take my soul and sell it to the Devil
To be revenged upon him! I'll get level. . . ."   180
So, weeping like a child that has been whipped,
He turned away; across the road he slipped
And called on Gervase. Gervase was a **smith**;
His forge was full of things for ploughing with. . . .
[Absalon] caught a [poker] up—the haft was cool—   185
And left the **smithy** softly with the tool,
Crept to the little window in the wall
And coughed. He knocked and gave a little call
Under the window as he had before.
Alison said, "There's someone at the door.   190
Who's knocking there? I'll warrant it's a thief."
"Why, no," said he, "my little flower-leaf,

It's your own Absalon, my sweety-thing!
Look what I've brought you—it's a golden ring. . . .
I'll give it to you, darling, for a kiss."   195
Now Nicholas had risen for a piss,
And thought he could improve upon the **jape**
And make him kiss his arse **ere** he escape,
And opening the window with a jerk,
Stuck out his arse, a handsome piece of work,   200
Buttocks and all, as far as to the **haunch**.
Said Absalon, all set to make a launch,
"Speak, pretty bird, I know not where thou art!"
This Nicholas at once let fly a **fart**
As loud as if it were a thunder-clap.   205
He was near blinded by the blast, poor chap,
But his hot iron was ready; with a thump
He [struck] him in the middle of the rump. . . .
"Help! Water! Water! Help! For Heaven's love!"
The carpenter, startled from sleep above,   210
And hearing shouts for water and a thud,
Thought, "Heaven help us! Here come's Nowel's Flood!"
And up he sat and with no more ado
He took his axe and [cut] the ropes in two
And down went everything. He didn't stop   215
To sell his bread and ale, but came down flop
Upon the floor and fainted right away.
Up started Alison and Nicholay
And shouted, "Help!" and "Murder!" in the street.
The neighbors all came running up in heat. . . .   220
[John's] arm in falling had been broken double.
But still he was obliged to face his trouble,
For when he spoke he was at once borne down
By Nicholas and his wife. They told the town
That he was mad, there'd got into his blood   225
Some sort of nonsense about "Nowel's Flood,"
That vain imaginings and fantasy
Had made him buy the kneading-tubs, that he
Had hung them in the rafter up above
And that he'd begged them both for heaven's love   230
To sit up in the roof for company.
All started laughing at this lunacy
And streamed upstairs to **gape** and pry and poke,
And treated all his sufferings as a joke.

No matter what the carpenter asserted   235
It went for nothing, no one was converted;
With powerful oaths they swore the fellow down
And he was held mad by all the town;
Even the learned said to one another,
"The fellow must be crazy, my dear brother."   240
So to a general laughter he succumbed.
That's how the carpenter's young wife was **plumbed**
For all the tricks his jealousy could try,
And Absalon has kissed her **nether** eye
And Nicholas is branded on the **bum**.   245
And God bring all of us to Kingdom Come.

Vocabulary

*arse *(n.)*   ass; buttocks (often considered vulgar)
*astrolabe *(n.)*   medieval instrument used to calculate the position of heavenly bodies
awry *(adv.)*   in a turned or twisted position
*bum *(n.)*   (chiefly British) buttocks (sometimes considered vulgar)
*cense *(v.)*   to perfume with a covered incense burner
clamber *(v.)*   to climb awkwardly; to scramble
clap *(v.)*   to slam
*codger *(n.)*   affectionate or mildly derogatory term for an old man
*ere *(conj.)*   before
fart (farting) *(n.)*   expulsion of intestinal gas (usually considered vulgar)
*fillet *(n.)*   ribbon or narrow strip of material used especially as a headband
*flounced *(adj.)*   trimmed with a wide ruffle
*gallant *(adj.)*   courteously and elaborately attentive, especially to ladies
gape *(v.)*   to look at stupidly or in open-mouthed surprise or wonder
*geomancy *(n.)*   practice of foretelling future events or discovering hidden knowledge by means of figures, lines, or geographic features
hack *(v.)*   to chop
hatch *(v.)*   to plan in secret
*haunch *(n.)*   hip
hose *(n.)*   stockings
*jape *(n.)*   joke
*kip *(n.)*   sleeping place
*kneading-trough/tub *(n.)*   container for making bread dough

*Denotes low-frequency word.

lecherous *(adj.)*   given to indulgence or sexual activity
lodger *(n.)*   roomer
make a pass *(v.)*   to make a sexually inviting gesture
***mead** *(n.)*   fermented beverage made of water, honey, malt, and yeast
nether *(adj.)*   situated under or below
***plumb** *(v.)*   to probe the depths of
proffer *(v.)*   to present for acceptance
saucy *(adj.)*   bold and impudent
***scud** *(n.)*   rain driven by wind
skittish *(adj.)*   nervous
smith *(n.)*   worker in metals
***smithy** *(n.)*   metal workshop
squeamish *(adj.)*   easily nauseated or disgusted
sting (stung) *(v.)*   to cheat
***thatching** *(n.)*   plant material, such as straw, used as a roof for a house
***tracery** *(n.)*   decorative openwork
***victuals** *(n.)*   food

Activities

1. As a class, read lines 60 through 88, which describe Absalon. What
    specific details about Absalon does Chaucer use to develop his charac-
    ter? What is your impression of him? How does Chaucer prepare us
    for what happens to Absalon?

2. With your study group, choose a second character from "The Miller's
    Tale." What is this character like? How does Chaucer's description of
    this character relate to what happens later in the tale? Record your
    ideas in your journal.

3. After 600 years, why do we still laugh at "The Miller's Tale"? What is
    the serious side or moral in this story? What makes this tale a satire of
    medieval society and literary conventions? Make notes in your jour-
    nal, using details from the story to support your ideas.

4. Write an essay on Chaucer's satire of medieval society.

5. Working alone or with your study group, write a short tale set in me-
    dieval times, using some of Chaucer's techniques, such as physically
    describing the characters, using humor, and teaching a moral lesson.
    You may want to use one of the following as a main character for your
    story: sailor, nun, student, lawyer, or physician.

6. If you have read "Bisclavret," write an essay comparing Absalon and
    Bisclavret as courtly lovers. What is the situation of each one at the
    end of his story?

*Denotes low-frequency word.

For Further Reading

Brewer, Derek, ed. *Chaucer: The Critical Heritage.* 2 vols. London: Routledge, 1978.

Chaucer, Geoffrey. *The Canterbury Tales.* Trans. Nevill Coghill. 1952. Baltimore: Penguin, 1975.

Coghill, Nevill. *The Poet Chaucer.* 2nd ed. New York: Oxford UP, 1968.

Howard, Donald R. *Chaucer: His Life, His Works, His World.* New York: Dutton, 1987.

CHAPTER **8**

From *Romeo and Juliet*

William Shakespeare (1564–1616)
Drama: Tragedy

Background

As the prolific author of poetry, history plays, tragedies, and comedies, Shakespeare continues to be regarded as one of the greatest writers in
the English language. Most of his life was spent under the reign of
Elizabeth I, a time when drama in England flourished. Shakespeare's career was unusual in that he managed his own London theater company,
wrote the plays that the company performed, and acted in them as well.
Moreover, he was an owner of two theaters, the Globe and the Blackfriars.

Romeo and Juliet is one of the greatest love tragedies of all time. The
story of tragic young lovers was a popular one in the plays and novels of
the Renaissance. Shakespeare's direct source for the play appears to have
been a poem in English, "The Tragical History of Romeus and Juliet," written by Arthur Brooke in 1562. Shakespeare adapts Brooke freely, and his
skill as a dramatist can be seen in the play resulting from the adaptation.

An inspiration for later musical compositions, ballets, and other
artistic interpretations, Romeo and Juliet are probably the world's most famous pair of star-crossed lovers.

Pre-Reading Activities

1. With your class, discuss the differences between traditional and mod-
    ern ways of contracting a marriage.
2. In your journal, make a list of reasons why, in your opinion, some

families cannot get along with other families. Then discuss your ideas
with your small group or class.

Key Terms

blood feud	heir/heiress
courtly love	London
Elizabeth I (1533–1603)	Renaissance
Elizabethan England	Shakespearean sonnet
empire	Stratford-on-Avon
Fate (the Stars)	"The Tragical History of Romeus and
Globe Theater	Juliet" (Arthur Brooke, 1562)

From *Romeo and Juliet*
William Shakespeare

Characters for These Scenes

Chorus
Juliet, a daughter of the Capulet family
Romeo, a son of the Montague family

Prologue

[*Enter*] Chorus: Two households, both alike in dignity,
    In fair **Verona**, where we lay our scene,
    From ancient grudge break new **mutiny**,
    Where **civil** blood makes **civil** hands unclean.
    From forth the fatal **loins** of these two **foes**   5
    A pair of **star-crossed** lovers take their life;
    Whose misadventured **piteous overthrows**
    Doth with their death bury their parents' strife.
    The fearful passage of their death-marked love,
    And the continuance of their parents' rage,   10
    Which, but their children's end, **nought** could remove,
    Is now the two hours' **traffic** of our stage;
    The which if you with patient ears attend,
    What here shall miss, our **toil** shall strive to **mend**.
[*Exit*]

Figure 13 • Balcony scene from *Romeo and Juliet,* as portrayed in the film by director Franco Zeffirelli *(Everett Collection)*

Act II, Scene II

[*Romeo advances*]

ROMEO: He **jests** at scars that never felt a wound.

[*Enter Juliet above at her window*]

But soft, what light through yonder window breaks?
It is the east, and Juliet is the sun.
Arise, fair sun, and kill the envious moon,
Who is already sick and pale with grief   5
That thou, her maid, art far more fair than she.
Be not her maid, since she is **envious**;
Her **vestal livery** is but **sick and green**,
And none but fools do wear it; **cast it off**.
It is my lady, O, it is my love!   10
O that she knew she were!
She speaks, yet she says nothing; what of that?

Her eye **discourses**, I will answer it.
I am too bold, 'tis not to me she speaks.
Two of the fairest stars in all the heaven,   15
Having some business, [do] entreat her eyes
To twinkle in their spheres till they return.
What if her eyes were there, they in her head?
The brightness of her cheek would shame those stars,
As daylight doth a lamp; her [eyes] in heaven   20
Would through the airy region stream so bright
That birds would sing and think it were not night.
See how she leans her cheek upon her hand!
O that I were a glove upon that hand,
That I might touch that cheek!   25

JULIET: Ay me!

ROMEO: She speaks!
     O, speak again, bright angel, for thou art
     As glorious to this night, being o'er my head,
     As is a winged messenger of heaven
     Unto the white-upturned wond'ring eyes
     Of mortals that fall back to gaze on him,   30
     When he **bestrides** the lazy puffing clouds,
     And sails upon the bosom of the air.

JULIET: O Romeo, Romeo, wherefore art thou Romeo?
     Deny thy father and refuse thy name;
     Or, if thou wilt not, be but sworn by my love,   35
     And I'll no longer be a Capulet.

ROMEO [*Aside*]: Shall I hear more, or shall I speak at this?

JULIET: 'Tis but thy name that is my enemy;
     Thou art thyself, though not a Montague.
     What's Montague? It is nor hand nor foot,   40
     Nor arm nor face, [nor any other part]
     Belonging to a man. O, be some other name!
     What's in a name? That which we call a rose
     By any other word would smell as sweet;
     So Romeo would, were he not Romeo called,   45
     Retain that dear perfection which he owes
     Without that title. Romeo, **doff** thy name,
     And for thy name, which is no part of thee,
     Take all myself.

ROMEO: I take thee at thy word.   50

    Call me but love, and I'll be new baptized;
    Henceforth I never will be Romeo.

JULIET: What man art thou that thus **bescreened** in night
    So stumblest on my **counsel**?

ROMEO: By a name
    I know not how to tell thee who I am.   55
    My name, dear saint, is hateful to myself,
    Because it is an enemy to thee;
    Had I it written, I would tear the word.

JULIET: My ears have yet not drunk a hundred words
    Of thy tongue's uttering, yet I know the sound.   60
    Art thou not Romeo, and a Montague?

ROMEO: Neither, fair maid, if either thee dislike.

JULIET: How camest thou **hither**, tell me and wherefore?
    The orchard walls are high and hard to climb,
    And the place death, considering who thou art,   65
    If any of my kinsmen find thee here.

ROMEO: With love's light wings did I **o'erperch** these walls.
    For stony limits cannot hold love out.
    And what love can do, that dares love attempt;
    Therefore thy kinsmen are no stop to me.   70

JULIET: If they do see thee, they will **murther** thee.

ROMEO: Alack, there lies more peril in thine eye
    Than twenty of their swords! Look thou but sweet,
    And I am **proof** against their **enmity**.

JULIET: I would not for the world they saw thee here.   75

ROMEO: I have night's **cloak** to hide me from their eyes,
    And but thou love me, let them find me here;
    My life were better ended by their hate,
    Than death [put off], wanting of thy love.

JULIET: By whose direction foundest thou out this place?   80

ROMEO: By love, that first did prompt me to inquire;
    He lent me counsel, and I lent him eyes.
    I am no pilot, yet wert thou as far
    As that vast shore [washed] with the farthest sea,
    I should adventure for such merchandise.   85

JULIET: Thou knowest the mask of night is on my face,
    Else would a maiden **blush bepaint** my cheek
    For that which thou hast heard me speak to-night.

Fain would I dwell on form, fain, fain, deny
What I have spoke, but farewell **compliment**!   90
Dost thou love me? I know thou wilt say, "Ay,"
And I will take thy word; yet, if thou swearest,
Thou mayest prove false: at lovers' **perjuries**
They say **Jove** laughs. O gentle Romeo,
If thou dost love, pronounce it faithfully;   95
Or if thou thinkest I am too quickly won,
I'll frown and be perverse, and say thee **nay**,
So thou wilt woo, but else not for the world.
In truth, fair Montague, I am too fond,
And therefore thou mayest think my behavior light,   100
But trust me, gentleman, I'll prove more true
Than those that have [more] **coying** to be **strange**.
I should have been more strange, I must confess,
But that thou overheardst, ere I was ware,
My true-love passion; therefore pardon me,   105
And not **impute** this yielding to light love,
Which the dark night hath so discovered.

ROMEO: Lady, by yonder blessed moon I vow,
    That tips with silver all these fruit-tree tops—

JULIET: O, swear not by the moon, the inconstant moon,   110
    That monthly changes in her [circled] orb,
    Lest that thy love prove likewise variable.

ROMEO: What shall I swear by?

JULIET: Do not swear at all;
    Or if thy wilt, swear by thy gracious self,
    Which is the god of my **idolatry**,   115
    And I'll believe thee.

ROMEO: If my heart's dear love—

JULIET: Well, do not swear. Although I joy in thee,
    I have no joy of this contract to-night,
    It is too rash, too unadvised, too sudden,
    Too like the lightning, which doth cease to be   120
    Ere one can say it lightens. Sweet, good night!
    This bud of love, by summer's ripening breath,
    May prove a beauteous flower when next we meet.
    Good night, good night! as sweet repose and rest
    Come to thy heart as that within my breast!   125

ROMEO: O, wilt thou leave me so unsatisfied?

JULIET: What satisfaction canst thou have to-night?

ROMEO: The exchange of thy love's faithful vow for mine.

JULIET: I gave thee mine before thou didst request it;
  And yet I would it were to give again.   130

ROMEO: Wouldst thou withdraw it? for what purpose, love?

JULIET: But to be frank and give it thee again,
  And yet I wish for but the thing I have.
  My **bounty** is as boundless as the sea,
  My love as deep; the more I give to thee,   135
  The more I have, for both are infinite.

[*Nurse calls within*]

  I hear some noise within; dear love, adieu!
  Anon, good nurse! Sweet Montague, be true.
  Stay but a little, I will come again.

[*Exit above*]

ROMEO: O blessed, blessed night! I am afeard,   140
  Being in night, all this is but a dream,
  Too flattering-sweet to be substantial.

[*Enter Juliet above*]

JULIET: Three words, dear Romeo, and good night indeed.
  If that thy **bent of love** be honorable,
  Thy purpose marriage, send me word tomorrow,   145
  By one that I'll procure to come to thee,
  Where and what time thou wilt perform the rite,
  And all my fortunes at thy foot I'll lay,
  And follow thee my lord throughout the world.

NURSE [*Within*]: Madam!   150

JULIET: I come, anon. –But, if thou meanest not well,
  I do **beseech** thee—

NURSE [*Within*]: Madam!

JULIET: **By and by**, I come—
  To cease thy strife, and leave me to my grief.
  To-morrow will I send.

ROMEO: So **thrive** my soul—

JULIET: A thousand times good night! [*Exit above*]   155

ROMEO: A thousand times the worse, to want thy light.
  Love goes toward love as schoolboys from their books,
  But love from love, toward school with heavy looks.

[*Retiring*]

Vocabulary

PROLOGUE

civil *(adj.)*   relating to citizens; civilized
foe *(n.)*   enemy
***loins** *(n. pl.)*   reproductive organs
mend *(v.)*   to correct; to set right
***mutiny** *(n.)*   bitter conflict
***nought** (also **naught**) *(n.)*   nothing
***overthrow** *(n.)*   upset
piteous *(adj.)*   arousing pity or compassion
***star-crossed** *(adj.)*   not favored by the stars; ill-fated
toil *(n.)*   labor; effort
***traffic** *(n.)*   business; dealings
***Verona** *(n.)*   city in northeastern Italy

ACT II, SCENE II

***anon** *(adv.)*   presently; soon
***bent of love** *(n.)*   love's intent or resolve
***bepaint** *(v.)*   to color; to tinge
***bescreened** *(adj.)*   screened; covered
***beseech** *(v.)*   to beg for urgently or earnestly
***bestride** *(v.)*   to walk across
blush *(n.)*   reddening of the face
bounty *(n.)*   generosity
***by and by** *(adv.)*   before long; soon
cast [something] off *(v.)*   to remove [something]
***cloak** *(n.)*   loose outer garment
***compliment** *(n.)*   social courtesy
***counsel** *(n.)*   guarded thoughts
***coying** *(n.)*   cute or coquettish playfulness
***discourse** *(v.)*   to talk
***doff** *(v.)*   to remove; to put aside
enmity *(n.)*   hatred; hostility
envious *(adj.)*   feeling or showing envy (the desire to possess something
    belonging to another)
***fain** *(adv.)*   with pleasure
***hither** *(adv.)*   here
idolatry *(n.)*   excessive devotion to a person or thing
***impute** *(v.)*   to charge; to attribute
jest *(v.)*   to make fun of; to mock
***Jove (Jupiter)** *(prop. n.)*   chief Roman god

*Denotes low-frequency word.

*lest *(conj.)*   for fear
*livery *(n.)*   clothing; garb
*murther *(n.)*   old form of *murder*
*nay *(n.)*   no
*o'erperch *(v.)*   to go over and rest on, as on a bird's perch or roost
perjury *(n.)*   false swearing
*proof *(adj.)*   able to resist
*sick and green *(adj. phrase)*   suffering a kind of anemia thought in
    Shakespeare's time to be found in single girls
*strange *(adj.)*   distant; external
thrive *(v.)*   to be successful; to flourish
*vestal *(adj.)*   pure; virginal

Activities

1. Read the Prologue closely. What is its function? Make notes in your journal and discuss your ideas with your class.

2. If you have read *Antigone,* compare its Prologue to that of *Romeo and Juliet.*

3. Read the dialogue aloud, with the entire class reading the chorus, male students reading Romeo's lines, and female students reading Juliet's lines.

4. Romeo and Juliet decide to marry against their parents' wishes. Do you agree or disagree with their decision? Justify your answer.

5. Alone or with a partner, write a dialogue in modern English between a young man and woman who are in love but do not have their parents' approval to marry. Have your characters decide what they are going to do about their situation.

6. Write an essay arguing for or against young people's marrying against their parents' wishes.

7. If you have read "Bisclavret," write an essay on Romeo and Juliet as courtly lovers.

For Further Reading

Burgess, Anthony. *Shakespeare.* New York: Knopf, 1970.
Cahn, Victor L. *Shakespeare the Playwright.* New York: Greenwood, 1991.
Shakespeare, William. *The Riverside Shakespeare.* Ed. G. Blakemore Evans.
    Boston: Houghton, 1974.

Additional Reading

Sonnet 29

William Shakespeare
Oral Tradition and Poetry: Sonnet

> When, in disgrace with Fortune and men's eyes,
> I all alone beweep my outcast state,
> And trouble deaf heaven with my bootless cries,
> And look upon myself and curse my fate,
> Wishing me like to one more rich in hope,   5
> Featured like him, like him with friends possessed,
> Desiring this man's art and that man's scope,
> With what I most enjoy contented least;
> Yet in these thoughts myself almost despising
> Haply I think on thee, and then my state,   10
> Like to the lark at break of day arising
> From sullen earth, sings hymns at heaven's gate:
> For thy sweet love remember'd such wealth brings
> That then I scorn to change my state with kings.

Activities

1. What is the state of mind of the speaker at the beginning of the sonnet? In which lines do his feelings change? Why do they change?
2. Compare the poet's attitude toward love in Sonnet 29 with his attitude in *Romeo and Juliet.*
3. Write an essay on love in Shakespeare's tragedy *Romeo and Juliet* and in Sonnet 29.

For Further Reading

Rougemont, Denis de. *Love in the Western World.* New York: Harper, 1974.

CHAPTER **9**

Romantic Poetry

Johann Friedrich von Schiller (1759–1805) and William Wordsworth (1770–1850)
Oral Tradition and Poetry: Ode and Sonnet

Key Terms

Beethoven, Ludwig van
   (1770–1827)
Enlightenment
individualism
metonymy
pathetic fallacy

personification
rational
Romanticism
Symphony No. 9, opus 125
   (by Beethoven)
universal brotherhood

Pre-Reading Activities

1. How do you think an artist, especially a poet, might react to a period in which reason and scientific thinking prevail?
2. Listen to the last movement of Beethoven's Ninth Symphony. Record your thoughts and feelings as you listen.
3. How are poetry and music related?

Background: Schiller

During Schiller's lifetime, Germany was a center of great intellectual activity in many fields. Important German trends are reflected in

79

Schiller's life as well as in his philosophical and literary works. Together, they embodied and helped to define major preoccupations of European culture in the Romantic period, which reached from the end of the eighteenth through much of the nineteenth century.

Living in a period of violent political upheaval that resulted in the overthrow of absolute monarchies, Schiller was concerned with supranational issues such as universal brotherhood, freedom, and humane government. He is best known as the author of dramatic tragedies such as *Mary Stuart* and *Don Carlos* (1787). Much of Schiller's literary work became the basis for musical interpretations, including operas. His poem "Ode to Joy" was set to music by Beethoven in his Ninth Symphony in 1824.

From "Ode to Joy"
Johann Friedrich von Schiller

Joy, thou source of heaven-sent light,
Daughter of **Elysium**.
Touched with fire, to the site
Of thy shining shrine we come.
What Custom's strength divides from others   5
Thy pure magic union brings;
Men throughout the world are brothers
In safety of thy wings.

Millions, turn and come together!
Share this universal kiss!   10
Brothers—over a heavenly **bliss**
Must reign our all-loving Father.

He who for achievement may long,
Of strong friendship may be sure,
He who has a wife to treasure,   15
Let him join our mighty song.
Yes—If exists a single being
Who on earth calls one heart his own,
And denies it—then, unseeing,
Let him go and weep alone.   20

Joy is drunk by all the creatures
From the Earth's abundant breast;
All things good and bad are Nature's,

And with blameless joy are blessed.
    Joy to us gives love and wine,   25
Friendship that will last 'til death;
    The lowly worm feels life divine,
As the angel near God's breast.

    Glad, as when the suns run glorious
Through the Heaven's dazzling skies,   30
Brothers, run with shining eyes
    Heroes, happy and victorious.

    Millions, turn and come together!
Share this universal kiss!
Brothers, over a heavenly bliss   35
    Must reign our all-loving Father.

    Do the millions, His creation,
Know Him and His works of love?
Find Him in the heights above.
    Brothers! Brothers!   40
    In the heights above
Is His starry **habitation**!

    Joy, O daughter of Elysium,
Thy pure magic union brings;
What Custom's strength divides from others   45
    Men throughout the world are brothers
In the safety of thy wings.
Joy, thou source of heaven-sent light,
Daughter of Elysium.

Vocabulary

bliss *(n.)*   spiritual joy
*Elysium *(n.)*   in Greek mythology, the place of ideal happiness; paradise
habitation *(n.)*   home

Background: Wordsworth

    Outstanding among the great English Romantic poets, Wordsworth is well known for his poetic collections *Lyrical Ballads* and *The Prelude*,

---

*Denotes low-frequency word.

which he continued reworking until his death. Like most of his poems, the ballads are autobiographical. With deeply personal detail, Wordsworth records in recollection his travels in England and on the European continent in the company of his sister Dorothy; together they encounter the wonders and permanence of nature and contemplate the brief, hard lives of human beings.

Wordsworth sympathized with the struggle for the common man to be free, and, at the beginning of the French Revolution in 1789, looked with favor on the overthrow of the monarchy. After the violence of the French mob got out of hand, however, he became more conservative. Still, these poems represent his enthusiasm for freedom and brotherhood as well as his love of nature. The years given for each poem are dates of publication. The date on the left is the first year the poem was published, and the date on the right is the year this version was published. The first poem is a sonnet.

"To Toussaint L'Ouverture"
William Wordsworth

Toussaint, the most unhappy man of men!
Whether the whistling Rustic tend his plough
Within thy hearing, or thy head be now

Figure 14 • *Summer Afternoon, Arundel Castle,* **by the Romantic painter George Cole (British, 1810–83)** *(©Sotheby Parke-Bernet)*

Pillowed in some deep **dungeon's earless den**:—
O miserable **Chieftain**! where and when   5
Wilt thou find patience? Yet die not; do thou
Wear rather in thy bonds a cheerful brow:
Though fallen thyself, never to rise again,
Live, and take comfort. Thou hast left behind
Powers that will work for thee; air, earth, and skies;   10
There's not a breathing of the common wind
That will forget thee; thou hast great allies;
Thy friends are exultations, agonies,
And love, and man's unconquerable mind.   14

1802   1803

"My Heart Leaps Up When I Behold"
William Wordsworth

My heart leaps up when I behold
    A rainbow in the sky;
So was it when my life began;
So is it now I am a man;
So be it when I shall grow old,   5
    Or let me die!
The child is father of the Man;
And I could wish my days to be
Bound each to each by natural **piety**.

1802   1807

"The World Is Too Much with Us; Late and Soon"
William Wordsworth

The world is too much with us; late and soon,
Getting and spending, we lay waste our powers:
Little we see in Nature that is ours;
We have given our hearts away, a **sordid boon**!
This Sea that bares her bosom to the moon;   5
The winds that will be howling at all hours,
And are up-gathered now like sleeping flowers;
For this, for everything, we are out of tune;

It moves us not.—Great God! I'd rather be
A **Pagan suckled** in a **creed** outworn;   10
So might I, standing on this pleasant **lea**,
Have glimpses that would make me less forlorn;
Have sight of **Proteus** rising from the sea;
Or hear old **Triton** blow his **wreathed** horn.

1802–1804   1807

Vocabulary

"To Toussaint L'Ouverture"

*chieftain *(n.)*   leader of a group, usually a clan or tribe
den *(n.)*   cave
dungeon *(n.)*   prison
*earless *(adj.)*   without ears; here, a metonym to indicate that no
human being is present to hear
L'Ouverture, Toussaint (1743–1803) *(prop. n.)*   Haitian general,
liberator, and governor of Haiti from 1801 to 1802

"My Heart Leaps Up When I Behold"

piety *(n.)*   devotion and reverence

"The World Is Too Much with Us; Late and Soon"

*boon *(n.)*   favor or blessing given to someone
creed *(n.)*   formal statement of religious belief
*lea *(n.)*   grassland; meadow
pagan *(n.)*   any non-Christian
*Proteus *(prop. n.)*   in Greek mythology, a sea god who could
change his shape
sordid *(adj.)*   dirty; morally degraded
suckled *(adj.)*   nursed or brought up, as a child
*Triton *(prop. n.)*   in Greek mythology, a sea god having a man's head
and a fish's tail
wreathed *(adj.)*   in a circle or spiral, like a conch shell

Activities

1. Read each poem aloud. What feelings are being conveyed by the poet?
    What images does he use to accomplish this? What is the rhyme
    scheme of the poem?

*Denotes low-frequency word.

2. A common theme of the Romantic poets is freedom. Select one poem, read it carefully, and note in your journal the images used by the poet to express his feelings and thoughts about freedom.

3. Write an essay on nature or brotherhood in the poetry of Schiller and Wordsworth. If you cite lines from the poetry, use quotation marks (". . .") around the quoted material and give the line number in parentheses. For example:

    Wordsworth believes that Toussaint L'Ouverture does not suffer alone, for he is accompanied by "exultations, agonies, / And love. . ." (13–14).

4. Write an essay comparing Romantic poetry and music.

For Future Reading

Johnson, Paul. *The Birth of the Modern: World Society 1815–1830*. New York: Harper, 1991.

Mahoney, John L. *The English Romantics: Major Poetry and Critical Theory.* Lexington, MA: Heath, 1978.

Ungar, Frederick. *Friedrich Schiller: An Anthology for Our Time*. New York: Ungar, 1959.

10

"Ain't I a Woman?"

Sojourner Truth (ca. 1797–1883)
Nonfiction: Autobiographical Essay

Background

An African-American born into slavery in New York State as
Isabella Van Wagener, Sojourner Truth fled to freedom in 1827 and renamed herself after experiencing religious visions. In 1850, she began her
courageous tours of the United States, speaking out for the abolition of
slavery. An eloquent speaker, Sojourner Truth drew large crowds.
Although she was illiterate most of her life, she dictated her autobiography, *The Narrative of Sojourner Truth* (1850), sales of which helped to earn
her living. She later supported an independent state for freed slaves and
joined the women's suffrage movement; spirituality continued to be one of
her major concerns.

"Ain't I a Woman?" is the title given to a speech made by
Sojourner Truth at the second annual Women's Rights Convention, which
was held in Akron, Ohio, in 1852, when she was over 50 years old. Men
and women gathered at this convention to discuss whether women should
have the same political and social rights as men. After formal speeches,
anyone who wished to get up and speak could do so. Most of the speakers
were men, because during the nineteenth century it was considered im-
proper for a woman to speak in public.

On the second day of the convention, several clergymen spoke
against women's rights. All of them gave reasons why the status of women
should be lower than that of men. For example, one minister said that
women deserved lower status than men because of the sin committed by
Eve in the Garden of Eden. After these men had spoken, Sojourner Truth

rose and moved to the front of the room. "Ain't I a Woman?" is her reply to their speeches.

Pre-Reading Activities

1. With your study group or class, discuss the meaning of democracy. Should all citizens be treated alike?
2. With your study group or class, discuss the ways in which human rights can be extended to include groups that did not have them before.

Key Terms

abolition	feminist movement
African-American	Liberia
American Civil War (1861–1865)	Underground Railroad
emancipation	women's suffrage movement

"Ain't I a Woman?"
Sojourner Truth

Well, children, where there is so much **racket** there must   1
be something out of **kilter**. I think that **'twixt** the negroes of the South and the women at the North, all talking about rights, the white men will be in a **fix** pretty soon. But what's all this here talking about?

That man over there says that women need to be helped into   2
carriages, and lifted over **ditches**, and to have the best place everywhere. Nobody ever helps me into carriages, or over mud-puddles, or gives me any best place! And **ain't** I a woman? Look at me! Look at my arm! I have **plowed** and planted, and gathered into barns, and no man could **head** me! And ain't I a woman? I could work as much and eat as much as a man—when I could get it—and **bear** the **lash** as well! And ain't I a woman? I have **borne** thirteen children, and seen them most all sold off to slavery, and when I cried out with my mother's grief, none but Jesus heard me! And ain't I a woman?

Figure 15   •   Sojourner Truth (d. 1883) *(Sophia Smith Collection, Smith College)*

Then they talk about this thing in the head; what's this they   3
call it? [Intellect, someone whispers.] That's it, honey. What's that
got to do with women's rights or negroes' rights? If my cup won't
hold but a pint, and yours holds a quart, wouldn't you be **mean** not
to let me have my little half-measure full?

Then that little man in black there, he says women can't have   4
as much rights as men, 'cause Christ wasn't a woman! Where did
your Christ come from? Where did your Christ come from? From
God and a woman! Man had nothing to do with Him.

If the first woman God ever made was strong enough to turn   5
the world upside down all alone, these women together ought to be
able to turn it back, and get it right side up again! And now they is
asking to do it, the men better let them.

Obliged to you for hearing me, and now old Sojourner ain't   6
got nothing more to say.

Vocabulary

ain't *(v.)*   aren't (nonstandard English)
bear (bore, borne) *(v.)*   to give birth to; to endure
ditch *(n.)*   long, narrow trench dug in the earth, usually for drainage
fix *(n.)*   difficult position
head *(v.)*   to be ahead of; to surpass
***kilter** *(n.)*   order
lash *(n.)*   whip
mean *(adj.)*   characterized by petty selfishness or malice
obliged to you *(v. phrase)*   a way to say "thank you"
plow *(v.)*   to work with a plow (an agricultural tool used to prepare the
    earth for planting)
racket *(n.)*   confused, clattering noise; clamor
***'twixt** *(prep.)*   between

Activities

1. Read the text closely. Who do you think is the speaker's audience?
    What parts of Sojourner Truth's speech give it an informal tone? What
    aspects make it formal?

2. What are the two arguments Sojourner Truth is making? How does
    she relate the two? How does she organize her thoughts to persuade
    her audience?

3. Notice that Sojourner Truth makes many references to religion in her
    speech. Why do you think she does this? Is it effective?

4. Write a summary of Sojourner Truth's argument for giving women the
    right to vote.

5. Write an essay to persuade an audience that a group of people who do
    not have a right to do something should be allowed to have that right.
    Before writing your essay, be sure to have a clear idea of who your au-
    dience is. This should help you to plan which facts and what tone you
    will use to convince your audience.

For Further Reading

Gilbert, Sandra M., and Susan Gubar, eds. *No Man's Land: The Place of the
    Woman Writer in the Twentieth Century*. Vol. 2: *Sexchanges*. New Haven:
    Yale UP, 1989.

*Denotes low-frequency word.

_____. *The Norton Anthology of Literature by Women: The Tradition in English.* New York: Norton, 1985.

Krass, Peter. *Sojourner Truth.* New York: Chelsea House, 1988.

Loewenberg, Bert James, and Ruth Bogin, eds. *Black Women in Nineteenth-Century American Life.* University Park: Pennsylvania State UP, 1976.

Rogers, Katherine, ed. *Early American Women Writers: From Anne Bradstreet to Louisa May Alcott, 1650–1865.* New York: Meridian, 1991.

11

From *Oliver Twist*

Charles Dickens (1812–1870)
Fiction: Novel

Background

The year of Charles Dickens's birth saw his native England en-gaged in war against Napoleon and against the United States. The cost of these wars was high, not only in human lives but in increased taxes that made life even more difficult for the starving poor. In 1824, Dickens's fa-ther went to debtors prison, forcing Charles to leave school and go to work in a factory. Thus, he experienced firsthand the sufferings of the poor. After his father's release from prison, he returned to school. But these events had greatly shocked him, and they influenced his writing and haunted him until his death.

As a young man, Dickens became a journalist who contributed well-received stories and essays to magazines and newspapers. Thereafter he began to write serial installments of what would become three of his major novels: *The Pickwick Papers, Oliver Twist,* and *Nicholas Nickleby.* Other well-known works by Dickens are *David Copperfield* (an autobiographical work), *A Christmas Carol, A Tale of Two Cities, Great Expectations,* and *Hard Times.* The realistic details of these works helped the cause of social reform in England. Even today, Dickens is regarded as one of the greatest English novelists.

Written in 1838, *Oliver Twist* was the second Dickens novel pub-lished in installments—that is, one small portion at a time. It is the story of an illegitimate orphan boy born in a workhouse and the trials this poor child suffers in nineteenth-century England. For many of the novel's real-istic and detailed descriptions of the period, Dickens drew on events from his own childhood. The novel was relevant to the times as a statement against the New Poor Law, passed three years earlier, which was tearing apart the family life of the poor.

Pre-Reading Activities

1. Discuss with your group what you think might happen to poor children whose parents have died.
2. What happens to the poor in an industrialized nation?

Key Terms

autobiographical	picaresque
"Boz"	New Poor Law
debtors prison	Realism
Industrial Revolution	Victorian England
irony	workhouse
novel	

From *Oliver Twist*
Charles Dickens

Although I am not disposed to maintain that the being born   1
in a workhouse is in itself the most fortunate and enviable circumstance that can possibly **befall** a human being, I do mean to say that in this particular instance it was the very best thing for Oliver Twist that could by possibility have occurred. The fact is, that there was considerable difficulty in inducing Oliver to take upon himself the **office of respiration**,—a troublesome practice, but one which custom has **rendered** necessary to our easy existence,—and for some time he lay gasping on a little flock mattress, rather unequally poised between this world and the next, the balance being decidedly in favour of the latter.

Now, if during this brief period, Oliver had been surrounded   2
by careful grandmothers, anxious aunts, experienced nurses, and doctors of **profound** wisdom, he would most inevitably and **indubitably** have been killed in no time. There being nobody by, however, but a **pauper** old woman, who was rendered rather misty by an **unwonted** allowance of beer, and a parish surgeon who did such

matters by contract, Oliver and Nature fought out the point between them.

The result was, that, after a few struggles, Oliver breathed, sneezed, and proceeded to advertise to the inmates of the workhouse the fact of a new burden having been imposed upon the **parish**, by setting up as loud a cry as could reasonably have been expected from a male infant who had not been possessed of that very useful **appendage**, a voice, for a much longer space of time than three minutes and a quarter.

As Oliver gave this first proof of the free and proper action of his lungs, the patchwork coverlet which was carelessly flung over the iron bedstead, rustled; the pale face of a young female was raised feebly from the pillow; and a faint voice imperfectly **articulated** the words, 'Let me see the child, and die.'

. . . The surgeon deposited it in her arms. She **imprinted** her cold white lips passionately on its forehead, passed her hands over her face, gazed wildly round, **shuddered**, fell back—and died. They **chafed** her breast, hands, and temples; but the blood had frozen for ever. They talked of hope and comfort. They had been strangers too long.

"It's all over, Mrs. Thingummy," said the surgeon at last.

"Ah, poor dear, so it is!" said the nurse, picking up the cork of a green bottle of drink which had fallen out on the pillow as she stooped to take up the child. "Poor dear!"

"You needn't **mind** sending up to me, if the child cries, nurse," said the surgeon, putting on his gloves with great deliberation. "It's very likely it *will* be troublesome. Give it a little **gruel** if it is." He put on his hat, and, pausing by the bedside on his way to the door, added, "She was a good-looking girl, too; where did she come from?"

"She was brought here last night," replied the old woman, "by the **overseer's** order. She was found lying in the street;—she had walked some distance, for her shoes were worn to pieces; but where she came from, or where she was going to, nobody knows."

The surgeon leant over the body, and raised the left hand. "The old story," he said, shaking his head: "no wedding-ring, I see. Ah! Good night!"

The medical gentleman walked away to dinner; and the nurse, having once more applied herself to the green bottle, sat down on a low chair before the fire, and proceeded to dress the infant.

What an excellent example of the power of dress young Oliver Twist was! Wrapped in the blanket which had **hitherto** formed his only covering, he might have been the child of a nobleman or a beggar;—it would have been hard for the **haughtiest** stranger to have fixed his **station** in society. But now that he was enveloped in the old calico robes, which had grown yellow in the same service, he was badged and ticketed, and fell into his place at once—a parish child—the orphan of a workhouse—the humble half-starved **drudge**—to be **cuffed** and **buffeted** through the world,—despised by all, and pitied by none.

Oliver cried **lustily**. If he could have known that he was an orphan, left to the tender mercies of **churchwardens** and overseers, perhaps he would have cried the louder.   13

For the next eight or ten months, Oliver was the victim of a systematic course of treachery and deception—he was brought up by hand. The hungry and **destitute** situation of the infant orphan was **duly** reported by the workhouse authorities to the parish authorities. The parish authorities inquired with dignity of the workhouse authorities, whether there was no female then **domiciled** in "the house" who was in a situation to **impart** to Oliver Twist the consolation and nourishment of which he stood in need.   14

The workhouse authorities replied with humility that there was not. Upon this, the parish authorities **magnanimously** and humanely resolved, that Oliver should be "farmed," or, in other words, that he should be dispatched to a branch-workhouse some three miles off, where twenty or thirty other juvenile offenders against the poor-laws rolled about the floor all day, without the inconvenience of too much food or too much clothing, under the parental superintendence of an elderly female who received the **culprits** at and for the consideration of a sevenpence-halfpenny per small head per week. Sevenpence-halfpenny's worth per week is a good round diet for a child; a great deal may be got for sevenpence-halfpenny—quite enough to overload its stomach, and make it uncomfortable.   15

The elderly female was a woman of wisdom and experience; she knew what was good for children, and she had a very accurate perception of what was good for herself. So, she **appropriated** the greater part of the weekly **stipend** to her own use, and **consigned** the rising **parochial** generation to even a shorter allowance than was originally provided for them; thereby finding in the lowest depth a deeper still, and proving herself a very great experimental philosopher.   16

Everybody knows the story of another experimental philosopher, who had a great theory about a horse being able to live without eating, and who demonstrated it so well, that he got his own horse down to a straw a day, and would have unquestionably have rendered him a very spirited and **rampacious** animal on nothing at all,   17 if he had not died, just four-and-twenty hours before he was to have had his first comfortable **bait** of air.

Unfortunately for the experimental philosophy of the female to whose protecting care Oliver Twist was delivered over, a similar result usually attended the operation of *her* system; for at the very moment when a child had **contrived** to exist upon the smallest possible portion of the weakest possible food, it did **perversely** happen in eight and a half cases out of ten, either that it sickened from **want** and cold, or fell into the fire from neglect, or got half **smothered** by accident; in any one of which cases, the miserable little being was usually summoned into another world, and there gathered to the fathers it had never known in this.   18

Vocabulary

appendage *(n.)*   subordinate part
appropriate *(v.)*   to take without authority or right
articulate *(v.)*   to utter; to speak
*bait *(n.)*   snack, taste
befall *(v.)*   to happen to, especially as if by fate
*buffet *(v.)*   to drive or move, as if by repeated blows
*chafe *(v.)*   to warm by rubbing
*churchwarden *(n.)*   church officer responsible for money or goods given to help the poor, and for church property
consign *(v.)*   to transfer; to deliver
contrive *(v.)*   to manage
*cuff *(v.)*   to strike with the palm of the hand
culprit *(n.)*   one guilty of a crime or fault
destitute *(adj.)*   lacking necessities of life; very poor
*domiciled *(adj.)*   provided with a home
*drudge *(n.)*   one who is obliged to do unpleasant work
duly *(adv.)*   properly
*gruel *(n.)*   thin porridge (a soft food made from grains or legumes)
haughtiest *(adj.)*   most scornfully proud
*hitherto *(adv.)*   up to this time
impart *(v.)*   to give or grant, as from a supply
imprint *(v.)*   to mark by pressure
indubitably *(adv.)*   unquestionably
lustily *(adv.)*   vigorously; heartily
magnanimously *(adv.)*   nobly and generously
mind *(v.)*   to be concerned about; to care

*Denotes low-frequency word.

*office of respiration *(n.)*   breathing
*overseer *(n.)*   supervisor
parish *(n.)*   area committed to one pastor (a Christian religious leader)
parochial *(adj.)*   of or relating to a parish
*pauper *(adj.)*   very poor
perversely *(adv.)*   contrarily
profound *(adj.)*   deep
*rampacious *(adj.)*   not easily controlled
render *(v.)*   to cause to become; to make
shudder *(v.)*   to shake or tremble suddenly and violently
smothered *(adj.)*   overcome or killed from lack of air
station *(n.)*   place; position
stipend *(n.)*   fixed sum of money paid periodically for services or expenses
*unwonted *(adj.)*   unusual; unaccustomed
*want *(n.)*   extreme poverty

Activities

1. How do we know from the first moment that Oliver Twist's life will be difficult?
2. Look closely at the text. Select one or two passages where Dickens uses strong irony—that is, where he says the direct opposite of what he means. What does he *really* mean in the passage?
3. What are the attitudes of the adults in charge of Oliver Twist's care? What tone does Dickens use to describe them?
4. With your study group or class, discuss what you think might happen to Oliver Twist as he grows up. Justify your views.
5. In *Oliver Twist*, Dickens shows negative effects of the Industrial Revolution in England. Write an essay discussing both the positive and the negative sides of industrialization.
6. Based on your notes and class discussion, write an essay on Dickens's use of irony to criticize his contemporary society.

For Further Reading

Ackroyd, Peter. *Dickens.* New York: Harper, 1990.
_____. *An Introduction to Dickens.* New York: Ballantine, 1991.
Mankowitz, Wolf. *Dickens of London.* New York: Macmillan, 1976.

---

*Denotes low-frequency word.

12

From *The Turn of the Screw*

Henry James (1843–1916)
Fiction: Novella

Background

Born into a distinguished family of writers from New York, Henry James grew up in close contact with European culture. He attended Harvard University, following his brother William, who later became a famous psychologist. After graduation, James began his career writing literary, theater, and art reviews and essays for monthly magazines. By 1875, he had moved permanently to England. In 1915, distressed by the slowness of the United States to enter World War I, James decided to become a British citizen. A master of the art of fiction, he was a radical experimenter who contributed to shaping the modern novel. His best-known novels are *The Portrait of a Lady* and *Daisy Miller*.

The Turn of the Screw shows a clear Romantic influence. It resembles the nineteenth-century literary form of the Gothic tale, a story combining realism and the supernatural. Such stories contain dark castles, the appearance of supernatural beings such as ghosts, and horrible and frightening events. A struggle between good and evil forces is a common Gothic theme, with one character representing the good and another figure, a double, symbolizing evil. Freudian critics see this threatening evil as disguised urges from a primitive, uncontrolled ego and generally trace these urges to the nineteenth-century repression of sexual feelings.

The main framed story of *The Turn of the Screw* is told by the governess, and we do not know whether or not she is a reliable narrator.

Therefore, the reader cannot judge what is real and what is imaginary. The ambiguity of the text suggests that the psychological state of the young Romantic protagonist may have an influence on her perceptions. Only if the reader considers what may be the governess's subconscious motives can he or she appreciate all the possible meanings of the story.

Pre-Reading Activities

1. What is the supernatural? Why do you think stories about the supernatural are popular?
2. What kind of setting or atmosphere would make for a good "ghost story"?

Key Terms

ambiguous meaning	good versus evil
consciousness	Gothic tale
double	indirect narration
framed story	literary conventions
Freud, Sigmund (1856–1939)	subconscious

From *The Turn of the Screw*
Henry James

The story had held us, round the fire, sufficiently breathless, but except the obvious remark that it was **gruesome**, as on Christmas Eve in an old house a strange tale should essentially be, I remember no comment **uttered** till somebody happened to note it as the only case he had met in which . . . a [ghost's] visitation had fallen on a child.   1

The case, I may mention, was that of an **apparition** in just such an old house as had gathered us for the occasion—an appearance, of a dreadful kind, to a little boy sleeping in the room with his mother and waking her up in the terror of it; waking her not to **dissipate** his dread and soothe him to sleep again, but to **encounter** also herself . . . the same sight that had shocked him.   2

It was this observation that drew from Douglas—not immediately, but later in the evening—a reply that had the interesting con-   3

Figure 16 • European Gothic castle

sequence to which I call attention. Some one else told a story not particularly effective, which I saw he was not following. This I took for a sign that he had himself something to produce and that we should only have to wait. We waited in fact till two nights later; but that same evening, before we **scattered**, he brought out what was in his mind.

"I quite agree—in regard to [that] ghost, or whatever it was   4
—that its appearing first to the little boy, at so **tender** an age, adds
a particular touch. But it's not the first occurrence of its charming kind that I know to have been concerned with a child. If the
child gives the effect another turn of the **screw**, what do you say to
two children—?"

"We say of course," somebody exclaimed, "that two children   5
give two turns! Also that we want to hear about them."

I can see Douglas there before the fire, to which he had got up   6
to present his back, looking down at this **converser** with his hands
in his pockets. "Nobody but me, till now, has ever heard. It's quite
too horrible." This was naturally declared by several voices to give
the thing the **utmost** price, and our friend, with quiet art, prepared
his triumph by turning his eyes over the rest of us and going on: "It's
beyond everything. Nothing at all that I know touches it."

"For sheer terror?" I remember asking.   7

He seemed to say it wasn't so simple as that; to be really at a   8
loss how to qualify it. He passed his hand over his eyes, made a little
wincing grimace. "For dreadful—dreadfulness!"

"Oh how delicious!" cried one of the women.   9

He took no notice of her; he looked at me, but as if, instead of   10
me, he saw what he spoke of. "For general **uncanny** ugliness and
horror and pain."

"Well, then," I said, "just sit right down and begin."   11

. . . Then as he faced us again: "I can't begin. I shall have to   12
send to town. . . . The story's written. It's in a locked drawer—it
has not been out for years. . . ."

"Your manuscript—?"   13

"Is in old faded ink and in the most beautiful **hand**." He **hung**   14
fire again. "A woman's. She has been dead these twenty years. She
sent me the pages in question before she died." They were all listening now. . . .

Let me say here distinctly, to **have done with** it, that this   15
narrative, from an exact transcript of my own made much later, is
what I shall presently give. Poor Douglas, before his death—when
it was in sight—**committed** to me the manuscript that reached him
. . . and with immense effort, he began to read to our **hushed** little
circle on the night of the fourth.

The departing ladies who had said they would stay didn't, of   16
course, thank heaven, stay: they departed, in consequence of arrange-
ments made, in a rage of curiosity . . . produced by the touches
with which he had already worked us up. But that only made his

little final **auditory** more compact and select, kept it, round the **hearth**, subject to a common thrill.

        . . . [H]is old friend, the youngest of several daughters of a   17
poor country **parson**, had at the age of twenty . . . come up to London, in **trepidation**, to answer an advertisement. . . . [T]he advertiser . . . proved . . . a gentleman, a bachelor in the **prime** of life, such a figure as had never risen, save in a dream or an old novel, before a **fluttered** anxious girl. . . . One could easily have fixed his type; it never, happily, dies out. He was handsome and bold and pleasant, off-hand and gay and kind. He struck her, **inevitably**, as gallant and splendid . . . rich . . . in a glow of high fashion, of good looks, of expensive habits, of charming ways with women. He had for his town residence a big house filled with the **spoils** of trav-els and trophies of the **chase**; but it was to his country home, an old family place in Essex, that he wished her immediately to proceed.

        He had been left . . . **guardian** to a small nephew [named   18
Miles] and a small niece [named Flora] . . . [whom he had] . . . sent . . . down to his other house, the proper place for them being the country. . . .

        There had been for the two children at first a young lady   19
whom they had had the misfortune to lose. She **had done for** them quite beautifully—she was a most respectable person—till her death. . . .

        So far had Douglas presented his picture when some one put a   20
question. "And what did the former governess die of? Of so much respectability?"

        Our friend's answer was prompt. "That will come out. I don't   21
anticipate."

        "Pardon me—I thought that was just what you *are* doing."   22

    ."You shall hear tomorrow what she learnt. Meanwhile of   23
course the prospect struck her as slightly **grim**. She was young, un-tried, nervous: it was a vision of serious duties and little company, of really great loneliness. . . . But the salary offered much exceeded her modest measure, and on a second interview, she **faced the mu-sic**, she **engaged**. . . . [H]is main condition was that she should never trouble him—but never, never: neither appeal nor complain nor write about anything . . . let him alone. She promised to do this, and she mentioned to me that when, for a moment, **disbur-dened**, delighted, he held her hand, thanking her for the sacrifice, she already felt rewarded."

        "But was that all her reward?" one of the ladies asked.   24
        "She never saw him again."   25

. . . Douglas had begun to read with a fine clearness that was   26
like a **rendering** to the ear of the beauty of his author's hand. . . .

[from the governess's tale]

[Some time after I arrived at the country house, Bly, I spent   27
the day with little Flora and arranged for her to show me the place.]
Young as she was I was struck, throughout our little tour, with her
confidence and courage, with the way, in empty chambers and dull
corridors, on crooked staircases that made me pause and even on the
summit of an old . . . square tower that made me dizzy, her morning music, her disposition to tell me so many more things than she
asked, rang out and led me on. I have not seen Bly since the day I
left it, and I dare say that to my present older and more informed
eyes, it would show a very reduced importance.

But as my little conductress, with her hair of gold and her   28
frock of blue, danced before me round the corners and pattered
down passages, I had the view of a castle of romance inhabited by a
rosy **sprite**, such a place as would somehow, for the diversion of the
young idea, take all color out of story-books and fairy-tales. Wasn't it
just a story-book over which I had fallen [asleep] and a-dream? No;
it was a big ugly antique but convenient house, embodying a few features of a building still older, half-displaced and half-used, in which I
had the fancy of our being almost as lost as a handful of passengers in
a great drifting ship. Well, I was strangely at the helm!

. . . One afternoon, . . . the children were tucked away and   29
I had come out for my stroll. One of the thoughts that, as I don't in
the least shrink now from noting, used to be with me in these
wanderings was that it would be as charming as a charming story
suddenly to meet someone. Some one would appear there at the
turn of a path and would stand before me and smile and approve. I
didn't ask more than that—I only asked that he should *know*; and
the only way to be sure he knew would be to see it, and the kind
light of it, in his handsome face. . . . What arrested me on the
spot—and with a shock much greater than any vision had allowed
for—was the sense that my imagination had, in a flash, turned real.
He did stand there!—but high up, beyond the lawn and at the very
top of the tower to which, on that first morning, little Flora had conducted me. . . .

It produced in me, this figure, in the clear twilight, I remem-   30
ber, two distinct gasps of emotion, which were, sharply, the shock of
my first and that of my second surprise. My second was a violent per-

ception of the mistake of my first: the man who met my eyes was not the man I expected, but . . . an unknown man.

The place, moreover, in the strangest way in the world, had on   31
the instant and by the very fact of its appearance become a solitude . . . . It was as if, while I took in what I did take in, all the rest of the scene had been stricken with death. I can hear again, as I write, the intense hush in which the sounds of evening dropped. The **rooks** stopped cawing in the golden sky and the friendly hour lost for the unspeakable minute all its voice. But there was no other change in nature, unless indeed it were a change that I saw with a stranger sharpness. The gold was still in the sky, the clearness in the air, and the man who looked at me over the battlements was as definite as a picture in a frame. That's how I thought, with extraordinary quickness, of each person he might have been and that he wasn't.

He was in one of the angles, the one away from the house,   32
very erect, as it struck me, and with both hands on the ledge. So I saw him as I see the letters I form on this page; then, exactly, after a minute . . . he slowly changed his place—passed, looking at me hard all the while, to the opposite corner of the platform. Yes, it was intense to me that during this transit he never took his eyes from me, and I can see at this moment the way his hand, as he went, moved from one of the **crenellations** to the next. He stopped at the other corner, but less long, and even as he turned away still markedly fixed me. He turned away; that was all I knew.

Vocabulary

anticipate *(v.)*   to speak or write in knowledge or expectation of something to come
apparition *(n.)*   ghostly figure
***auditory** *(n.)*   audience
chase *(n.)*   hunt
commit *(v.)*   to give in charge or trust; to entrust
***converser** *(n.)*   one who is talking or carrying on a conversation
***crenellation** *(n.)*   upthrust portion of a battlement (a wall used for defense on top of a castle, fort, or tower)
***disburdened** *(adj.)*   unburdened; unworried
dissipate *(v.)*   to dispel
***do [for]** *(v.)*   to care [for]

*Denotes low-frequency word.

encounter *(v.)*   to meet
*engage *(v.)*   to agree to employment
face the music *(v. phrase)*   to meet an unpleasant situation directly
*fluttered *(adj.)*   agitated; disturbed
grim *(adj.)*   frightful; sinister
grimace *(n.)*   facial expression usually of disgust or disapproval
gruesome *(adj.)*   inspiring horror or repulsion
guardian *(n.)*   person legally placed in charge of the affairs of a minor
*hand *(n.)*   handwriting
hang fire *(v.)*   to hesitate
*have done with [it] *(v. phrase)*   to bring [something] to an end
hearth *(n.)*   area in front of a fireplace
hushed *(adj.)*   quiet
inevitably *(adv.)*   inescapably; unavoidably
*parson *(n.)*   clergyman or minister in charge of a parish
prime *(n.)*   most active, thriving, or successful period
*rendering *(n.)*   imparting; giving
*rook *(n.)*   large, crowlike bird
scatter *(v.)*   to go in various directions; to disperse
screw *(n.)*   spirally grooved pin used to fasten parts of something
   together; also, instrument of torture applied to the thumbs of a
   prisoner. Both meanings are intended here.
spoils *(n., usually pl.)*   goods or objects resulting from a special effort
*sprite *(n.)*   small supernatural being
tender *(adj.)*   young
trepidation *(n.)*   apprehension
uncanny *(adj.)*   strange; weird
utmost *(adj.)*   highest; greatest
uttered *(adj.)*   spoken
wincing *(adj.)*   flinching; shrinking back

Activities

1. Reread the story closely, noting in your journal the setting and atmo-
    sphere that James creates. What specific vocabulary does he use to cre-
    ate these? Discuss your ideas with your group.
2. Who is James's audience for the story within the story? How does
    James secure their attention?
3. What is the governess like? What images show her state of mind?
    Why might a Freudian psychologist doubt the governess's story?
4. Discuss what you think is the meaning of the title of the story.

*Denotes low-frequency word.

5. Write an essay summarizing the important qualities of a good ghost story.

6. A complex structure is typical of many modern stories and novels. Look closely at how James has assembled *The Turn of the Screw*. Who is telling the story? Make notes in your journal and discuss your findings with your group.

7. Based on your notes and your discussion, write an essay on the complex structure of *The Turn of the Screw*.

8. Using your imagination, write an ending to *The Turn of the Screw*. Be sure to use the characters introduced by James. (Note that the governess has no name.)

For Further Reading

Edel, Leon. *Henry James: A Life.* New York: Harper, 1985.

MacAndrew, Elizabeth. *The Gothic Tradition in Fiction.* New York: Columbia UP, 1979.

Purdy, Strother B. *The Hole in the Fabric: Science, Contemporary Literature, and Henry James.* Pittsburgh: U of Pittsburgh P, 1977.

Schug, Charles. *The Romantic Genesis of the Modern Novel.* Pittsburgh: U of Pittsburgh P, 1979.

13

From *Uncle Vanya*

Anton Chekhov (1860–1904)
Drama: Comedy

Background

At the end of the nineteenth century, most of the writers in Russia were members of the nobility. However, Anton Chekhov came from a family of emancipated serfs—that is, his forefathers had been bound to their masters' land but were later freed. In spite of his modest background, Chekhov succeeded in getting an education. While he was studying medicine at Moscow University, he supported himself and his family by writing comic stories.

Chekhov practiced medicine throughout his life. His medical training and professional experiences provided him with a scientific, objective view of the world. Furthermore, as a doctor he met many types of people, and he lived in the environments of both the city and the countryside. These varied experiences were incorporated as realistic details into Chekhov's works.

Although Chekhov wrote more than 50 stories, he is best remembered for his dramas *The Sea Gull* (1896), *Uncle Vanya* (1899), *The Three Sisters* (1902), and *The Cherry Orchard* (1904). These plays have earned Chekhov a reputation as an outstanding representative of the late-nineteenth-century Realist school. His observations of Russian life are presented on stage in a spare and concentrated form. With dramatic characters representing diverse classes, professions, and individual personalities, Chekhov's work provides a panoramic view of the Russia of his time.

Pre-Reading Activities

1. In your journal, note your ideas about life in the country as opposed to life in the city. Which do you think is preferable? Why? Discuss your ideas with your group.
2. Why do you believe science and social traditions sometimes come into conflict? What do you think might be the result?

Key Terms

czar/czarist Russia

Flaubert, Gustave (1821–1880)

indirect method

Maupassant, Guy de (1850–1893)

Moscow Art Theater

Naturalism

objectivity

serf

Tolstoy, Leo (1828–1910)

Zola, Émile (1840–1902)

From *Uncle Vanya*
Anton Chekhov

Characters for This Scene

ALEXANDER SEREBRAKOFF, a retired professor

SONIA, his daughter by a former marriage

IVAN [VANYA] VOITSKI, son of a **privy councilor** and brother-in-law to Serebrakoff

MICHAEL ASTROFF, a medical doctor

ILIA [WAFFLES] TELEGIN, an **impoverished** landowner

MARINA, an old nurse

The scene is laid on Serebrakoff's country place.

Act I

A country house on a terrace. In front of it, a garden. In an avenue of trees, under an old poplar, stands a table set for tea, with a **samovar**, etc. Some benches and chairs stand near the table. On one of them is lying a guitar. A **hammock** is swung near the table. It is three o'clock in the afternoon of a cloudy day. MARINA, a quiet, gray-haired, little old woman, is sitting at the table knitting a stocking. ASTROFF is walking up and down near her.

Figure 17 • **Around the samovar, late nineteenth century** *(Culver Pictures, Inc.)*

ASTROFF: . . . [T]en years have made me another man. And why? Because I am overworked. Nurse, I am on my feet from dawn till dusk. I know no rest; at night I **tremble** under my blankets for fear of being dragged out to visit one who is sick; I have **toiled** without **repose** or a day's freedom since I have known you; could I   5 help growing old? And then, existence is tedious, anyway; it is a senseless, dirty business, this life, and goes heavily. Every one about here is silly, and after living with them for two or three years one grows silly oneself. It is inevitable. [*Twisting his mustache*] See what a long mustache I have grown. A foolish, long mustache. Yes,   10 I am as silly as the rest, nurse, but not as stupid; no, I have not grown stupid. Thank God, my brain is not **addled** yet, though my feelings have grown **numb**. I ask nothing, I need nothing, I love no one, unless it is yourself alone. [*He kisses her head*] I had a nurse just like you when I was a child.   15

MARINA: Don't you want a bite of something to eat?

ASTROFF: No. During the third week of **Lent** I went to the epidemic
at Malitskoi. It was . . . **typhoid**. The peasants were all lying
side by side in their huts, and the calves and pigs were running
about the floor among the sick. Such dirt there was, and smoke!   20
Unspeakable! I slaved among those people all day, not a crumb
passed my lips, but when I got home there was still no rest for me;
a switchman was carried in from the railroad; I laid him on the op-
erating table and he went and died in my arms under **chloroform**,
and then my feelings that should have been dead awoke again, my   25
conscience tortured me as if I had killed the man. I sat down
and closed my eyes—like this—and thought: will our descendants two hundred years from now, for whom we are breaking the
road, remember to give us a kind word? No, nurse, they will forget.

MARINA: Man is forgetful, but God remembers.   30

ASTROFF: Thank you for that. You have spoken the truth.

[*Enter VOITSKI from the house. He has been asleep after dinner and looks
rather **disheveled**. He sits down on the bench and straightens his collar*]

VOITSKI: H'm. Yes. [*A pause*] Yes.

ASTROFF: Have you been asleep?

VOITSKI: Yes, very much so. [*He yawns*] Ever since the professor and
his wife have come, our daily life seems to have jumped the track. I   35
sleep at the wrong time, drink wine, and eat all sorts of messes for
luncheon and dinner. It isn't **wholesome**. . . .

MARINA [*shakes her head*]: Such a confusion in the house! The professor gets up at twelve, the samovar is kept boiling all the morning
and everything has to wait for him. Before they came we used to   40
have dinner at one o'clock, like everybody else, but now we have
it at seven. The professor sits up all night writing and reading, and
suddenly, at two o'clock, there goes the bell! Heavens, what is
that? The professor wants some tea! Wake the servants, light the
samovar! Lord, what disorder!   45

ASTROFF: Will they be here long?

VOITSKI: A hundred years! The professor has decided to make his
home here.

MARINA: Look at this now! The samovar has been on the table for two
hours, and they are all out walking!   50

VOITSKI: All right, don't get excited; here they come.

[*Voices are heard approaching. SEREBRAKOFF, SONIA, and TELEGIN come in from the depths of the garden, returning from their walk*]

SEREBRAKOFF: Superb! Superb! What beautiful views!

TELEGIN: They are wonderful, your Excellency.

SONIA: Tomorrow we shall go into the woods, shall we, papa?

VOITSKI: Ladies and gentlemen, tea is ready.   55

SEREBRAKOFF: Won't you please be good enough to send my tea into the library? I still have some work to finish.

SONIA: I am sure you will love the woods.

[. . . SEREBRAKOFF *and* SONIA *go into the house*]

VOITSKI: There goes our learned scholar on a hot, **sultry** day like this, in his overcoat and **galoshes** and carrying an umbrella!   60

ASTROFF: He is trying to take good care of his health. . . .

ASTROFF: Come, Ivan, tell us something.

VOITSKI: [**indolently**] What shall I tell you?

ASTROFF: Haven't you any news for us?

VOITSKI: No, it is all **stale**. I am just the same as usual, or perhaps   65
worse, because I have become lazy. I don't do anything now but **croak** like an old **raven**. My mother, the old **magpie**, is still **chattering** about the **emancipation** of woman, with one eye on her grave and the other on her **learned** books, in which she is always looking for the dawn of a new life.   70

ASTROFF: And the professor?

VOITSKI: The professor sits in his library from morning till night, as usual—

> **Straining** the mind, **wrinkling** the **brow**,
> We write, write, write,   75
> Without **respite**
> Or hope of praise in the future or now.

Poor paper! He ought to write his autobiography; he would make a really splendid subject for a book! Imagine it, the life of a retired professor, as stale as a piece of hardtack, tortured by gout, headaches,   80
and rheumatism, his liver bursting with jealousy and envy, living on the estate of his first wife, although he hates it, because he can't afford to live in town. He is **everlastingly whining** about his hard lot, though, as a matter of fact, he is extraordinarily lucky. He is the son of a common **deacon** and has attained the professor's chair,   85

become the son-in-law of a senator, is called "your Excellency," and so on. But I'll tell you something; the man has been writing on art for twenty-five years, and he doesn't know the very first thing about it. For twenty-five years he has been chewing on other men's thoughts about realism, naturalism, and all such foolishness;   90 for twenty-five years he has been reading and writing things that clever men have long known and stupid ones are not interested in; for twenty-five years he has been **making** his imaginary **mountains out of molehills**. And just think of the man's self-conceit and presumption all this time! For twenty-five years he has been   95 **masquerading** in false clothes and has now retired, absolutely unknown to any living soul; and yet see him! **stalking** across the earth like a **demi-god**!

ASTROFF: I believe you envy him.

VOITSKI: Yes, I do. Look at the success he has had with women! . . .   100 His first wife, who was my sister, was a beautiful, gentle being. . . . His mother-in-law, my mother, adores him to this day. . . . His second wife is, as you see, a brilliant beauty, she married him in his old age and has surrendered all the glory of her beauty and freedom to him. Why? What for?   105

ASTROFF: Is she faithful to him?

VOITSKI: Yes, unfortunately she is.

ASTROFF: Why "unfortunately"?

VOITSKI: Because such fidelity is false and unnatural, **root and branch**. It sounds [good], but there is no logic in it. It is thought immoral   110 for a woman to deceive an old husband whom she hates, but quite moral for her to strangle her youth in her breast and **banish** every vital desire from her heart.

TELEGIN [*in a tearful voice*]: Vanya, I don't like to hear you talk so. Listen, Vanya; every one who betrays husband or wife is faithless, and   115 could also betray his country.

VOITSKI [*crossly*]: **Turn off the tap**, Waffles.

Vocabulary

*****addle** *(v.)*   to confuse
banish *(v.)*   to drive out

*Denotes low-frequency word.

brow *(n.)*   forehead
chatter *(v.)*   to talk rapidly or idly
*chloroform *(n.)*   anesthesia used in earlier times to prevent pain during
   surgery
*croak *(v.)*   to speak in a hoarse, throaty voice
*deacon *(n.)*   subordinate officer in a Christian church
*demi-god *(n.)*   person regarded as partly divine
disheveled *(adj.)*   untidy; rumpled
emancipation *(n.)*   freeing from the power or control of another
*everlastingly *(adv.)*   eternally
*galoshes *(n.)*   boots
*hammock *(n.)*   swinging bed made of netting and hung from two poles
impoverished *(adj.)*   made poor
*indolently *(adv.)*   lazily
learned *(adj.)*   having or showing good education
Lent *(n.)*   the 40 weekdays from Ash Wednesday to Easter observed by
   Christians as a period of penitence and fasting
*magpie *(n.)*   kind of bird that makes rapidly succeeding sounds; a person
   who talks in such a way
*make a mountain out of a molehill *(v. phrase)*   to make more of
   something than is necessary or required
   *molehill *(n.)*   little mound of dirt pushed up by a mole, an animal
   that lives underground
masquerade *(v.)*   to go about disguised
numb *(adj.)*   without feeling or emotion; deadened
*privy councilor *(n.)*   confidential advisor appointed by a ruler
*raven *(n.)*   large black bird
repose *(n.)*   state of rest
respite *(n.)*   interval of rest or relief
*root and branch *(adv.)*   completely; entirely
*samovar *(n.)*   metal container with an internal tube for heating water to
   make tea, used especially in Russia
stale *(adj.)*   having lost freshness or originality
stalking *(adj.)*   walking stiffly or haughtily
straining *(adj.)*   exerting to the utmost
sultry *(adj.)*   sweltering; hot and humid
toil *(v.)*   to work long and hard
tremble *(v.)*   to shake
*turn off the tap *(v. phrase)*   to stop crying
   *tap *(n.)*   spout and valve at the end of a pipe that control the flow of
   a liquid
*typhoid *(n.)*   serious disease contracted from polluted water and marked
   by high fever
whine *(v.)*   to complain in a childish, undignified way
wholesome *(adj.)*   promoting health or well-being
wrinkling *(adj.)*   creasing; making small ridges

Activities

1. Taking the parts of the characters, read the play aloud. Note the tensions and conflicts between the characters.

2. Alone or with a partner, look closely at the text. What does Voitski think of the professor? Why do you think he feels this way? Make notes in your journal about what he is saying about Russian education. Discuss your views with your class.

3. Describe the marriage between Professor Serebrakoff and his second wife. What does Voitski think of this marriage?

4. Like Chekhov, Astroff is a medical doctor. Make notes in your journal about his view of Russia. Share your ideas with your class.

5. How does living in the country affect Dr. Astroff? Do you think this is the usual effect it has on people? Why might he feel the way he does?

6. Write an essay on Chekhov's view of his contemporary Russia.

7. Do you think young women should marry older men? (These are sometimes called May-December marriages.) Write an essay defending your point of view.

8. If you have read "The Miller's Tale," compare and contrast the way Chaucer presents the marriages of John the Carpenter and Alison with the way Chekhov presents the marriage of Professor Serebrakoff and his second wife.

For Further Reading

Barricelli, Jean-Pierre, ed. *Chekhov's Great Plays: A Critical Anthology.* New York: New York UP, 1981.

Chekhov, Anton. *Anton Chekhov's Life and Thought: Selected Letters and Commentary.* Trans. Michael H. Heim with Simon Karlinsky. Berkeley: U of California P, 1975.

Jackson, Robert L., ed. *Chekhov.* Englewood Cliffs, NJ: Prentice, 1967.

Mechinger, Siegfried. *Anton Chekhov.* New York: Ungar, 1972.

Priestly, J. B. *Anton Chekhov.* Cranbury, NJ: Barnes, 1970.

14

From "Roman Fever"

Edith Wharton (1862–1937)
Fiction: Short Story

Background

Born in the North during the American Civil War, Edith Jones was fortunate enough to enjoy the luxuries of an old New York family. The Jones family went to Europe on what Americans called "the Grand Tour" and later stayed for prolonged visits. They spent summers vacationing at their large second home in Newport, Rhode Island. However, like most young women of her day, Edith received no formal education; her travels and her reading in her father's library formed the bases of her knowledge. Through her governess she learned German and French and thus was able to read great European literature in the original languages.

After her marriage to Edward Wharton in 1885, Edith traveled extensively to Greece, Italy, and other parts of Europe, as well as to North Africa. In 1891 she published her first short story, "The Bunner Sisters." Her 1897 book *The Decoration of Houses*, written with Ogden Codman, is still a classic on interior decoration.

Although she received the Pulitzer Prize in fiction for her novel *The Age of Innocence* (1921), Edith Wharton also excelled as a short-story writer. Her stories include Gothic tales as well as many more realistic ones, a number of which focus on the city of her birth, New York. Wharton left the United States in 1909 for permanent exile in Paris. But she continued to write critically of the nouveaux riches—that is, the newly rich Americans who made their fortunes on railroads and other developing industries and displaced the traditional Eastern aristocratic families. A close friend of Henry James, she frequently wrote on international themes, especially about Americans living in or visiting Europe.

While her fiction is usually considered realistic, it also contains many references to biblical, Greek, and Roman mythology. Understanding these references greatly expands the surface meaning of Wharton's fiction. It is important to note that in "Roman Fever" a dramatic dialogue between two goddesslike Americans takes place overlooking the ruins of Rome. Meanwhile, their innocent daughters have flown off to Tarquinia with two airplane pilots in Mussolini's Fascist air force. The ruins of the past hint at a sinister future both for the daughters and for Italy of the 1930s.

Pre-Reading Activities

1. With your study group, discuss the reasons why, in your opinion, a visitor would want to go to an ancient city such as Rome. What kinds of things might a visitor do and think about there?

2. How might an author show that two characters are different from each other? What techniques might she use?

Key Terms

Colosseum
dramatic technique
Etruscan
Fascism
Forum
the Grand Tour
international themes

irony
nouveau riche (*pl.* nouveaux riches)
Palatine Hill
Pulitzer Prize
Roman fever
Tarquinia

From "Roman Fever"
Edith Wharton

From the table at which they had been lunching two American   1
ladies of ripe but well-cared-for middle age moved across the **lofty** terrace of the Roman restaurant and, leaning on its **parapet**, looked first at each other, and then down on the outspread glories of the Palatine and the Forum. . . .

As they leaned there a girlish voice echoed up gaily from the   2
stairs. . . . "Well, come along, then," it cried, not to them but to an invisible companion, "and let's leave the young things to their

Figure 18   •   Roman Forum and Colosseum *(The Bettmann Archive)*

knitting . . . after all, we haven't left our poor parents much else to
do. . . . "

"Barbara!" [the smaller and paler one] murmured, sending an   3
unheard **rebuke** after the **mocking** voice in the stairway.

The other lady, who was fuller, and higher in color, with a   4
small determined nose supported by vigorous black eyebrows, gave a
good-humoured laugh. "That's what our daughters think of us!"

Her companion replied . . . , "Not of us individually. We must   5
remember that. It's just the collective modern idea of Mothers. And
you see—" Half guiltily she drew from her handsomely mounted
black hand-bag a twist of crimson silk run through by fine knitting
needles. "One never knows," she murmured. "The new system has
certainly given us a good deal of **time to kill**; and sometimes I get
tired just looking—even at this." Her gesture was now addressed to
the **stupendous** scene at their feet. . . .

"Well, I don't see why we shouldn't just stay here," said Mrs.   6
Slade, the lady of the high color and energetic brows. . . .   "After
all, it's still the most beautiful view in the world."

"It always will be, to me," assented her friend Mrs. Ansley,   7 with a slight stress on the "me" that Mrs. Slade, though she noticed it, wondered if it were not merely accidental. . . .

"Grace Ansley was always old-fashioned," she thought; and   8
added aloud, with a **retrospective** smile: "It's a view we've both been familiar with for a good many years. When we first met here we were younger than our girls are now. . . ."

[Alida] Slade's black brows drew together. . . . But she   9
smiled away her frown. . . . "Well, why not? We might do worse. There's no knowing, I suppose, when the girls will be back. Do you even know from *where*? I don't."

Mrs. Ansley again colored slightly. "I think those young Italian   10
aviators we met at the Embassy invited them to fly to Tarquinia for tea. I suppose they'll want to wait and fly back by moonlight."

"Moonlight—moonlight! What a part it still plays. Do you   11
suppose they're as sentimental as we were?"

"I've come to the conclusion that I don't in the least know   12
what they are," said Mrs. Ansley. "And perhaps we didn't know much more about each other."

. . . Each one, of course, had a label ready to attach to the   13
other's name; Mrs. Delphin Slade, for instance, would have told herself, or any one who asked her, that Mrs. Horace Ansley, twenty-five years ago, had been exquisitely lovely—no, you wouldn't believe it, would you? . . . though, of course, still charming, distinguished. . . . Well, as a girl she had been exquisite; far more beautiful than her daughter Barbara, though certainly **Babs**, according to the new standards at any rate, was more effective—had more *edge*, as they say. Funny where she got it, with those two **nullities** as parents. Yes; Horace Ansley was—well, the duplicate of his wife. . . .

A few years later, and not many months apart, both ladies   14
lost their husbands. . . . The similarity of their lot had again drawn them together. . . .

. . . [B]eing *the* Slade's widow was dullish business. . . . In   15
living up to such a husband all her **faculties** had been engaged; now she had only her daughter to live up to. . . . There was nothing left but to mother her daughter; and dear Jenny was such a perfect daughter that she needed no excessive mothering. . . . She wished that Jenny would fall in love—with the wrong man, even; that she might have to be watched, **outmaneuvered**, rescued. And instead, it was Jenny who watched her mother, kept her out of **draughts**, made sure she had taken her **tonic**. . . .

Mrs. Ansley was much less **articulate** than her friend, and her   16
mental portrait of Mrs. Slade was slighter, and drawn with fainter
touches. "Alida Slade's awfully brilliant; but not as brilliant as she
thinks," would have summed it up. . . .

"I was just thinking," [Mrs. Slade] said slowly, "what different   17
things Rome stands for to each generation of travellers. To our grandmothers, Roman fever; to our mothers, sentimental dangers—how
we used to be guarded!—to our daughters, no more dangers than
the middle of Main Street. They don't know it—but how much
they're missing!"

. . . "The sun's set. You're not afraid, my dear?" [said Mrs.   18
Slade].

"Afraid—"   19

"Of Roman fever or pneumonia? I remember how ill you were   20
that winter. As a girl you had a very delicate throat, hadn't you? . . .
There's no more Roman fever, but the Forum is deathly cold after
sunset—especially after a hot day. And the Colosseum's even colder
and damper."

"The Colosseum—?"   21

"Yes. It wasn't easy to get in, after the gates were locked for   22
the night. Far from easy. Still in those days it could be managed; it
was managed, often. Lovers met there who couldn't meet elsewhere.
You knew that?"

"I—I **daresay**. I don't remember."   23

"You don't remember? You don't remember going to visit some   24
ruins or other one evening, just after dark, and catching a bad chill?
People always said that expedition was what caused your illness."

There was a moment's silence; then Mrs. Ansley **rejoined**:   25
"Did they? It was all so long ago."

. . . "I've always known why you went. . . . Well, you   26
went to meet the man I was engaged to—and I can repeat every
word of the letter that took you there. . . . Listen, if you don't
believe me. 'My one darling, things can't go on like this. I must see
you alone. Come to the Colosseum immediately after dark tomorrow.
There will be somebody to let you in. No one whom you need fear
will suspect'—but perhaps you've forgotten what the letter said?"

Mrs. Ansley met the challenge with an unexpected **compo-**   27
sure. Steadying herself against the chair she looked at her friend,
and replied: "No; I know it by heart too."

"And the signature? 'Only *your* D.S.' Was that it? I'm right,   28
am I? That was the letter that took you out that evening after

dark? . . . Well, my dear, I know what was in that letter because I wrote it! . . . I hated you, hated you. I knew you were in love with Delphin—and I was afraid; afraid of you, of your quiet ways, your sweetness . . . your . . . well, I wanted you out of the way, that's all. Just for a few weeks; just till I was sure of him. . . . I had no reason to think you'd ever taken it seriously. How could I, when you were married to Horace Ansley two months afterward? As soon as you could get out of bed your mother rushed you off to Florence and married you. . . ."

At length Mrs. Slade began again: "I suppose I did it as a sort of joke—"   29

"A joke?"   30

"Well, girls are ferocious sometimes, you know. Girls in love especially. And I remember laughing to myself all that evening at the idea that you were waiting around there in the dark. . . . Of course I was upset when I heard you were so ill afterward."   31

Mrs. Ansley had not moved for a long time. But now she turned slowly toward her companion. "But I didn't wait. He'd arranged everything. He was there. We were let in at once," she said. . . . "I answered the letter. I told him I'd be there. So he came."   32

Mrs. Slade **flung** her hands up to her face. "Oh, God—you answered! I never thought of your answering. . . ."   33

"It's odd you never thought of it, if you wrote the letter."   34

. . . Mrs. Ansley rose, and drew her fur scarf about her. "It is cold here. We'd better go. . . . I'm sorry for you," she said. . . .   35

The unexpected words sent a **pang** through Mrs. Slade. "Yes; we'd better go." She gathered up her bag and cloak. "I don't know why you should be sorry for me," she muttered.   36

Mrs. Ansley stood looking away from her toward the **dusky** secret mass of the Colosseum. "Well—because I didn't have to wait that night."   37

Mrs. Slade gave an unquiet laugh. "Yes; I was beaten there. But I oughtn't to **begrudge** it to you, I suppose. At the end of all these years. After all, I had everything; I had him for twenty-five years. And you had nothing but that one letter that he didn't write."   38

Mrs. Ansley was again silent. At length she turned toward the door of the terrace. She took a step, and turned back, facing her companion.   39

"I had Barbara," she said, and began to move ahead of Mrs. Slade toward the stairway.   40

Vocabulary

articulate *(adj.)* able to express oneself readily, clearly, and effectively
*Babs *(prop. n.)* short for *Barbara*
begrudge *(v.)* to look upon with disapproval
composure *(n.)* calmness
*daresay *(v.)* to suppose
*draught *(n.)* a current of air (chiefly British; a variation of *draft*)
*dusky *(adj.)* shadowy
faculty *(n.)* ability
fling (flung) *(v.)* to move suddenly
lofty *(adj.)* impressively high
lose someone *(v.)* to have someone who is close die
mocking *(adj.)* ridiculing; treating with contempt
*nullity *(n.)* something that has no value or significance
outmaneuver *(v.)* to defeat by more skillful manipulation or management
pang *(n.)* sharp attack of pain
*parapet *(n.)* wall or railing to protect people from falling off the edge, as on a balcony or terrace
rebuke *(n.)* expression of strong disapproval; reprimand
rejoin *(v.)* to say in response
retrospective *(adj.)* looking back to the past
steady oneself *(v.)* to make oneself stable or fixed
stupendous *(adj.)* overwhelming; astonishingly great
time to kill *(n.)* time to waste or to use up
*tonic *(n.)* medicine

Activities

1. What is the setting for the story "Roman Fever"? What is the Colosseum? Why is it important to the story?

2. Wharton carefully builds her story to show us what her characters are like. Find specific lines in "Roman Fever" that tell us about these two characters, and note them in your journal. Discuss your ideas with your class.

3. Look at the structure of the short story. How does the author show us what Mrs. Slade and Mrs. Ansley are like?

4. Based on your notes and classroom discussion, write an essay comparing and contrasting Mrs. Slade and Mrs. Ansley.

*Denotes low-frequency word.

5. Write an essay on the multiple meanings of "Roman fever." Include the significance of "Roman fever" to the three generations involved in the story.

For Further Reading

Fryer, Judith. *Felicitous Space: The Imaginative Structures of Edith Wharton and Willa Cather.* Chapel Hill: U of North Carolina P, 1986.

Lewis, R. W. B. *Edith Wharton: A Biography.* New York: Harper, 1975.

McDowell, Margaret B. *Edith Wharton.* Boston: Twayne, 1976.

Wolff, Cynthia Griffin. *A Feast of Words: The Triumph of Edith Wharton.* New York: Oxford, 1977.

15

From "The Metamorphosis"

Franz Kafka (1883–1924)
Fiction: Short Story

Background

Although he died at an early age, Kafka wrote many novels, novellas, and short prose pieces. Among his most well-known works are *The Trial* (1925), *The Castle* (1926), *America* (1927), and "The Metamorphosis" (1912). He is regarded as one of the great modern writers because of his psychoanalytic approach—that is, his deep exploration of the psychology of his characters.

Kafka's fiction reflects his strong sense of isolation and melancholy as a German-speaking Jew in Prague, Czechoslovakia, and as the artist son of an overbearing father who wished his son to become a businessman. Fathers and other authority figures play an important role in his stories, especially in the mind of the main character. Frequently, the protagonist is a young male ridden with feelings of guilt who is being judged by the powerful father figure.

The influence of Freud's psychoanalysis and his concept of the "Oedipus complex" is evident in both the content and the tone of Kafka's work. With the voice of a matter-of-fact narrator that reveals the inner workings of his character's mind, Kafka explores a bizarre world that still shocks modern readers.

"The Metamorphosis" is the story of Gregor Samsa, a traveling salesman who has been working very hard at a boring job to support his parents and sister. In Existential terms, his life is meaningless. One morning he awakens and believes himself transformed into a huge insect. He is confined to his room as much as possible. He is persecuted by his father; his mother pleads for him; his sister tries to feed him. After much suffering, to the relief of his family, Gregor dies.

As a comic tragedy about the isolation, alienation, inadequacy, and guilt of modern life, "The Metamorphosis" has become one of the most widely read and discussed works of twentieth-century literature.

Pre-Reading Activities

1. Discuss what influence you think a very strong father figure might have on a young man. How do you think the young man might rebel?
2. What techniques might an author use to reveal the innermost thoughts of a character? Would we know whether or not these thoughts were "normal"? How?

Key Terms

alienation   Prague Circle
Austro-Hungarian Empire   psychoanalysis
Existentialism   psychology
Freud, Sigmund (1856–1939)   subconscious
isolation   vermin
metaphor

From "The Metamorphosis"
Franz Kafka

As Gregor Samsa awoke one morning from uneasy dreams he   1
found himself transformed in his bed into a gigantic insect. He was
lying on his hard, as it were **armor-plated**, back and when he lifted
his head a little he could see his **dome-like** brown belly divided into
stiff arched segments on top of which the bed quilt could hardly keep
in position and was about to slide off completely. His numerous legs,
which were pitifully thin compared to the rest of his **bulk**, waved
helplessly before his eyes.

What has happened to me? he thought. It was no dream. His   2
room, a regular human bedroom, only rather too small, lay quiet between the four familiar walls. Above the table on which a collection

of cloth samples was unpacked and spread out—Samsa was a **commercial traveler**—hung the picture which he had recently cut out of an illustrated magazine and put into a pretty **gilt** frame. It showed a lady, with a fur cap on and a fur **stole**, sitting upright and holding out to the spectator a huge fur **muff** into which the whole of her arm had vanished!

Gregor's eyes turned next to the window, and the overcast sky—one could hear rain drops beating on the window gutter—made him quite melancholy. What about sleeping a little longer and forgetting all this nonsense, he thought, but it could not be done, for he was accustomed to sleeping on his right side and in his present condition he could not turn himself over. However violently he forced himself towards his right side he always rolled on his back again. He tried it at least a hundred times, shutting his eyes to keep from seeing his struggling legs, and only **desisted** when he began to feel in his side a faint dull ache he had never experienced before. . . . 3

He slid down again into his former position. This getting up early, he thought, makes one quite stupid. A man needs his sleep. Other commercials live like **harem women**. For instance, when I come back to the hotel [in the] morning to write up the orders I've got, these others are only sitting down to breakfast. Let me just try that with my chief; I'd be **sacked on the spot**. Anyhow, that might be quite a good thing for me, who can tell? If I didn't have to hold my hand because of my parents, I'd have **given notice** long ago, I'd have gone to the chief and told him exactly what I think of him. . . . For the moment, though, I'd better get up, since my train goes at five. 4

He looked at the alarm clock ticking on the chest. Heavenly Father! he thought. It was half-past six o'clock and the hands were quietly moving on, it was even past the half-hour, it was getting on toward a quarter to seven. Had the alarm clock not gone off? From the bed one could see that it had been properly set for four o'clock; of course it must have gone off. . . . 5

But what was he to do now? The next train went at seven o'clock; to catch that he would need to hurry like mad and his samples weren't even packed up, and he himself wasn't feeling particularly fresh and active. And even if he did catch the train he wouldn't avoid a **row** with the chief, since the firm's porter would have been waiting for the five o'clock train and would have long since reported his failure to turn up. The porter was a creature of the chief's, **spineless** and stupid. Well, supposing he were to say he was sick? But that 6 would be most unpleasant and would look suspicious, since during his five years' employment he had not been ill once. . . .

As all this was running through his mind at top speed without   7
his being able to decide to leave his bed—the alarm clock had just struck a quarter to seven—there came a cautious tap at the door behind the head of his bed. "Gregor," said a voice—it was his mother's—"it's a quarter to seven. Hadn't you a train to catch?" That gentle voice!

Gregor had a shock as he heard his own voice answering hers,   8
unmistakably his own voice, it was true, but with a persistent horrible **twittering squeak** behind it like an undertone. . . . Gregor wanted to answer at length, but in the circumstances he confined himself to saying: "Yes, yes, thank you, Mother, I'm getting up now."

The wooden door between them must have kept the change   9
in his voice from being noticeable outside, for his mother contented herself with this statement and **shuffled** away. Yet this brief exchange of words had made the other members of the family aware that Gregor was still in the house, as they had not expected, and at one of the side doors his father was already knocking, gently, yet with his fist. "Gregor, Gregor," he called, "what's the matter with you?" And after a little while he called again in a deeper voice: "Gregor! Gregor!" At the other side door his sister was saying in a low, **plaintive** tone: "Gregor? Aren't you well? Are you needing anything?"

He answered them both at once: "I'm just ready," and did his   10
best to make his voice sound as normal as possible by enunciating the words very clearly. . . . His immediate intention was to get up quietly without being disturbed, to put on his clothes and above all eat his breakfast, and only then to consider what else was to be done, since in bed, he was well aware, his meditations would come to no sensible conclusion. . . .

"Gregor," said his father now from the left-hand room, "the   11
chief clerk has come and wants to know why you didn't catch the early train. We don't know what to say to him. Besides, he wants to talk to you in person. So open the door, please. He will be good enough to excuse the **untidiness** of your room."

"Good morning, Mr. Samsa," the chief clerk was calling **ami-**   12
ably meanwhile. "He's not well," said his mother to the visitor, while his father was still speaking through the door, "he's not well, sir, believe me. What else would make him miss a train! The boy thinks about nothing but his work. It makes me almost **cross** the way he never goes out in the evenings; he's been here the last eight days and

has stayed at home every single evening. He just sits there quietly at the table reading a newspaper or looking through railway timetables. The only amusement he gets is doing **fretwork**. For instance, he spent two or three evenings cutting out a little picture frame; you would be surprised to see how pretty it is; it's hanging in his room; you'll see it in a minute when Gregor opens the door. . . . "

"Well, can the chief clerk come in now?" asked Gregor's father   13
impatiently, again knocking on the door. "No," said Gregor. In the left-hand room a painful silence followed this refusal; in the right-hand room his sister began to **sob**. . . .

[W]hy was she crying? Because he wouldn't get up and let the   14
the chief clerk in, because he was in danger of losing his job, and because the chief would begin **dunning** his parents again for the old debts? Surely these were things one didn't need to worry about for the present. Gregor was still at home and not in the least thinking of **deserting** his family. At the moment, true, he was lying on the carpet and no one who knew the condition he was in could seriously expect him to **admit** the chief clerk. . . . And it seemed to Gregor that it would be much more sensible to leave him in peace for the present than to trouble him with tears and **entreaties**.

Vocabulary

admit *(v.)* to allow to enter
amiably *(adv.)* in a friendly manner; sociably
*armor-plated *(adj.)* covered with defensive material or protective covering such as is used in combat
bulk *(n.)* massive size
*commercial traveler *(n.)* nineteenth-century traveling salesman
*cross *(adj.)* marked by bad temper; grumpy
deserting *(n.)* leaving; abandoning
desist *(v.)* to stop
*dome-like *(adj.)* arched
dun *(v.)* to make persistent demands for payment
entreaty *(n.)* plea; earnest request
*fretwork *(n.)* kind of ornamental work
gilt *(adj.)* made of gold; gold-colored
*give notice *(v.)* to announce to an employer that one is going to leave a position

*Denotes low-frequency word.

*harem women *(n.)*   women living together in an isolated room, as in a Muslim household
*muff *(n.)*   tube-shaped warm covering for women's hands, often made of fur
on the spot *(adv.)*   immediately; at once
plaintive *(adj.)*   expressive of suffering or melancholy
*row *(n.)*   quarrel; argument
*sack *(v.)*   to dismiss or fire from a position
shuffle *(v.)*   to walk in a sliding, dragging manner without lifting the feet
sob *(v.)*   to cry with a catching of the breath
spineless *(adj.)*   lacking strength of character
squeak *(n.)*   sharp, shrill cry or sound
stole *(n.)*   long, wide scarf worn by women, usually across the shoulders
twittering *(adj.)*   trembling; quivering
untidiness *(n.)*   disorder; disorganized state

Activities

1. From whose point of view is the story told? Do we know whether it is true or not?
2. Look closely at the text. How does Kafka make full use of the central metaphor (the insect) in his story? Make notes in your journal and discuss your ideas with your group or class.
3. What is Gregor's relationship with his family? What is his relationship with figures of authority besides his parents? Do you believe this is normal? Note lines from the text that support your view.
4. Using your notes, write an essay on Kafka's use of metaphor to show Gregor Samsa's suffering.
5. Write an essay arguing for or against a young person's taking a job selected by his/her parents.

For Further Reading

Anderson, Mark, ed. *Reading Kafka: Prague, Politics, and the Fin de Siècle.* New York: Schocken, 1989.
Carrouges, Michel. *Kafka versus Kafka.* University: U of Alabama P, 1962.
Robertson, Ritchie. *Kafka: Judaism, Politics, and Literature.* New York: Oxford UP, 1987.
Sandbank, Shimon. *After Kafka: The Influence of Kafka's Fiction.* Athens: U of Georgia P, 1989.

*Denotes low-frequency word.

16

From *O Pioneers!*

Willa Cather (1873–1947)
Fiction: Novel

Background

Although she was born in Virginia, Willa Cather and her extended family moved to the Nebraska prairie in 1883 during the great nineteenth-century migration to the American West. The stark contrast between the older, more settled East and the open prairie of Nebraska made a lasting impression on the developing author. For Cather, the Midwest landscape possessed an almost mystical quality; she associated its richness and productivity with ancient myths of fertility gods and goddesses. The land and its magical powers became the setting for many of her novels.

While growing up in the Midwest, Willa Cather strongly identified with masculine tradition. Sometimes calling herself William, Cather wore extremely short hair and dressed in men's clothing. However, her nonconformist appearance did not hide her talents. Cather attended the University of Nebraska, where she began writing reviews of cultural events for newspapers. Convinced that she could earn a living as a writer, Cather took a magazine job in Pittsburgh, Pennsylvania, in 1896. Ten years later, she moved to New York, where she worked for *McClure's Magazine*.

Especially in her early work, Cather values the Romantic ideal of the exalted individual and his sensations and impressions. Under the guidance of the American writer Sarah Orne Jewett, Cather learned that one can seek universal truths in the particular experience and that one person's struggle to survive can symbolize human efforts everywhere.

In 1923, Cather received the Pulitzer Prize in fiction for *One of Ours*, her World War I novel, which demonstrates a woman's view of war and its mindless destruction of idealistic youth. But her most memorable heroine is Alexandra Bergson, the protagonist of her 1913 novel *O Pioneers!* The story takes its title from Walt Whitman's poem "Pioneers! O Pioneers!" and is a combination of two short stories Cather had written: one the tragic love story of Marie Shabata and Emil Bergson, and the other the saga of the Bergson family and their relationship with the land. Unmarried and alone for much of the novel, Alexandra Bergson directs her reproductive energies into the land. But her imagination of the powers of the land reminds her of her own body's needs. *O Pioneers!* is Cather's most popular novel; in 1992 it was made into a television film. This portion of the novel is from Part III, "Winter Memories."

Pre-Reading Activities

1. With your class or study group, define *pioneer*. What do you imagine the personality of a pioneer might be like?
2. In your journal, make a list of your ideas about "the myth of the American West." Discuss your ideas with your class.

Key Terms

American Midwest   personification
corn god   prairie
Great (or Continental) Divide   saga
journalist   sod house
migration

From *O Pioneers!*
Willa Cather

Winter has settled down over the **Divide** again; the season in   1
which Nature **recuperates**, in which she sinks to sleep between the
fruitfulness of autumn and the passion of spring. The birds have
gone. The **teeming** life that goes on down in the long grass is **exterminated**. The prairie-dog keeps in his hole. The rabbits run **shivering** from one frozen garden patch to another. . . .

The **variegated** fields are all one color now; the pastures, the   2
stubble, the roads, the sky are the same leaden gray. The
hedgerows and trees are scarcely **perceptible** against the bare
earth, whose **slaty hue** they have taken on. . . . It is like an iron
country, and the spirit is oppressed by its rigor and melancholy. One

Figure 19 • Sod house on the American prairie, Nebraska, 1892 *(Historical Pictures Service)*

could easily believe that in that dead landscape the germs of life and fruitfulness were extinct forever. . . .

Marie sat sewing or crocheting . . . but she was always   3
thinking about the fields outside . . . where the snow was falling and packing. . . . She seemed to feel the weight of all the snow that lay down there. The branches had become so hard that they wounded your hand if you tried to break a twig. And yet, down un-der the frozen **crusts**, at the roots of the trees, the secret of life was still safe, warm as the blood in one's heart; and the spring would come again! Oh, it would come again!

If Alexandra had had much imagination she might have guessed   4
what was going on in Marie's mind, and she would have seen long before what was going on in [brother] Emil's. But that, as Emil him-self had more than once **reflected**, was Alexandra's blind side, and her life had not been of the kind to sharpen her vision. Her training had all been toward the end of making her **proficient** in what she had undertaken to do.

Her personal life, her own realization of herself, was almost a   5
subconscious existence; like an underground river that came to the surface only here and there, at intervals months apart, and then sank again to flow on under her own fields. Nevertheless, the under-ground stream was there, and it was because she had so much per-

sonality to put into her **enterprises** and succeeded in putting it into them so completely, that her [farming] affairs **prospered** better than those of her neighbors.

There were certain days in her life, outwardly uneventful,   6 which Alexandra remembered as peculiarly happy; days when she was close to the flat, **fallow** world about her, and felt, as it were, in her own body the joyous **germination** in the soil. There were days, too, which she and Emil had spent together, upon which she loved to look back. There had been such a day when they were down on the river in the dry year, looking over the land. They had made an early start one morning and had driven a long way before noon. When Emil said he was hungry, they drew back from the road . . . and climbed up to the top of a grassy **bluff** to eat their lunch. . . .

The river was clear there, and shallow, since there had been no   7 rain, and it ran in ripples over the sparkling sand. Under the over-hanging willows of the opposite bank there was an inlet where the water was deeper and flowed so slowly that it seemed to sleep in the sun. In this little bay a single wild duck was swimming and diving and **preening** her feathers, **disporting herself** very happily in the **flickering** light and shade.

They sat for a long time, watching the solitary bird take its   8 pleasure. No living thing had ever seemed to Alexandra as beautiful as that wild duck. Emil must have felt about it as she did, for after-ward, when they were at home, he used sometimes to say, "Sister, you know our duck down there—" Alexandra remembered that day as one of the happiest in her life. Years afterward she thought of the duck as still there, swimming and diving all by herself in the sunlight, a kind of **enchanted** bird that did not know age or change.

Most of Alexandra's happy memories were as impersonal as   9 this one; yet to her they were very personal. Her mind was a white book, with clear writing about weather and beasts and growing things. Not many people would have cared to read it; only a happy few. She had never been in love, she had never indulged in senti-mental **reveries**. Even as a girl she had looked upon men as workfel-lows. She had grown up in serious times.

There was one **fancy**, indeed, which persisted through her girl-   10 hood. It most often came to her on Sunday mornings, the one day in the week when she lay abed listening to the familiar morning sounds; the windmill singing in the brisk breeze, Emil whistling as he blacked his boots down by the kitchen door.

Sometimes, as she lay thus luxuriously idle, her eyes closed,   11 she used to have an illusion of being lifted up bodily and carried lightly by someone very strong. It was a man, certainly, who carried her, but he was like no man she knew; he was much larger and stronger and swifter, and he carried her as easily as if she were a **sheaf** of wheat. She never saw him, but, with eyes closed, she could feel that he was yellow like the sunlight, and there was the smell of ripe cornfields about him.

She could feel him approach, bend over her and lift her, and   12
then she could feel herself being carried swiftly off across the fields. After such a reverie she would rise hastily, angry with herself, and go down to the bath-house that was partitioned off the kitchen shed. There she would stand in a tin tub and **prosecute** her bath with vigor, finishing it by pouring buckets of cold well-water over her gleaming white body which no man on the Divide could have carried very far.

As she grew older, this fancy more often came to her when   13
she was tired than when she was fresh and strong. Sometimes, after she had been in the open all day, overseeing the **branding** of the cattle or the loading of the pigs, she would come in chilled . . . and go to bed with her body actually **aching** with fatigue. Then, just before she went to sleep, she had the old sensation of being lifted and carried by a strong being who took from her all bodily weariness.

Vocabulary

aching *(adj.)*   suffering pain
bluff *(n.)*   cliff
branding *(n.)*   marking with a hot iron to show ownership
crust *(n.)*   hard surface layer, as of snow
***disporting herself** *(adj.)*   amusing herself
***Divide (Continental or Great Divide)** *(n.)*   ridge of the Rocky
   Mountains that separates rivers flowing toward the Atlantic from those
   flowing toward the Pacific
enchanted *(adj.)*   bewitched
enterprise *(n.)*   project; undertaking
exterminate *(v.)*   to destroy entirely
***fallow** *(adj.)*   dormant; inactive
***fancy** *(n.)*   mental image
flickering *(adj.)*   wavering; moving unsteadily
germination *(n.)*   beginning of growth
***hedgerow** *(n.)*   row of bushes enclosing or separating fields

*Denotes low-frequency word.

hue *(n.)* color
perceptible *(adj.)* capable of being observed
***preen** *(v.)* to clean and trim [feathers]
proficient *(adj.)* skilled; adept
***prosecute** *(v.)* to perform
prosper *(v.)* to succeed
recuperate *(v.)* to regain a former state; to recover
reflect *(v.)* to think seriously; to ponder
reverie *(n.)* daydream
***sheaf** *(n.)* stack or bundle, as of corn
shivering *(adv.)* shaking; trembling
***slaty** *(adj.)* gray like slate (a kind of rock)
***stubble** *(n.)* stems of plants remaining in the soil after harvest
***teeming** *(adj.)* abundant
***variegated** *(adj.)* having different colors

Activities

1. Look closely at the text. How does Cather describe the effect of the seasons on the life of the prairie? Make notes in your journal and discuss your ideas with your class.
2. What effect do the seasons have on the people living on the prairie? Compare their feelings with what is happening in nature.
3. Discuss with your class the symbolism of the male figure that Alexandra imagines carries her away. Why do you think she imagines such a figure?
4. Write an essay comparing the effect of winter and spring on the characters in the story.
5. Describe a significant experience you have had with nature. Try to make your audience feel the effect this experience had on you.

For Further Reading

Arnold, Marilyn. *Willa Cather's Short Fiction*. Athens: Ohio UP, 1986.

Randall, John H. *The Landscape and the Looking Glass*. Boston: Houghton, 1960.

Woodress, James. *Willa Cather: A Literary Life*. Lincoln: U of Nebraska P, 1987.

*Denotes low-frequency word.

17

From *Rickshaw*

Lao She (1899–1966)
Fiction: Novel

Background

Fatherless at an early age, Lao She had to work to support himself and his mother. Life was even more difficult because his family were Manchus, members of an ethnic minority from Manchuria in northeast China. Because of their non-Chinese ethnicity, Manchus were called "barbarians" by the ruling majority and were not given equal educational opportunities. Nevertheless, Lao She was an outstanding student who impressed his professors. Eventually he graduated from Beijing Teachers' College as a teacher of Chinese.

In 1924 he went to London, where he taught the Chinese language. During his stay he became familiar with Charles Dickens's nineteenth-century novels about the life of the London poor. It was also during this period that Lao She began to write his own novels, in part because he was so lonely and nostalgic for China. Ultimately Lao She returned to China, where he became a victim of the so-called "Great Cultural Revolution." Like many of China's intellectuals, he received rough treatment by the young revolutionary Red Guards. Directly or indirectly, Lao She's encounter with the Red Guards led to his death in 1966.

The novel *Rickshaw* takes place in 1934, when the Japanese occupied Manchuria, and ends shortly before the outbreak of war between China and Japan. Influenced by the Western Realism of Dickens, Lao She tells the story of a poor country boy, Hsiang Tzu. The orphaned young man has ambitions of leading a better life in the capital city, Beijing. Lao She's sympathetic picture of the tragic struggle of the urban poor in *Rickshaw* has led critics to regard this as his best novel.

Pre-Reading Activities

1. Why do you think people leave rural areas to live in large cities? In a country as densely populated as China, how could a poor person coming from a rural area to a large city make a living?
2. Keeping the issue of overpopulation in mind, what do you think transportation might be like in a large city in a nonindustrialized country? What kinds of vehicles do you think might be used?
3. What do you think an author could do in his writing to show his readers the need for social reform for the poor?

Key Terms

Beijing (formerly Peking)

Chiang Kai-shek (1888–1975)

Cultural Revolution (1966–1976)

Dickens, Charles (1812–1870)

Hsiang Tzu

Manchu/Manchuria

Mao Zedong (1893–1976)

People's Republic of China (Communist)

Puyi

Red Guards

Republic of China (Nationalist)

Taiwan

From *Rickshaw*
Lao She

When Hsiang Tzu rented someone else's rickshaw, he ran   1
from dawn till dark, from east to west, from south to north. He had
no say in the matter. He was like a **top** someone else was **spinning**.
But in the midst of all this twirling his eyes certainly had no spots before them nor was his mind confused. His thoughts were fixed on
that distant rickshaw, the rickshaw that would make him free and independent, the rickshaw that would be like his own hands and feet.
He would no longer have to put up with the bad temper of rickshaw
agency owners or be hypocritically polite to others when he had his
own rickshaw. With his own strength and his own rickshaw, he
would have something to eat when he opened his eyes in the morning.

He did not fear hardship and had none of the bad habits of the   2
other rickshaw men, habits which all of them could understand and
pardon but were certainly not to be taken as examples of proper be-

Figure 20 • **Chinese rickshaw**

havior. His intelligence and exertions were enough to realize his ambitions. Had his environment been a little better, had he had a little education, he certainly would not have ended up in the "**rubber tire corps**."

Furthermore, no matter what he worked at, he certainly 3 would never have failed to make the most of his opportunities. Unfortunately, he was compelled to pull a rickshaw. All right, he could prove his ability and intelligence in this occupation, too. He seemed to be just the sort of person who would even be a good **demon** in hell if he had to.

Born and reared in a village, he lost both his parents and the 4 few pieces of family land as well. He came to the city when he was eighteen. Bringing with him a country boy's muscles and **forthrightness**, he earned his keep by selling his strength in one day-labor job after another. But he realized before long that pulling a rickshaw was the easiest way of all to earn money. There are limits to the income from other laboring jobs.

There was more variety and opportunity in pulling a rickshaw; 5 you never knew when you might gain a reward greater than you had ever hoped for. Naturally he was aware that such an encounter did not come about entirely by chance. It was essential that both man and rickshaw have a handsome air. You can do business with a man who recognizes quality when you have the goods to sell.

After thinking it over, he believed that he did have the quali-   6
fications. He was strong and the right age. The trouble was he had
never done the running. He didn't dare just grab hold and take off
with a fine-looking rickshaw. But this was no **insurmountable** difficulty. With his **physique** and strength as a foundation, he would
need only ten or fifteen days of practice to be able to run with style.
Then he would rent a new rickshaw. Perhaps he'd get hired on a private basis very quickly and then, after eating **sparingly** and spending
very little for one year, or two years, or even three or four years, he
would certainly be able to get his own rickshaw, and one of the best!
Looking at his youthful muscles, it seemed to him it was only a question of time until he achieved his ambitions and reached his goal. It
was no dream at all. . . .

He was almost like a tree; **sturdy**, silent, and yet alive. He had   7
his own plans and some insight, but he did not enjoy conversation.
Each man's grievances and difficulties were topics of public discussion among the rickshaw pullers. They all reported, or described, or
yelled about their affairs at the rickshaw stands, in the small tea-
houses, and in front of mixed courtyards, the horizontal **tenements**
of Peking.

Afterwards these tales became everyone's property and like a   8
song were passed along from one place to another. Hsiang Tzu was a
peasant; his speech was not as **glib** as the city fellows'. Assuming that
cleverness of speech comes from **innate** ability, what was innate
with him was an unwillingness to talk. He was also, therefore, not
inclined to copy the **spiteful** lips and wicked tongues of the city folk.
He minded his own business and did not enjoy discussing it with others. Because his mouth was often **idle**, he had plenty of time to
think; his eyes seemed always to be peering at his mind. He needed
only to decide; then he would follow the road his mind had opened.
If it happened that his path was blocked, he would remain silent for
several days, **grinding** his teeth, just as if he were chewing up his
heart.

Vocabulary

corps *(n.)*   group of people under a common direction
    *****"rubber tire corps"** *(n.)*   another name for the rickshaw pullers
demon *(n.)*   devil
forthrightness *(n.)*   directness; frankness

*Denotes low-frequency word.

*glib *(adj.)*   smooth; fluent
*grinding *(adj.)*   pressing together with a turning motion, as when grinding one's teeth
idle *(adj.)*   not active
innate *(adj.)*   natural; inborn (as opposed to acquired)
insurmountable *(adj.)*   incapable of being overcome or conquered
*physique *(n.)*   form of the body
sparingly *(adv.)*   in a very limited way
spin *(v.)*   to cause to rotate quickly
spiteful *(adj.)*   full of evil or meanness
sturdy *(adj.)*   strong
tenement *(n.)*   apartment building (usually not a comfortable one)
*top *(n.)*   a child's toy shaped somewhat like an inverted cone, with a point upon which it is spun, as when released from a string

Activities

1. Working with your study group, make notes in your journal about the background of the main character, Hsiang Tzu. Why do you think the author describes these details? Who is the audience for the novel?

2. What is Hsiang Tzu's personal goal? Given his background, why do you think this goal is important for him?

3. Using your journal notes and what you learned from class, write an essay predicting Hsiang Tzu's future.

4. Write an essay on Lao She's portrayal of Chinese society before the Chinese Revolution. What is his purpose?

5. *Library research:* In an encyclopedia or literary biography, read about the English author Charles Dickens and his work. Write an essay comparing Dickens and Lao She.

For Further Reading

Fairband, John King. *China: A New History.* Cambridge, MA: Harvard UP, 1992.

Meskill, John, et al. *An Introduction to Chinese Civilization.* New York: Columbia UP, 1973.

Spence, Jonathan D. *The Search for Modern China.* New York: Norton, 1990.

Vohra, Ranbir. *Lao She and the Chinese Revolution.* Cambridge, MA: Harvard UP, 1974.

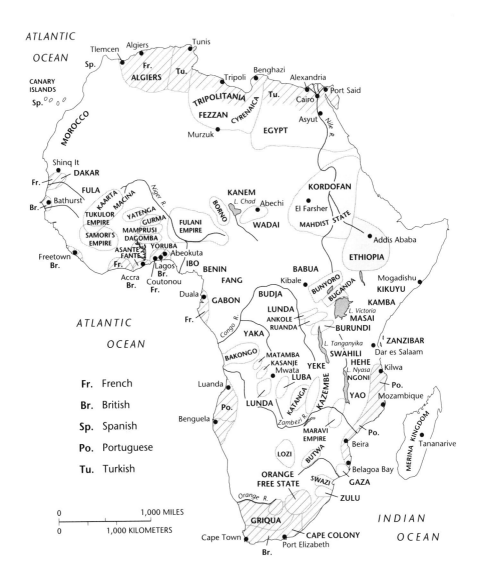

Figure 21A • Map of precolonial Africa

18

From *Things Fall Apart*

Chinua Achebe (b. 1925)
Fiction: Novel

Background

Nigerian author Chinua Achebe is an accomplished novelist, short-story writer, poet, and critic. He also has taught and lectured widely in Africa, Europe, and North America. His novel *Things Fall Apart*, first published in England in 1958, is a classic of modern Anglo-African writing and one of the most widely read works by an African.

Africa as a whole and Nigeria in particular are ethnically very diverse. For example, more than 200 languages are spoken in Nigeria. Modern political divisions in Africa were largely determined by imperialist European nations during the Berlin Conference in 1885. These divisions were unrelated to the areas occupied by the various African peoples. As a result, distinct ethnic groups were forced together into one area and conflicts such as the Biafran War (1965–1970) broke out. In this struggle, the Ibo, one of the three main ethnic groups in Nigeria and the group to which Chinua Achebe belonged, tried to become independent. Although they failed, Achebe gained an international reputation speaking out for his people. It is this specific ethnic background that Achebe drew upon for *Things Fall Apart* and the novels that followed it.

Furthermore, *Things Fall Apart* is biographical—that is, Achebe incorporates his own family's history into the book. He describes what Ibo life was like for his grandfather's generation and the "falling apart" of traditional society after British colonial forces arrived in the "Scramble for Africa." The novel describes the precolonial Ibo society and its later conflict with British imperialism by focusing on an important leader, Okonkwo, and his family. Okonkwo's personal tragedy symbolizes the end of traditional Ibo life.

Figure 21B   •   Map of colonial Africa

Pre-Reading Activities

1. With your study group, review what you know about oral tradition.
    You may wish to look back at earlier chapters in your book.
2. Chinua Achebe's native language is an African language, Ibo. Why do
    you think he writes in English?
3. Why do you think Europeans went to Africa in the late nineteenth
    century? Why do you think they later left?

Key Terms

Berlin Conference (1885)

Biafra; Biafran War (1965–1970)

colonize/colonization/colonial

ethnic group

Ibo (Igbo)

Ikemefuna (Okonkwo's adopted son)

imperialism

Nigeria

Nwoye (Okonkwo's son)

Okonkwo

precolonial

"Scramble for Africa"

secession

Umuofia

From *Things Fall Apart*
Chinua Achebe

For three years Ikemefuna lived in Okonkwo's household and 1
the elders of Umuofia seemed to have forgotten about him. He grew
rapidly like a **yam tendril** in the rainy season, and was full of the
sap of life. He had become wholly absorbed into his new family. He

Figure 22 • Ibo artisans carving wooden masks *(Peter Buckley/Photo Researchers)*

was like an elder brother to Nwoye, and from the very first seemed to have **kindled** a new fire in the younger boy. He made him feel grown-up; and they no longer spent the evenings in mother's hut while she cooked, but now sat with Okonkwo in his *obi*, or watched him as he tapped his palm tree for the evening wine. Nothing pleased Nwoye now more than to be sent for by his mother or another of his father's wives to do one of those difficult and masculine tasks in the home, like splitting wood, or **pounding** food. On receiving such a message through a younger brother or sister, Nwoye would **feign** annoyance and **grumble** aloud about women and their troubles.

Okonkwo was inwardly pleased at his son's development, and and he knew it was due to Ikemefuna. He wanted Nwoye to grow into a tough young man capable of ruling his father's household when he was dead and gone to join the ancestors. He wanted him to be a **prosperous** man, having enough in his barn to feed the ancestors with regular sacrifices. And so he was always happy when he heard him grumbling about women. That showed that in time he would be able to control his women-folk. No matter how prosperous a man was, if he was unable to rule his women and his children (and especially his women) he was not really a man. He was like the man in the song who had ten and one wives and not enough soup for his **foo-foo**.

So Okonkwo encouraged the boys to sit with him in his *obi*, and he told them stories of the land—masculine stories of violence and **bloodshed**. Nwoye knew that it was right to be masculine and to be violent, but somehow he still preferred the stories that his mother used to tell, and which she no doubt still told to her younger children—stories of the **tortoise** and his **wily** ways . . . and of the quarrel between Earth and Sky long ago, and how Sky **withheld** rain for seven years, until crops **withered** and the dead could not be buried because the **hoes** broke on the stony Earth. At last **Vulture** was sent to **plead** with Sky, and to soften his heart with a song of the suffering of the sons of men. Whenever Nwoye's mother sang this song he felt carried away to the distant scene in the sky where Vulture, Earth's **emissary**, sang for mercy.

At last Sky was moved to pity, and he gave to Vulture rain wrapped in leaves of coco-yam. But as he flew home his long **talons** pierced the leaves and the rain fell as it had never fallen before. And so heavily did it rain on Vulture that he did not return to deliver his message but flew to a distant land, from where he had espied a fire.

And when he got there he found it was a man making a sacrifice. He warmed himself in the fire and ate the **entrails**.

That was the kind of story that Nwoye loved. But he now   5
knew that they were for foolish women and children, and he knew that his father wanted him to be a man. And so he feigned that he no longer cared for women's stories. And when he did this he saw that his father was pleased and no longer **rebuked** him or beat him. So Nwoye and Ikemefuna would listen to Okonkwo's stories about tribal wars, or how, years ago, he had stalked his victim, overpowered him, and obtained his first human head.

Vocabulary

bloodshed *(n.)*   killing; spilling of human blood
emissary *(n.)*   person or agent sent on a specific mission
***entrails** *(n.)*   internal organs, especially the intestines
***feign** *(v.)*   to pretend
***foo-foo** *(n.)*   Ibo food prepared from mashed manioc root
grumble *(v.)*   to mutter or complain in an angry manner
***hoe** *(n.)*   tool with a thin blade set across the end of a long handle, used for loosening the earth
kindle *(v.)*   to light a fire
***obi** *(n.)*   Ibo living quarters for the head of the family
plead *(v.)*   to beg
pounding *(n.)*   beating to a pulp or powder
prosperous *(adj.)*   successful; well off
rebuke *(v.)*   to criticize sharply
sap *(n.)*   any fluid vital to the life of an organism; vigor; energy
***talon** *(n.)*   claw of a bird such as a vulture
***tendril** *(n.)*   threadlike part of a climbing plant that supports it as it climbs
***tortoise** *(n.)*   turtle
***vulture** *(n.)*   large bird, related to eagles and hawks, that lives on dead flesh
***wily** *(adj.)*   sly; crafty
***wither** *(v.)*   to dry up, as from great heat
withhold (withheld) *(v.)*   to hold back; to keep back
yam *(n.)*   sweet potato having red flesh

* Denotes low-frequency word.

Activities

1. In your study group or alone, make notes in your journal about the roles of men and women in traditional Ibo society as shown in *Things Fall Apart.*

2. Based on your reading, what other values do you believe are important in the Ibo culture? Discuss them with your study group or your class.

3. What evidence of oral tradition do you see in the story? How does the mother's oral tradition differ from the father's?

4. Choose one of the Ibo cultural values discussed above and write an essay explaining why the Ibo would consider this value important.

5. Every novel written by Chinua Achebe is about Nigeria, yet he has chosen to write in English. Since this is the language of the colonial power that controlled Nigeria before 1965, his choice has definite political implications. Write an essay discussing the advantages and disadvantages of writing a nation's literature in the language of a former colonial power.

6. In your study group, try to identify the framed story or story within the story. Discuss the relationship between humans and the gods as portrayed in the framed story. Make notes in your journal.

7. Write an essay comparing the sacrifice to Vulture in *Things Fall Apart* and the sacrifice to Poseidon in *The Odyssey* (Chapter 3).

For Further Reading

Achebe, Chinua. *Hopes and Impediments: Selected Essays.* New York: Doubleday, 1989.

Chinweizu et al. *Toward the Decolonization of African Literature.* Vol. 1. Washington, DC: Howard UP, 1983.

Pakenham, Thomas. *The Scramble for Africa: The White Man's Conquest of the Dark Continent from 1876 to 1912.* New York: Random, 1991.

CHAPTER **19**

From *Out of Africa*

Isak Dinesen (1885–1962)
Fiction: Novel

Background

Isak Dinesen is one of the pseudonyms, or pen names, of Baroness Karen Dinesen von Blixen-Finecke, who was born to a wealthy Danish family. As a young woman she emigrated from Denmark to the British colony in Kenya, East Africa, with her fiancé, Baron Bror von Blixen-Finecke. They were part of the emigration that followed the division of Africa by imperialist European governments. The 1890 Anglo-German Treaty divided East Africa into English and German colonies where European settlers were encouraged to set up businesses, plantations, and mines.

The Blixens purchased a farm on which they tried to grow coffee. Seventeen years later, both the farm and the marriage were in ruins. Suffering physically and psychologically, Isak Dinesen returned to her family in Denmark at age 46. It was through her writing that she managed to survive this painful experience.

The publication of her collection of stories, *Seven Gothic Tales* (1934), established her as one of the most significant European women writers of the mid-1930s. The earliest versions of these stories were begun in Africa. Her next work, *Out of Africa* (1937), has been considered an important landmark in colonial literature. A Romantic memoir of Dinesen's years in Africa, it was conceived and written after her return to Denmark. Like Wordsworth, she recreates the African landscape in recollection, focusing on her sensations and impressions. Her views of the African ethnic groups she encountered, especially the Kikuyu and the Muslim Somali, are Eurocentric—that is, colored by a European perspective.

149

With the publication of *Out of Africa*, Dinesen made her name as a modern classical writer. Further African reminiscences followed with *Shadows on the Grass* (1961). In 1985 the award-winning film *Out of Africa* was released, resulting in a renewed interest in the life and works of Isak Dinesen.

Pre-Reading Activities

1. With your study group or class, discuss what you think might be the attitudes of a colonial power toward the people of its colonies.
2. Romantic (nineteenth-century) European writers are interested in exotic places. What might they focus on when writing about Africa?

Key Terms

Anglo-German Treaty (1890)   Muslim
colonial literature   nostalgia
East Africa   pseudonym
Eurocentric view   simile
Kenya   Somali
Kikuyu   Swaheli

From *Out of Africa*
Isak Dinesen

I had a farm in Africa, at the foot of the Ngong Hills. The Equator runs across these highlands, a hundred miles to the North, and the farm lay at an altitude of over six thousand feet. In the day-time you felt that you had got high up, near to the sun, but the early mornings and evenings were **limpid** and restful, and the nights were cold.   1

The geographical position and the height of the land combined to create a landscape that [was not like anything] in all the world. There was no fat on it and no **luxuriance** anywhere; it was Africa **distilled** up through six thousand feet, like the strong and refined **essence** of a continent. The colors were dry and burnt, like the colors in pottery. The trees had a light delicate foliage, the structure of which was different from that of the trees in Europe; it did not grow in **bows** or **cupolas**, but in horizontal layers, and the formation gave   2 to the tall solitary trees a likeness to the palms, or a heroic and romantic air like **fullrigged** ships with their sails **clewed up**, and to the edge of a wood a strange appearance as if the whole wood were faintly **vibrating**. Upon the grass of the great plains the crooked bare old thorn-trees were scattered, and the grass was spiced like **thyme** and **bogmyrtle**; in some places the scent was so strong, that it **smarted** in the nostrils. . . . The views were immensely wide. Everything that you saw made for greatness and freedom, and unequalled nobility.

The chief feature of the landscape, and of your life in it, was   3
the air. Looking back on a **sojourn** in the African highlands, you are struck by your feeling of having lived for a time up in the air. The sky was rarely more than pale blue or violet, with a **profusion** of mighty, weightless, ever-changing clouds towering up and sailing on it, but it has a blue **vigor** in it, and at a short distance it painted the ranges of hills and the woods a fresh deep blue. In the middle of the day the air was alive over the land, like a flame burning; it **scintillated**, waved and shone like running water, mirrored and doubled all objects, and created great **Fata Morgana**. Up in this high air you breathed easily, drawing in a vital assurance and lightness of heart. In the highlands you woke up in the morning and thought: Here I am, where I ought to be. . . .

I had six thousand acres of land, and had thus got much spare   4
land besides the coffee-plantation. Part of the farm was native forest, and about one thousand acres were squatters' land, what [the Kikuyu] called their *shambas*. The squatters are Natives, who with their families hold a few acres on a white man's farm, and in return have to work for him a certain number of days in the year. My squatters, I think, saw the relationship in a different light, for many of them were born on the farm, and their fathers before them, and they very likely regarded me as a sort of superior squatter on their estates. The squatters' land was more intensely alive than the rest of the farm, and was changing with the seasons the year round. The **maize** grew up higher than your head as you walked on the narrow **hard-trampled** footpaths in between the tall green rustling **regiments**. . . . The beans ripened in the fields, were gathered and **thrashed** by the women, and the stalks and pods were collected and burned, so that in certain seasons thin blue columns of smoke rose here and there all over the farm. The Kikuyu also grew the sweet potatoes, that have a vinelike leaf and spread over the ground like a dense **entangled** mat, and many varieties of big yellow and green **speckled** pumpkins. . . .

Nairobi was our town, twelve miles away. . . . Here were the   5
Government House and the big central offices; from here the country
was ruled. . . . The quarters of the Natives and of the colored immigrants were very extensive compared to the European town.

The Swaheli town . . . had not a good name in any way, but   6
was a lively, dirty and **gaudy** place, with, at any hour, a number of
things going on in it. It was built mostly out of old paraffin tins hammered flat, in various states of rust, like the coral rock, the fossilized
structure, from which the spirit of the advancing civilization was
steadily fleeing.

The Somali town was farther away from Nairobi, on account,   7
I think, of the Somalis' system of **seclusion** of their women. There
were in my day a few beautiful young Somali women, of whom all
the town knew the names, who went and lived in the Bazaar and led
the Nairobi Police a great dance; they were intelligent, and **bewitching** people. But the honest Somali women were not seen in the
town. The Somali town lay exposed to all winds and was shadeless
and dusty, it must have recalled to the Somali their native deserts.

Europeans, who live for a long time, even for several genera-   8
tions, in the same place, cannot **reconcile themselves** to the
complete indifference to the surroundings of their homes, of the **nomadic** races. The Somalis' houses were irregularly **strewn** on the
bare ground, and looked as if they had been nailed together with a
bushel of four-inch nails, to last for a week. It was a surprising thing,
when you entered one of them, to find it inside so neat and fresh,
scented with Arab incenses, with fine carpets and hangings, **vessels**
of brass and silver, and swords with ivory **hilts** and noble blades.

The Somali women themselves had dignified, gentle ways, and   9
were hospitable and gay, with a laughter like silver bells. I was much
at home in the Somali village through my Somali servant Farah
Aden, who was with me all the time that I was in Africa, and I went
to many of their feasts. A big Somali wedding is a magnificent, traditional festivity. As a guest of honor I was taken into the bridal chamber, where the walls and bridal bed were hung with old gently glow-
ing weavings and **embroideries**, and the dark-eyed young bride
herself was stiff, like a **marshal's baton** with heavy silks, gold and
amber.

The Somali were cattle-dealers and traders all over the coun-   10
try. For the transport of their **goods** they kept a number of little grey
donkeys in the village, and I have seen camels there as well:
haughty, hardened products of the desert, beyond all earthly sufferings, like Cactus, and like the Somali.

Vocabulary

bewitching *(adj.)*   attractive as if by the power of witchcraft

***bogmyrtle** *(n.)*   fragrant plant that grows in wet, spongy ground

bow *(n.)*   something bent into a simple curve; arch

***clewed up** *(adj.)*   rolled or hauled up

***cupola** *(n.)*   arched structure resting on a circular base forming a covering

distilled *(adj.)*   concentrated

***embroidery** *(n.)*   needlework done with thread on cloth

entangled *(adj.)*   twisted together

essence *(n.)*   real or ultimate nature of a thing

***Fata Morgana** *(n.)*   mirage; illusion

***fullrigged** *(adj.)*   having the maximum number of sails and masts (used in describing a ship)

gaudy *(adj.)*   flashy; tastelessly ornamented

goods *(n. pl.)*   wares; merchandise

***hard-trampled** *(adj.)*   heavily walked on

haughty *(adj.)*   scornfully proud

***hilt** *(n.)*   handle of a sword

limpid *(adj.)*   clear

***luxuriance** *(n.)*   lushness

***maize** *(n.)*   corn

***marshal's baton** *(n.)*   slender stick carried by a high military officer as a symbol of office

nomadic *(adj.)*   wandering from place to place, usually seasonally in order to get food

profusion *(n.)*   great quantity

reconcile oneself *(v.)*   to make oneself accept

regiment *(n.)*   ordered rows, usually military

scintillate *(v.)*   to sparkle

seclusion *(n.)*   isolation; removal from outside influence

***smart** *(v.)*   to cause sharp pain

sojourn *(n.)*   temporary stay

***speckled** *(adj.)*   spotted

***strew (strewed, strewn)** *(v.)*   to scatter

***thrash** *(v.)*   to separate the seeds from the rest of a plant

***thyme** *(n.)*   plant of the mint family with fragrant leaves

vessel *(n.)*   container such as a cup, bowl, or kettle

vibrate *(v.)*   to move back and forth quickly; to quiver

vigor *(n.)*   force

*Denotes low-frequency word.

Activities

1. Dinesen refers many times to nature in her story. Read the story closely, making notes in your journal of the images she uses to describe nature. Discuss your notes with your group.
2. Based on your notes and discussion, write a summary of the way Isak Dinesen presents nature in her story.
3. What is Dinesen's attitude toward the native Africans in the story? Does she portray the Somali and the Kikuyu in the same way?
4. In an essay, compare life in Africa as shown in *Things Fall Apart* (Chapter 18) with how it is shown in *Out of Africa*. Why are the two depictions different?

For Further Reading

Johannesson, Eric O. *The World of Isak Dinesen.* Seattle: U of Washington P, 1961.

Langbaum, Robert. *The Gayety of Vision: A Study of Isak Dinesen's Art.* New York: Random, 1964.

Thurman, Judith. *Isak Dinesen, The Life of a Storyteller.* New York: St. Martin's, 1982.

Trzebinski, Errol. *Silence Will Speak: Denys Finch Hatton and Karen Blixen.* Chicago: U of Chicago P, 1977.

20

From *The Woman in the Dunes*

Kobo Abe (1924–1993)
Fiction: Philosophical Novel

Background

Perhaps Kobo Abe's early sense of alienation derived from his growing up in Japanese-occupied Manchuria, China, outside of his native Japan. As a young man, he entertained his classmates by reciting the Gothic tales of the American writer Edgar Allan Poe. Like the male protagonist of *The Woman in the Dunes*, he also enjoyed doing mathematical puzzles and collecting insects.

After returning to Tokyo, Japan, he developed tuberculosis and during his hospitalization devoured the works of the Russian Existentialist novelist Fyodor Dostoevsky. As Japan became more deeply involved in World War II, Abe felt a further sense of alienation from his culture and continued to read the work of Western philosophers such as Nietzsche, Jaspers, and Heidegger, and of the Existentialist author Franz Kafka.

The end of the war found Abe again in Manchuria, where his father died during a typhus epidemic. Although suffering poverty and ill health, Abe studied to become a medical doctor like his father and graduated in 1948. But he soon decided to undertake a career as a writer.

Like many intellectuals in the 1950s, Abe was shocked at the destructive horror of the dropping of two atomic bombs on Japan in order to end World War II. The cost of the war was tremendous, not only in human lives but in the devastation of traditional Japanese life. In an interview in the 1960s, Abe stated, "I will never forget that my adolescence began amidst death and ruin."

The Woman in the Dunes is a strange story that shows strong Western philosophical influence. Neither of the important characters—the man and the woman—has a personal name in the story.

Pre-Reading Activities

1. With your study group, discuss your feelings about the meaning of life. Do you think your ideas are different from your parents' or grandparents' ideas? In what way are they different (or the same)?
2. Do you believe that science and technology make our lives better than our grandparents' lives were? Are any of the changes made by technology causing our lives to be worse? How?

Key Terms

Camus, Albert (1913–1960)
cross-cultural influence
dehumanization
Dostoevsky, Fyodor (1821–1881)
Existentialism/Existentialist

Manchuria
metamorphosis
philosophy/philosophical novel
Sartre, Jean-Paul (1905–1980)

From *The Woman in the Dunes*
Kobo Abe

When he had finished carrying the kerosene cans over the 1 second time, he heard the sound of voices, and on the road above a hand lamp **flickered**.

The woman spoke rather sharply. "It's the lift basket. I've al- 2 ready finished over here. Give me some help over there, will you?"

For the first time he **grasped** the meaning of the sandbags 3 that lay buried at the top of the ladder: by running the ropes around them, the baskets could be raised and lowered. Four men managed each basket, and there were two or three groups in all. For the most part, they appeared to be young men who worked briskly and efficiently. By the time the basket of one group was full, the next group was already waiting to take over. In six hauls, the sand which had been piled up was completely leveled off.

"Those fellows are amazing!" 4

His tone was friendly as he wiped away the sweat with his 5

shirt sleeve. The young men, who **uttered** not a word of ridicule at his helping with the sand, appeared to devote themselves energetically to their work. He felt **well-disposed** toward them.

"Yes. In our village we really follow the motto 'Love Your Home'."   6

"What sort of love is that?"   7

"It's the love you have for where you live."   8

"Great!"   9

He laughed, and she laughed with him. But she did not seem   10
to understand the reason for her laughter herself.

From afar came the sound of a three-wheeled truck starting   11
up.

"Well now, shall we take a rest?" [he said].   12

"Oh no. When they finish with one round they come right   13
back again with the basket."

"Oh, let it go. The rest can wait until tomorrow and . . ."   14

He arose unconcerned and began walking toward the   15
earthen floor, but she showed no signs of coming along with him.

"You can't do things that way! We've got to work at least once   16
all around the house."

"What do you mean, 'all around'?"   17

"Well, we can't let the house be smashed, can we? The sand   18
comes down from all sides."

"But it'll take until morning to do that."   19

As though challenged, she turned abruptly and hurried off.   20
She apparently intended to return to the base of the cliff and continue her work. Quite like the behavior of the **beetle**, he thought.

Now that he understood this, he certainly wouldn't be taken   21
in again.

"I'm **dumbfounded**! Is it like this every night?"   22

"The sand never stops. The baskets and the three-wheeler keep   23
going the whole night through."

"I suppose they do." And indeed they did. The sand never   24
stopped falling. The man was completely at a loss. He was bewildered, rather as if he had casually stepped on the tail of a snake that he had thought to be small but had turned out to be surprisingly large; by the time he had realized this, its head was already threatening him from behind.

"But this means you exist only for the purpose of clearing   25
away the sand, doesn't it?"

"Yes, but we just can't sneak away at night, you know."   26

He was more and more upset. He had no intention of becom-   27
ing involved in such a life.

"Yes, you can. It would be simple, wouldn't it? You can do   28
anything if you want to."

"No, that wouldn't be right at all." She spoke casually, breath-   29
ing in rhythm with her shoveling. "The village keeps going because
we never let up clearing away the sand like this. If we stopped, in ten
days the village would be completely buried. Next it will be the
neighbor's turn in back. See, there."

"Very praiseworthy, I'm sure. And do the basket gangs work so   30
hard for the same reason?"

"Well, they do get some pay from the town."   31

"If they have that much money, why don't they build a more   32
permanent hedge of trees against the sand?"

"It seems to be cheaper to do it this way . . . when you fig-   33
ure the costs."

"This way? Is this really a way?" Suddenly a feeling of anger   34
welled up in him. He was angry at the things that bound the woman
. . . and at the woman who let herself be bound. "Why must you
cling so to such a village? I really don't understand. This sand is not a
trifling matter. You're greatly mistaken if you think you can set
yourself up against it with such methods. It's preposterous! Absurd! I
give up. I really give up. I have absolutely no sympathy for you."

Tossing the shovel on the kerosene cans which had been left   35
out, he abruptly returned to the room, ignoring the expression on
the woman's face.

He spent a sleepless night, turning and tossing. He **pricked up**   36
his ears, sensing the woman's presence. He felt somewhat guilty.
Taking such a stand in front of her was actually an expression of jealousy at what **bound** her; and was it not also a desire that she should
put aside her work and come secretly to his bed? Actually, his strong
feelings were apparently not simply anger at female stupidity. There
was something more **unfathomable**.

[Although he had laughed at her unscientific observation that   37
sand absorbed water, now he saw that] his mattress was getting
damper and damper, and the sand more and more **clammy** to his
skin. It was all too unreasonable, too **eerie**.

There was no need to blame himself for having thrown the   38
shovel aside and come in. He did not have to take that much responsibility. Besides, the obligations he had to assume were already more
than enough. In fact, his involvement with the sand and his insect
collecting were, after all, simply ways to escape, however temporarily, from his obligations and the inactivity of his life.

No matter how he tried, he could not sleep.   39

Vocabulary

*beetle *(n.)*   insect with hard outer wings
bind (bound, bound) *(v.)*   to hold; to restrain
*clammy *(adj.)*   damp; moist; sticky
dumbfounded *(adj.)*   astonished; amazed
eerie *(adj.)*   frightening because of strangeness
flicker *(v.)*   to burn or shine unsteadily
grasp *(v.)*   to understand
*prick up one's ears *(v. phrase)*   to listen intensely
*trifling *(adj.)*   unimportant
unfathomable *(adj.)*   not understandable
utter *(v.)*   to speak
well-disposed *(adj.)*   positive; favorable

Activities

1. Read aloud the dialogue between the woman and the man. Have a narrator read the man's inner thoughts.

2. The protagonist is a science teacher who tries to find a rational explanation for everything. Alone or with a partner, make a note of passages from the text that show him using his reason.

3. Look again at the text; make a note of passages where the scientist's reason does *not* explain what is happening. What do you think is the author's purpose in showing this?

4. Notice that the two characters have no personal names, but are "the man" and "the woman." In what way is this symbolic?

5. Write an essay contrasting the man's existentialist view of life with the simple view of the woman in the dunes.

6. Write an essay on the limits of reason in this selection from Kobo Abe's novel *The Woman in the Dunes.*

For Further Reading

Barnes, Hazel. *The Literature of Possibility; A Study of Humanistic Existentialism.* Lincoln: U of Nebraska P, 1959.

Currie, William. *Abe Kobo's Nightmare World of Sand.* New York: Knopf, 1976.

Hibbett, Howard, ed. *Contemporary Japanese Literature.* New York: Knopf, 1983.

*Denotes low-frequency word.

21

From *Chronicle of a Death Foretold*

Gabriel García Márquez (b. 1928)
Fiction: Novella

Background

In the first half of the twentieth century, the fiction of Latin America largely mirrored various regional and national customs. However, the 1940s saw the translation into Spanish of important international authors such as Proust, Joyce, Woolf, and Faulkner. As a result, that decade saw the appearance of several Central and South American writers, such as Guatemalan Miguel Angel Asturias, who took the novel in new directions.

The next generation of Latin American novelists brought a new and important feature to their Modernist work: the role of the imaginative world. Mimesis, or the imitation of reality, was replaced with invention. By the 1960s, the creativity and brilliance of Latin American novelists had produced a so-called "boom" that was internationally recognized. Works coming out of this period, characterized by the fantastic and inventive reality called Magical Realism, included Julio Cortazar's *Hopscotch* (1963) and Manuel Puig's 1968 work, *Betrayed by Rita Hayworth*. It was in this prolific period that Gabriel García Márquez began to write.

García Márquez was born in the small village of Aracataca in Colombia, South America. From his grandparents he heard the local oral tradition and myths. García Márquez recreated this tiny, forgotten inland port of call in his fictional and mythological village, Macondo, which appears in many of his works. García Márquez studied law after graduating from high school but soon became an international journalist for a Colombian newspaper.

García Márquez spent some years living and visiting abroad, and, after the Cuban Revolution in 1959, joined Prensa Latina, a Cuban news agency, first in Bogotá, Colombia, and then in New York. His left-wing political views have been widely publicized, making him unwelcome in anti-Communist circles. Since 1975 he has lived mostly in Mexico, where he continues to write. His most famous novel, *One Hundred Years of Solitude*, was published in 1967 and took the international literary world by storm. It has been translated from Spanish into more than 30 languages. For his years of consistently outstanding literary production, García Márquez was awarded the Nobel Prize in literature in 1982.

In his novella *Chronicle of a Death Foretold*, García Márquez tells of the murder of an innocent young man, Santiago Nasar, in a small Colombian village. The end of the story is told first. Then the details are recreated by an unnamed omniscient narrator through the recollections of a number of the villagers; as each person tells his or her story, the same moments are relived over and over but are seen from a different perspective. Thus the story compresses time and does not follow normal chronological order.

García Márquez uses a stream of consciousness to reveal his characters in a state of stagnation, decay, and solitude. The close reader will also note the religious symbolism in the names of the story's characters and their parallels with the New Testament story of Christ.

Pre-Reading Activities

1. With your study group, discuss what you believe is the role of a man's honor in traditional family life. What is the role of a woman's honor?

2. How do you think someone who is accused of a crime should be treated? Discuss your ideas with your group or class.

Key Terms

Colombia	omniscient narrator
Latin American "boom" of the 1960s	perspective
Magical Realism	South America
Modernist	stream of consciousness
Nobel Prize in Literature	symbolism

Figure 23 • **Modern Central American village with church** *(Carole M. Shaffer-Koros)*

From *Chronicle of a Death Foretold*
Gabriel García Márquez

On the day they were going to kill him, Santiago Nasar got up   1
at five-thirty in the morning to wait for the boat the **bishop** was
coming on. . . .

[Santiago Nasar] had slept little and poorly, without getting   2
undressed, and he woke up with a headache and a **sediment** of cop-
per stirrup on his palate, and he interpreted them as the natural
havoc of the wedding **revels** that had gone on until after midnight.
Furthermore: all the many people he ran into after leaving his house
at five minutes past six and until he was carved up like a pig an hour
later remembered him as being a little sleepy but in a good mood,
and he remarked to all of them in a casual way that it was a very
beautiful day. No one was certain if he was referring to the state of
the weather.

Many people **coincided** in recalling that it was a radiant   3
morning with a sea breeze coming in through the banana groves, as

was to be expected in a fine February of that period. But most agreed
that the weather was **funereal**, with a cloudy, low sky and the thick
smell of still waters, and that at the moment of the misfortune a thin
drizzle was falling like . . . one Santiago Nasar had seen in his
dream. . . . I was recovering from the wedding revels in the **apostolic** lap of Maria Alejandrina Cervantes, and I only awakened with
the **clamor** of the alarm bells, thinking they had turned them loose
in honor of the bishop. . . .

    I saw [Santiago] in [his mother's] memory. He had just turned   4
twenty-one the last week in January, and he was slim and pale and
had his father's Arab eyelids and curly hair. He was the only child
of a **marriage of convenience** without a single moment of happiness. . . . From her he had inherited a sixth sense. From his father
he learned at a very early age the manipulation of **firearms**, his love
for horses, and the mastery of high-flying birds of prey, but from him
he also learned the good arts of **valor** and **prudence**. They spoke
Arabic between themselves, but not in front of [his mother] Placida
Linero, so that she wouldn't feel **excluded**.

    They were never seen armed in town, and the only time they   5
brought in their trained birds was for a demonstration of **falconry** at
a charity bazaar. The death of his father had forced him to abandon
his studies at the end of secondary school in order to take charge of
the family ranch. By his nature, Santiago Nasar was merry and
peaceful, and openhearted. . . .

    It had struck six and the street lights were still on. In the   6
branches of the almond trees and on some balconies the colored
wedding decorations were still hanging and one might have thought
they'd just been hung in honor of the bishop. . . . When Santiago
Nasar left his house, several people were running toward the docks,
hastened along by the **bellowing** of the boat.

    The only place open on the square was a milk shop on one   7
side of the church, where the two men were who were waiting for
Santiago Nasar in order to kill him. . . . They were twins: Pedro and
Pablo Vicario. They were twenty-four years old, and they looked so
much alike that it was difficult to tell them apart. "They were hard-
looking, but of a good sort," the report said. I, who had known them
since grammar school, would have written the same thing. That
morning they were still wearing their dark wedding suits, too heavy
and formal for the Caribbean, and they looked **devastated** by so
many hours of bad living, but they'd done their duty and shaved. . . .

    Angela Vicario was the youngest daughter of a family of **scant**   8
resources. Her father, Poncio Vicario, was a poor man's goldsmith,

and he'd lost his sight from doing so much fine work in gold in order to maintain the honor of the house. Purisima del Carmen, her mother, had been a schoolteacher until she married for ever. Her **meek** and somewhat **afflicted** look hid the strength of her character quite well. "She looked like a **nun**," my wife Mercedes recalls. She devoted herself with such spirit of sacrifice to the care of her husband and the rearing of her children that at times one forgot that she still existed. . . . The brothers were brought up to be men. The girls had been reared to get married. . . .

"Any man will be happy with them because they've been raised   9
to suffer," [my mother said]. . . . No one would have thought, nor did anyone say, that Angela Vicario wasn't a virgin. She hadn't known any previous fiancé and she'd grown up along with her sisters under the **rigor** of a mother of iron. Even when it was less than two months before she would be married, Pura Vicario wouldn't let her go alone with [her husband-to-be] Bayardo San Roman to see the house where they were going to live, but she and the blind father accompanied her to watch over her honor. . . .

[On the wedding night] Pura Vicario had fallen into a deep   10
sleep, when there was knocking on the door. "They were three very slow knocks," she told my mother, "but they had that strange touch of bad news about them." . . . [She] saw Bayardo San Roman in the glow of the street light, his silk shirt unbuttoned and his fancy pants held up by elastic suspenders. "He had that green color of dreams," Pura Vicario told my mother. Angela Vicario was in the shadows. . . . Her satin dress was in **shreds** and she was wrapped in a towel up to the waist. Pura Vicario thought they'd gone off the road in the car. . . .

"Holy Mother of God," she said in terror. "Answer me if you're   11
still of this world."

Bayardo San Roman didn't enter, but softly pushed his wife   12
into the house without speaking a word. Then he kissed Pura Vicario on the cheek and spoke to her in a very deep, **dejected** voice, but with great tenderness. "Thank you for everything, Mother," he told her. "You're a saint."

. . . The twins returned home a short time before three, ur-   13
gently summoned by their mother. . . . Pedro Vicario, the more forceful of the brothers, picked [Angela] up by the waist and sat her on the dining room table.

"All right, girl," he said to her, **trembling** with rage, "tell us   14
who it was."

She took the time necessary to say the name. She looked for   15 it in the shadows, she found it at first sight among the many, many easily confused names from this world and the other, and she nailed it to the wall with her well-aimed **dart**, like a butterfly with no will whose sentence has always been written.

"Santiago Nasar," she said.   16

Vocabulary

afflicted *(adj.)* troubled; distressed

*apostolic *(adj.)* relating to an apostle (one sent on a mission), especially any of the 12 apostles of Christ

*bellowing *(n.)* loud, deep, hollow sound characteristic of a bull

bishop *(n.)* member of the Christian clergy who supervises other clergy, typically governing a diocese

clamor *(n.)* loud, continuous noise

coincide *(v.)* to be in agreement; to concur

dart *(n.)* small missile, usually with a pointed tip at one end and feathers at the other

dejected *(adj.)* disheartened; discouraged

devastated *(adj.)* overwhelmed; overcome

drizzle *(n.)* fine, misty rain

excluded *(adj.)* barred from participation or inclusion

*falconry *(n.)* art and sport of training hawks to hunt in cooperation with a person

firearm *(n.)* weapon from which a shot is fired by gunpowder

*funereal *(adj.)* suggesting a funeral or burial

hastened *(adj.)* hurried

havoc *(n.)* confusion; disorder

*marriage of convenience *(n.)* marriage contracted for social, political, or economic advantage rather than for mutual affection

meek *(adj.)* submissive

nun *(n.)* woman belonging to a religious order, especially one under the vows of poverty, chastity, and obedience

prudence *(n.)* ability to exercise sound judgment in practical matters

*revel *(n.)* wild party or celebration

rigor *(n.)* strictness

scant *(adj.)* barely sufficient

*sediment *(n.)* deposited material

shred *(n.)* long, narrow strip cut or torn off

trembling *(adj.)* shaking involuntarily; shivering

valor *(n.)* personal bravery

*Denotes low-frequency word.

Activities

1. Magical Realism combines reality with fantastic, inventive events. Look closely at the text. Alone or with a partner, make notes about important events that seem realistic and those that are fantastic.

2. Look closely at the text. Who is telling the story? What do we know about the narrator?

3. What is the crime of which Santiago Nasar is accused? What is his punishment? Who punishes him? Write an essay agreeing or disagreeing with the punishment.

4. In your journal, make notes on the roles of both women and men in García Márquez's story. In an essay, analyze the roles of men and women in the story.

5. Write an essay on the treatment of honor in *Chronicle of a Death Foretold*.

6. Write an essay on Magical Realism in *Chronicle of a Death Foretold*.

For Further Reading

Byk, John. "From Fact to Fiction: Gabriel García Márquez and the Short Story." *Mid-American Review* 6 (1986): 111–16.

McMurray, George, ed. *Critical Essays on Gabriel García Márquez.* Boston: Houghton, 1987.

Williams, Raymond L. *Gabriel García Márquez.* Boston: Twayne, 1984.

22

From "Boys and Girls"

Alice Munro (b. 1931)
Fiction: Short Story

Background

Alice Munro was born Alice Laidlaw to a family of Scots descent in Ontario, Canada. Her father, Robert Laidlaw, became a breeder of silver foxes shortly before he married Anne Chamney, a schoolteacher. Their daughter Alice spent her youth in small-town Wingham and from 1949 to 1951 attended the University of Western Ontario, where she majored in English and began to write. In 1951 Alice married James Munro; she spent the next 20 years living on the west coast of Canada, where their three daughters were born. In 1971 she returned to Ontario to be close to her father and her former home. Following a second marriage, she moved to her present home in Clinton, Ontario.

Munro is widely recognized as a major North American author and has won several Canadian Governor-General's Awards for her outstanding fiction. "Boys and Girls" is from her first collection, *Dance of the Happy Shades*, which appeared in Canada in 1968 and was dedicated to her father. In this early story, the conflict between mother and daughter is readily apparent.

Pre-Reading Activities

1. With your study group or class, discuss ways in which adults treat girls and boys differently. Why do you think they do this?
2. How do you think family life on a farm is different from life in the city? Discuss your ideas with your class.

Key Terms

autobiographical   provincial
feminist   Realism
gender role   rural
Ontario, Canada   sexist
postmodern

From "Boys and Girls"
Alice Munro

My father was a fox farmer. That is, he raised **silver foxes**, in   1
pens; and in the fall and early winter, when their fur was **prime**, he
killed them and skinned them and sold their pelts to the Hudson's
Bay Company or the Montreal Fur Traders. These companies sup-
plied us with heroic calendars to hang, one on each side of the
kitchen door. . . .

[M]y father worked after supper in the cellar of our house. The   2
cellar was **white-washed**, and lit by several hundred-watt bulbs
over the worktable. My brother Laird and I sat on the top step and
watched. My father removed the pelt inside-out from the body of the
fox, which looked surprisingly small, mean and ratlike, **deprived** of
its arrogant weight of fur.

The naked, slippery bodies were collected in a **sack** and buried   3
at the **dump**. One time the hired man, Henry Bailey, had taken a
swipe at me with this sack, saying, "Christmas present!" My mother
thought that was not funny. In fact she disliked the whole pelting operation—that was what the killing, skinning, and preparation of the
furs was called—and wished it did not have to take place in the
house. . . .

Alive, the foxes inhabited a world my father made for them.   4
It was surrounded by a high guard fence, like a medieval town, with
a gate that was **padlocked** at night. Along the streets of this town
were ranged large, sturdy pens. . . . Everything was tidy and **ingenious**; my father was tirelessly inventive and his favorite book in the
world was *Robinson Crusoe*. He had fitted a tin **drum** on a **wheelbarrow**, for bringing water down to the pens. This was my job in
summer, when the foxes had to have water twice a day. . . .

Besides carrying water I helped my father when he cut the   5
long grass. . . . He cut with the **scythe** and I **raked** into piles. Then

he took a **pitchfork** and threw fresh-cut grass all over the tops of the pens, to keep the foxes cooler and shade their coats. . . . My father did not talk to me unless it was about the job we were doing.

In this he was quite different from my mother, who, if she was   6
feeling cheerful, would tell me all sorts of things—the name of a dog she had had when she was a little girl, the names of boys she had gone out with later on when she was grown up, and what certain dresses of hers had looked like—she could not imagine now what had become of them.

Whatever thoughts and stories my father had were private,   7
and I was shy of him and would never ask him questions. Nevertheless I worked willingly under his eyes, and with a feeling of pride. One time a **feed** salesman came down into the pens to talk to him and my father said, "Like to have you meet my new hired man." I turned away and raked furiously, red in the face with pleasure.

"Could [have] fooled me," said the salesman. "I thought it was   8
only a girl."

. . . I hated the hot dark kitchen in summer, the green **blinds**   9
and the **flypapers**, the same old oilcloth table and wavy mirror and bumpy **linoleum**. My mother was too tired and **preoccupied** to talk to me, she had no heart to tell about the Normal School Graduation Dance; sweat **trickled** over her face and she was always counting under her breath, pointing at jars, **dumping** cups of sugar. It seemed to me that work in the house was endless, dreary and peculiarly depressing; work done out of doors, and in my father's service, was **ritualistically** important.

I **wheeled** the tank up to the barn, where it was kept, and I   10
heard my mother saying, "Wait till Laird gets a little bigger, then you'll have a real help."

What my father said I did not hear. I was pleased by the way   11
he stood listening, politely as he would to a salesman or a stranger, but with an **air** of wanting to get on with his real work. I felt my mother had no business down here and I wanted him to feel the same way. What did she mean about Laird? He was no help to anybody. Where was he now? Swinging himself sick on the swing, going around in circles, or trying to catch **caterpillars**. He never once stayed with me till I was finished.

"And then I can use her more in the house," I heard my mother   12
say. She had a dead-quiet, **regretful** way of talking about me that always made me uneasy. "I just get my back turned and she runs off. It's not like I had a girl in the family at all."

I went and sat on a feed bag in the corner of the barn, not   13 wanting to appear when this conversation was going on. My mother, I felt, was not to be trusted. She was kinder than my father and more easily fooled, but you could not depend on her, and the real reasons for the things she said and did were not to be known. She loved me, and she sat up late at night making a dress of the difficult style I wanted, for me to wear when school started, but she was also my enemy.

She was always **plotting**. She was plotting now to get me to   14
stay in the house more, although she knew I hated it (*because* she knew I hated it) and keep me from working for my father. It seemed to me she would do this simply out of **perversity**, and to try her power. It did not occur to me that she could be lonely, or jealous. No grown-up could be; they were too fortunate. I sat and kicked my heels **monotonously** against a feedbag, raising dust, and did not come out till she was gone.

At any rate, I did not expect my father to pay any attention to   15
what she said. Who could imagine Laird doing my work—Laird remembering the padlock and cleaning out the watering-dishes with a leaf on the end of a stick, or even wheeling the tank without it tumbling over? It showed how little my mother knew about the way things really were.

Vocabulary

air *(n.)*   look; appearance
blind *(n.)*   window shade
*caterpillar *(n.)*   wormlike larva of a butterfly or moth
deprived *(adj.)*   marked by loss
*drum *(n.)*   container in the shape of a cylinder
dump *(n.)*   place where garbage is brought
dump *(v.)*   to throw down
*feed *(n.)*   food for farm animals
*flypaper *(n.)*   sticky paper that catches flies
ingenious *(adj.)*   clever
*linoleum *(n.)*   kind of floor covering
monotonously *(adv.)*   without varying or changing
padlock *(n.)*   lock with a particular kind of lock
pen *(n.)*   enclosed space for animals
perversity *(n.)*   stubborn contrariness; obstinacy
*pitchfork *(n.)*   long-handled fork for use in farm work
plot *(v.)*   to plan secretly; to scheme

*Denotes low-frequency word.

preoccupied *(adj.)*   lost in thought; absorbed mentally in some other matter

prime *(adj.)*   of the highest quality

rake *(v.)*   to gather together using a rake (a tool with a long handle and short prongs)

regretful *(adj.)*   sorrowful; remorseful

***ritualistically** *(adv.)*   ceremonially

***Robinson Crusoe** *(n.)*   the name of a book written by Daniel Defoe in 1719; also the name of its hero. Crusoe, an English sailor, managed to live for years by making clever inventions after being shipwrecked on a tropical island.

sack *(n.)*   bag

***scythe** *(n.)*   tool with a long handle and curved blade, used for cutting grass

***silver fox** *(n.)*   a phase of the common red fox, which at a certain time of year has black fur tipped with white

***swipe** *(n.)*   strong, sweeping blow

trickle *(v.)*   to flow slowly in a thin stream; to fall in drops

wheel *(v.)*   to push something on wheels

wheelbarrow *(n.)*   type of cart having a single wheel and handles for moving small loads

***white-washed** *(adj.)*   covered with a white, paintlike liquid

Activities

1. Look closely at the text. What is life on the farm like for each of the characters? Make notes from the text to prove your point. Discuss your ideas with your class.

2. Look closely at the story. From whose point of view is the story being told? Make notes from the text to support your opinion.

3. How is the girl treated by each of her parents? What are their expectations of the boy Laird? How are these different from their expectations of the girl? Refer to specific passages in the story to support your opinion.

4. What are the girl's feelings toward her mother and her father? How does she feel about her brother Laird?

5. Write an essay describing the traditional roles for men and women in "Boys and Girls." Agree or disagree with this division of responsibilities by gender.

6. Using your notes, write an essay on the difficulties of farm life.

For Further Reading

Blodgett, E. D. *Alice Munro.* Boston: Twayne, 1988.

MacKendrick, Louis K., ed. *Probable Fictions: Alice Munro's Narrative Acts.* Downsview, ON: ECW, 1983.

Redekop, Magdalene. *Mothers and Other Clowns: The Stories of Alice Munro.* New York: Routledge, 1992.

Stouck, David. *Major Canadian Authors.* 2nd ed. Lincoln: U of Nebraska P, 1988.

23

From *Fire on the Mountain*

Anita Desai (b. 1937)
Fiction: Novel

Background

India is both a nation and a subcontinent. It is a multicultural area of at least 20 major language groups and three principal religious groups, Hindu, Muslim, and Buddhist. Since the early nineteenth century, this diverse area had been held together as a political unit by the British Empire. After a long period of struggle under the nonviolent leadership of Mohandas Gandhi, India gained independence from the British in 1947.

It was during the period of struggle against British rule that Anita Desai was born in 1937. She is representative of her multicultural nation in that her father was a Bengali and her mother a German. Fluent in both her parents' languages, Desai writes in English. In this way she gains a broad audience, since even in postcolonial India English is still the most commonly spoken language.

One of her country's leading contemporary women novelists, Desai added a new dimension to Anglo-Indian fiction by writing about the inner lives of her characters. That is, she focuses on the psychology of her characters, especially females, and reveals their private thoughts through unspoken monologues. In her work Desai also raises questions about the role of women in contemporary Indian society.

In addition, her novels and short stories frequently deal with aspects of the multicultural heritage of India. She is also concerned with the conflict between traditional Indian life, which is guided by Hindu and

Buddhist principles, and postindependence modern life. While the Indian leader Mohandas Gandhi encouraged a return to native Indian values, the impact of foreign occupation, especially under the British, has been enormous.

Desai's personal experiences mirror the multicultural situation of modern India. The autobiographical references and feminist perspective of her work echo an individual and national struggle for independence and identity.

In addition to *Fire on the Mountain* (1975), Anita Desai has written other successful novels such as *Clear Light of Day* (1980), *In Custody* (1980), and *Baumgartner's Bombay* (1988). In 1978 she received the National Academy of Letters Award. She presently lives and teaches in the United States.

Fire on the Mountain is the story of Nanda Kaul, an Indian great-grandmother who lives alone high in a Himalayan hill station. With only a servant to attend her, she fulfills her *dharma*, or destiny, with her solitary existence. Nanda Kaul is unable to understand the values of the younger generation and is quite disturbed when she learns that her great-granddaughter Raka will be coming to stay with her. The novel describes their attempt to live together and their alienation from each other.

Pre-Reading Activities

1. With your study group, discuss what you think is the traditional role of women in the family. How do you see this traditional role changing?
2. With your study group, discuss the role of the elderly in traditional society. How is this role changing?

Key Terms

British Raj   Himalayan Mountains
Buddhism   Hindu/Hinduism
feminism/feminist   Indian independence (1947)
Gandhi, Mohandas (1869–1948)   Punjab

From *Fire on the Mountain*
Anita Desai

[Nanda Kaul] felt an enormous reluctance to open this letter.   1
She looked at it with **distaste** and **foreboding** for a long time before

Figure 24 • Indian woman in a garden
(Courtesy of Rita Narang)

she finally tore it open and drew out the bundle of dark blue pages across which [her daughter] Asha's large writing **pranced**. This writing had none of the writer's loveliness—it **sprawled** and spread and **shrieked** out loud an aggressive **assurance** and **aplomb**.

In this writing she conveyed a series of disasters and tragedies to her mother who read it through with her lips pressed so tightly together that it made deep lines **furrow** the skin from the corners of her nostrils to the corners of her mouth, dark **runnels** of disapproval.

2

"Darling Mama" (wrote Asha, and Nanda Kaul could scarcely believe that there had been a time when she was actually addressed as such and heard it quite naturally and calmly), "just a note this time as I'm in a mad rush. Now that I've persuaded Tara into going to Geneva [Switzerland] and Rakesh into taking her . . . well, I have to get Tara ready. This year's she's done *nothing*, Mama, just let herself go to **rack and ruin**, as well as her house—and poor little Raka, as you well know. . . .

3

"Poor little Raka looks like a ghost and hasn't quite got over her **typhoid** yet. She is very weak and the heat and humidity of

4

Bombay will do her no good. Everyone who sees her says she should go to the hills to recuperate. So Tara and I have decided it will be best to send her to you for the summer. Later, when Tara is settled in Geneva and has set up house, she will send for Raka.

"At the moment it is not possible for the child to travel or live   5
in an hotel. . . . We can't think of a better way for her to recuperate than spend a quiet summer with you in [Carignano]. And I know how happy it will make you to have your great-grandchild for company in that lonely house. . . ."

. . . Nanda Kaul narrowed her eyes as she went over the de-   6
tails of her great-grandchild's journey. Then she folded the blue sheets firmly, as if **suppressing** the hurry and rush of her daughter's excited plans, and slipped them back into the envelope. Placing it on her lap again, she looked out into the apricot trees, down the path to the gate, the cloudy **hydrangeas**, the pines scattering and hissing in the breeze. . . .

One long finger moved like a searching insect over the letter   7
on her lap, moved **involuntarily** as she struggled to suppress her anger, her disappointment and her total **loathing** of her daughter's meddling, **busybody** ways, her granddaughter [Tara's] **abject** helplessness, and her great-granddaughter's **impending** arrival here at Carignano.

She tried to divert her mind from these thoughts and concen-   8
trate on this well known and **perpetually** soothing scene. She tried to look on it as she had before the letter arrived, with pleasure and satisfaction. But she was too distracted now.

All she wanted was to be alone, to have Carignano to herself,   9
in this period of her life when stillness and calm were all that she wished to entertain.

Getting up at last, she went slowly round to the back of the   10
house and leant on the wooden railing on which the yellow rose creeper had blossomed so youthfully last month but was now reduced to an exhausted mass of grey creaks and groans again. She gazed down the **gorge** with its **gashes** of red earth, its rocks and **gullies** and sharply spiked **agaves**, to the Punjab plains—a silver haze in the summer heat—stretching out to a dim yellow horizon, and said Is it wrong? Have I not done enough and had enough? I want no more. I want nothing. Can I not be left with nothing? But there was no answer and of course she expected none.

Looking down, over all those years she had survived and   11
borne, she saw them, not bare and shining as the plains below, but like the gorge, **cluttered**, choked and blackened with the heads of

children and grandchildren, servants and guests, all restlessly surging, clamoring about her. . . .

Looking down at her knuckles, two rows of yellow bones on the railing, she thought of her sons and daughters, of her **confinements**, some in great discomfort at home and others at the small **filthy** missionary-run hospital . . . and the different nurses and doctors who had wanted to help her but never could, and the **slovenly**, neurotic **ayahs** she had had to have because there was such a deal of washing and ironing to do and Mr. Kaul had wanted her always in silk, at the head of the long **rosewood** table in the dining-room, entertaining his guests. 12

Mentally she **stalked** through the rooms of that house—his house, never hers—very carefully closing the wire-screen doors behind her to keep out the flies, looking sharply to see if the dark furniture, all rosewood, had been properly polished and the doors of the gigantic cupboards properly shut. . . . 13

Now, to **bow** again, to let that **noose** slip once more round her neck that she had thought was freed fully, finally. Now to have those **wails** and **bawls** shatter and rip her still house to pieces, to clutter the bare rooms. . . . 14

It seemed hard, it seemed unfair, when all she wanted was the sound of the **cicadas** and the pines, the sight of this gorge plunging, blood-red, down to the silver plain. 15

An eagle swept over it, far below her, a thousand feet below, its wings outspread, gliding on currents of air without once moving its great muscular wings which remained in **repose**, in control. She had wished, it occurred to her, to imitate that eagle—gliding with eyes closed. 16

Then a **cuckoo** called, quite close, here in her garden, very softly, very musically, but definitely calling—she recognized its domestic tone. 17

She gave that ironic **bow** again, very, very slightly, and went to the kitchen to see what Ram Lal had for lunch and tell him about the great-grandchild's visit. 18

Vocabulary

abject *(adj.)*   miserable; wretched
***agave** *(n.)*   plant in the amaryllis family having tall flower stalks
***aplomb** *(n.)*   complete, confident self-possession; poise

*Denotes low-frequency word.

assurance *(n.)*   confidence; certainty
*ayah *(n.)*   nurse or maid native to India
*bawl *(n.)*   loud cry that goes on for a long time
bow *(n.)*   bending in submission
bow *(v.)*   to yield; to submit
*busybody *(adj.)*   concerned with other people's affairs
*cicada *(n.)*   large, flylike insect, the male of which makes a loud, shrill
   sound
cluttered *(adj.)*   filled or covered with scattered things
*confinement *(n.)*   state of being kept in bed or indoors because of
   illness or childbirth
*cuckoo *(n.)*   bird whose call sounds somewhat like its name
distaste *(n.)*   dislike; aversion
filthy *(adj.)*   disgustingly dirty
*foreboding *(n.)*   prediction, especially of something bad or harmful
*furrow *(v.)*   to groove
*gash *(n.)*   deep, narrow depression in the earth
*gorge *(n.)*   narrow, steep-walled passage through land; canyon
*gully *(n.)*   trench worn in the earth by running water after rains
*hydrangea *(n.)*   plant with large, showy groups of white, pink, or blue
   flowers
impending *(adj.)*   about to occur
involuntarily *(adv.)*   not consciously controlled; automatically
loathing *(n.)*   great dislike
noose *(n.)*   loop formed in a rope that tightens as the rope is pulled; used
   to hang people
perpetually *(adv.)*   continuing forever
prance *(v.)*   to move in a spirited way
*rack and ruin *(n.)*   poor state or condition
repose *(n.)*   state of rest
*rosewood *(n.)*   valuable dark red or purplish wood used to make
   furniture
*runnel *(n.)*   small stream
shriek *(v.)*   to cry out in a sharp, shrill sound; to suggest such a sound
slovenly *(adj.)*   untidy, especially in personal appearance
*sprawl *(v.)*   to take up more space than is necessary
stalk *(v.)*   to walk stiffly or haughtily
suppress *(v.)*   to check; to keep back
*typhoid *(n.)*   serious disease contracted from polluted water and marked
   by high fever
wail *(n.)*   cry expressing dissatisfaction or complaint that goes on for a
   long time

*Denotes low-frequency word.

Activities

1. Look closely at the text. With your group or alone, make notes on how Nanda Kaul feels about her great-grandchild's visit. How does the author reveal Nanda Kaul's feelings to the reader? Support your answer with specific lines from the text. Discuss your ideas with the class.

2. How does the author use nature in this passage? In what way is it Romantic?

3. Based on your notes and discussion, write an essay on the conflict Nanda Kaul feels over her role as a woman.

4. Based on your notes and discussion, write an essay on the role of the elderly in modern society. Support your points with specific details.

For Further Reading

Bande, Usha. *The Novels of Anita Desai.* New Delhi: Prestige, 1988.

Dhawan, R. K., ed. *The Fiction of Anita Desai.* New Delhi: Bahri, 1989.

Embree, Ainslie T. *India's Search for National Identity.* New Delhi: Chanakya, 1980.

Watson, Francis. *A Concise History of India.* London: Thames, 1979.

Zimmer, Heinrich. *Myths and Symbols in Indian Art and Civilization.* Ed. Joseph Campbell. 2nd ed. Princeton: Princeton UP, 1974.

24

From *The Thief and the Dogs*

Naguib Mahfouz (b. 1911)
Fiction: Novel

Background

The son of middle-class Muslim parents, Naguib Mahfouz lived for the first six years of his life in the crowded, conservative Islamic old quarter of Cairo, Egypt. His family then moved to the modern, Europeanized suburb of Abbasiyah, where he witnessed firsthand the Egyptian struggle for independence from the British. He later attended the University of Cairo, where he studied philosophy and read the works of Western intellectuals such as Darwin, Marx, Nietzsche, and Freud. All of these contrasting experiences have influenced Mahfouz's novels.

Mahfouz combined a long career as an Egyptian civil servant with serious writing, earning a reputation as one of the most outstanding and gifted novelists in the Arabic-speaking world today. Mahfouz has been a highly prolific author, writing an average of one book per year, dozens of movie scripts, and a weekly political column in an Egyptian-language newspaper.

Although Arabic literature has a long history, its major forms have been the short story and poetry, both closely associated with a rich oral tradition. Mahfouz was the first successful creator of the modern Arabic novel. His early literary influences were drawn from important European sources such as the Romanticism of Victor Hugo, the Realism of Charles Dickens, and the internal monologue of James Joyce and Virginia Woolf. In 1988 he received the Nobel Prize in literature and was cited as forming "an Arabic narrative art that applies to all mankind."

The earliest novels written by Mahfouz were historical works about the rich ancient Egyptian past. But for some time after the 1952 Egyptian revolution led by Colonel Gamal Abdel Nasser, Naguib Mahfouz did not write fiction. He first received broad public recognition in the Arab world after the publication of his 1,200-page *Cairo Trilogy* (1956–1957). Mahfouz's 1959 Existentialist novel, *Children of Gebelawi*, was an allegorical story of religious crisis that reflected the pessimism of Egypt's intellectuals at that time. The work was poorly received by traditional Islamic readers. His next novel, *The Thief and the Dogs*, was published in 1961 and was well received. Using the stream-of-consciousness technique and interior mono-logue in this novel, Mahfouz reveals the mind of an Egyptian man seeking to destroy the individuals and the society he believes have condemned him to damnation. Although the protagonist, Said, tries to save himself by returning to the mystic influence of a sheikh and his childhood religion, his complete alienation and desire for revenge make it impossible for him to renew his faith.

Pre-Reading Activities

1. Why do you think people sometimes return to the places and memo-ries of their childhood? Discuss your ideas with your group.
2. What is moral behavior? How do you believe children learn about moral behavior? Discuss your ideas with your group.

Key Terms

allusion
Arab/Arabic
Cairo Trilogy
Egyptian revolution (1952)
historical novel
Islam

Koran
Muslim
mystic
Said [sah-eed] Mahran
sheikh
stream-of-consciousness technique

From *The Thief and the Dogs*
Naguib Mahfouz

At the **threshold** of the open door [Said] paused, trying to   1
remember when he'd crossed it last. The simplicity of the house, which could hardly be different from those of Adam's day, was **strik-ing**. At the left corner of the big, open courtyard stood a tall palm

Figure 25 • Moslem holy man reading the Koran *(© 1984 Eugene Gordon/Photo Researchers)*

tree with a crooked top; to the right an entrance corridor led by an open door—in this strange house no door was ever closed—to a single room.

His heart beat fast, carrying him back to a distant, gentle time of childhood, dreams, a loving father, and his own innocent **yearning**. He recalled the men filling the courtyard, **swaying** with their **chanting**, God's praise echoing from the depths of their hearts. "Look and listen, learn and open your heart," his father used to say.

Besides a joy like the joy of Paradise that was aroused in him by faith and dreams, there had also been the joy of singing and green tea. . . .

From inside the room he could hear a man concluding his prayers. Said smiled, slipped in carrying his books, and saw the Sheikh sitting cross-legged on the prayer carpet, absorbed in quiet

recitation. The old room had hardly changed. The **rush mats** had been replaced by new ones, thanks to his **disciples**, but the Sheikh's sleeping mattress still lay close to the western wall, pierced by the window through which the rays of the declining sun were pouring down at Said's feet. The other walls of the room were half covered with rows of books on shelves. The odor of incense **lingered** as if it were the same he remembered, never **dissipated**, from years ago. Putting down his load of books, he approached the Sheikh.

"Peace be upon you, my lord and master."   5

Having completed his recitation, the Sheikh raised his head,   6 disclosing a face that was **emaciated** but radiant with overflowing vitality, framed by a white beard like a **halo**, and surmounted by a white **skullcap** that **nestled** in thick **locks** of hair showing silvery at his temples.

The Sheikh **scrutinized** him with eyes that had been viewing   7 this world for eighty years and indeed had **glimpsed** the next, eyes that had not lost their appeal, acuteness, or charm. Said found himself bending over his hand to kiss it, suppressing tears of nostalgia for his father, his boyish hopes, the innocent purity of the distant past.

"Peace and God's compassion be upon you," said the Sheikh   8 in a voice like Time.

What had his father's voice been like? He could see his father's   9 face and his lips moving, and tried to make his eyes do the service of ears, but the voice had gone. . . .

Did the Sheikh remember him? "Forgive my coming to your   10 house like this. But there's nowhere else in the world for me to go." . . . [N]ot knowing what to say, [Said] sighed, then quietly remarked, "I got out of jail today."

"Jail?" said the Sheikh, his eyes closed.   11

"Yes. You haven't seen me for more than ten years, and dur-   12 ing that time strange things have happened to me. . . . In any case, I didn't want to meet you under **false pretenses**, so I'm telling you I got out of jail, only today."

The Sheikh slowly shook his head, then, opening his eyes, said,   13 "You have not come from jail." The voice was sorrowful.

Said smiled. This was the language of old times again, where   14 words had a double meaning. . . .

Fairly certain that he was remembered, Said asked for **reas-**   15 **surance**: "And do you remember my father, Mr. Mahran, God have mercy upon his soul?"

"May God have mercy upon all of us."   16

"What wonderful days those were!"   17
"Say that, if you can, about the present."   18
"But . . ."   19
"God have mercy upon all of us."   20
"I was saying, I just got out of jail today."   21

he was **impaled** on the stake he smiled and said, 'It was God's will
that I should meet Him thus.' "

    . . . "Master, I have come to you now when my own daughter   23
has **rejected** me."

The Sheikh sighed. "God reveals His secrets to His tiniest crea-   24
tures!"

"I thought that if God had granted you long life, I would find   25
your door open."

"And the door of Heaven? How have you found that?"   26

"But there is nowhere on earth for me to go. And my own   27
daughter has rejected me."

"How like you she is!"   28
"In what way, Master?"   29
"You seek a roof, not an answer."   30
    . . . "I am in need of a kind word," Said pleaded.   31

"Do not tell lies." The Sheikh spoke gently, then bowed his   32
head, his beard **fanning out** over his chest, and seemed lost in
thought. . . . Suddenly the Sheikh said, "Take a copy of the **Koran**
and read."

A little confused, Said explained apologetically, "I just got out   33
of jail today, and I have not performed the prayer **ablutions**."

"Wash yourself now and read."   34

"My own daughter has rejected me. She was scared of me, as   35
if I was the devil. And before that her mother was unfaithful to me."

"Wash and read," replied the Sheikh gently.   36

"She committed adultery with one of my men, a **layabout**, a   37
mere pupil of mine, utterly **servile**. She applied for divorce on
grounds of my imprisonment and went and married him."

"Wash and read."   38

"And he took everything I owned, the money and the jewelry.   39
He's a big man now, and all the local crooks have become followers
and **cronies** of his."

"Wash and read."   40

"It wasn't thanks to any sweat by the police that I was ar-   41
rested." Said went on, the veins in his forehead **pulsing** with anger.
"No, it wasn't. I was sure of my safety, as usual. It was that dog who

betrayed me, in **collusion** with her. Then disaster followed disaster until finally my daughter rejected me."

     "Wash and read the verses: 'Say to them: if you love God, then   42
follow me and God will love you' and 'I have chosen thee for
Myself.' Also repeat the words: 'Love is acceptance, which means
obeying His commands and refraining from what He has prohibited
and contentment with what He **decrees** and **ordains**.' "

     . . . *[T]he sun is not yet set. The last golden thread is **receding** from*   43
the window. A long night is waiting for me, the first night of freedom. I am
alone with my freedom, or rather I'm in the company of the Sheikh, who is
lost in heaven, repeating words that cannot be understood by someone ap-
*proaching hell. What other **refuge** have I?*

Vocabulary

*ablution *(n.)*   washing of one's body or part of it, as in a religious
     ceremony
chanting *(n.)*   reciting in a repetitive way
collusion *(n.)*   secret agreement or cooperation
*crony *(n.)*   close friend
decree *(v.)*   to command
disciple *(n.)*   one who accepts and assists in spreading the doctrines of
     another
dissipate *(v.)*   to dissolve; to spread out to the point of vanishing
emaciated *(adj.)*   very thin
*false pretense *(n.)*   deliberate misrepresentation of fact
*fanning out *(adj.)*   spreading out like a fan
glimpse *(v.)*   to get a brief look at
halo *(n.)*   circle of light, especially around the head, showing holiness
impale *(v.)*   to kill or torture by fixing on a sharp, pointed stick
Koran *(n.)*   book of sacred writings accepted by Muslims as revelations to
     Mohammed by Allah through the angel Gabriel
*layabout *(n.)*   lazy person
linger *(v.)*   to remain although in a weakened form
lock *(n.)*   tuft; clump
mere *(adj.)*   being nothing more than
nestle *(v.)*   to sit comfortably or snugly
ordain *(v.)*   to order
pulsing *(adj.)*   beating; throbbing
reassurance *(n.)*   new assurance
recede *(v.)*   to move back or away

*Denotes low-frequency word.

recitation *(n.)*   the act of reading or repeating aloud
refuge *(n.)*   shelter or protection from distress or danger
reject *(v.)*   to refuse to accept
***rush mat** *(n.)*   rug made of grasses
scrutinize *(v.)*   to examine closely
servile *(adj.)*   slavelike; exhibiting submissive behavior
***skullcap** *(n.)*   close-fitting cap without a brim
striking *(adj.)*   attracting attention because of remarkable qualities
swaying *(adj.)*   moving from side to side
***threshold** *(n.)*   doorsill
yearning *(n.)*   deep or anxious longing or desire

Activities

1. In your journal, make notes about Said's feelings as he returns to the Sheikh's house. How are the feelings he had as a child different from those he feels now?

2. Said is a criminal pursued by the police. Why do you believe he has returned to the Sheikh's house? What does he want?

3. What is the "double meaning" of the Sheikh's words? Why are the Sheikh and Said not communicating?

4. Write an essay explaining or elaborating on the importance of religious or moral education. Give specific examples to support your argument.

5. Write an essay on the reasons for the lack of communication between the Sheikh and Said in Mahfouz's story.

For Further Reading

Beard, Michael, and Adnan Haydar, eds. *Naguib Mahfouz: From Regional Fame to Global Recognition.* Syracuse: Syracuse UP, 1992.

Gordon, Hayim. *Naguib Mahfouz's Egypt: Existential Themes in His Writings.* New York: Greenwood, 1990.

Kessler, Brad. "Laureate in the Land of the Pharaohs." *New York Times Magazine* 3 June 1990: 38+.

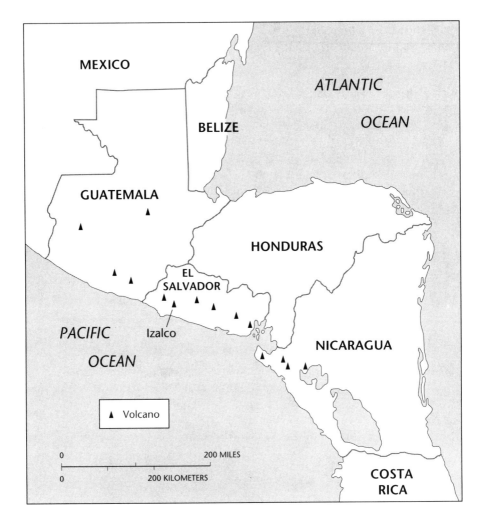

MEXICO

ATLANTIC

OCEAN

BELIZE

GUATEMALA

HONDURAS

EL
SALVADOR

PACIFIC

Izalco

OCEAN

NICARAGUA

▲ Volcano

0   200 MILES

0   200 KILOMETERS

COSTA
RICA

Figure 26   •   Map of Central America with volcanoes

CHAPTER 25

From *Flowers from the Volcano*

Claribel Alegría (b. 1924)
Oral Tradition and Poetry: Free Verse

Background

Born in Nicaragua, Central America, Claribel Alegría experienced political exile at the age of nine when her father was forced to leave their country and moved his family to El Salvador. At age 19 she arrived in the United States to study philosophy at George Washington University. After graduating, she married Darwin Flakoll.

Violence plays an important role in much of Alegría's work. She identifies the violence of the volcanic Meso-American landscape with a tradition of human violence. She acknowledges the violent behavior of pre-Columbian indigenous cultures such as the Aztec as well as the violence and destruction associated with the arrival of Christopher Columbus in the New World. Although sixteenth-century Spanish priests such as Fray Diego de Landa tried to protect the native culture, the European presence has had a major impact. As a result, the native Indian population finds itself marginalized in its own land. The present violence continues not only in the giant volcano Izalco, threatening to explode at any moment, but in the torture and mass murder of Indian peasants by terrorists.

In reaction to the horrors of Central American government terrorism against poor peasants seeking a better life, Claribel Alegría has looked to socialist and Marxist philosophy. In her life and in her writing, she has consistently spoken out about the struggle for liberation of the oppressed in Central America.

Alegría has published 14 books of poetry, as well as novellas and children's stories. Much of her work has been translated from Spanish into English by her husband. Claribel Alegría and her husband presently live in Managua, Nicaragua, and Mallorca, Spain.

Pre-Reading Activities

1. With your class, discuss the role of the poet in politics. Should the poet write only about "beauty," or about real-life issues as well?
2. Locate Central America on a map. What is the area like? How could the geography influence life there?

Key Terms

Aztecs and Incas

Central America

chacmol

Columbus, Christopher (1451–1506)

de Landa, Fray Diego (1524–1579)

human sacrifice

indigenous culture

marginal/marginalized

Marxism/Marxist

Maya/Mayan

Meso-America

mestizo

pre-Columbian

Tlaloc (also called Chac)

"Flowers from the Volcano"

Claribel Alegría

To Roberto and Ana Maria

Fourteen volcanos rise
in my remembered country
in my mythical country.
Fourteen volcanos of **foliage** and stone
where strange clouds hold back   5
the **screech** of a homeless bird.
Who said that my country was green?
It is more red, more gray, more violent:
Izalco roars,
taking more lives.   10
Eternal **Chacmol** collects blood,
the gray **orphans**
the volcano spitting bright lava

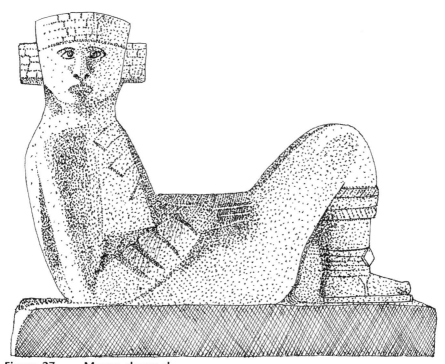

Figure 27 • Mayan chacmol

and the dead *guerrillero*
and the thousand **betrayed** faces,   15
the children who are watching
so they can tell of it.
Not one kingdom was left us.
One by one they fell
through all the Americas.   20
Steel rang in palaces,
in the streets,
in the forests
and the **centaurs sacked** the temple.
Gold disappeared and continues   25
to disappear on *yanqui* ships,
the golden coffee mixed with blood.
The priest flees screaming
in the middle of the night
he calls his followers   30
and they open the *guerrillero's* chest

so as to offer the **Chac**
his smoking heart.
No one believes in Izalco
that **Tlaloc** is dead   35
despite television,
refrigerators,
Toyotas.
The cycle is closing,
strange the volcano's silence   40
since it last drew breath.
Central America trembled,
Managua collapsed.
In Guatemala the earth sank
Hurricane Fifi flattened Honduras.   45
They say the *yanquis* turned it away,
that it was moving toward Florida
and they forced it back.
The golden coffee is unloaded
in New York where   50
they roast it, grind it
can it and give it a price.
Siete de Junio
noche fatal
bailando el tango   55
la capital.
[Seventh of June
fatal night
dancing the tango
in the capital.]
From the shadowed terraces
San Salvador's volcano rises.
Two-story **mansions**
protected by walls   60
four meters high
march up its **flanks**
each with **railings** and gardens,
roses from England
and dwarf *araucarias*,   65
Uruguayan pines.
Farther up, in the **crater**
within the crater's walls
live peasant families

who cultivate flowers   70
their children can sell.
The cycle is closing,
Cuscatlecan flowers
thrive in volcanic ash,
they grow strong, tall, brilliant.   75
The volcano's children
flow down like lava
with their bouquets of flowers,
like roots they **meander**
like rivers the cycle is closing.   80
The owners of two-story houses
protected from thieves by walls
peer from their balconies
and they see the red waves descending
and they drown their fears in whiskey.   85
They are only children in rags
with flowers from the volcano,
with *Jacintos* and *Pascuas* and *Mulatas*
but the wave is **swelling**,
today's Chacmol still wants blood,   90
the cycle is closing,
Tlaloc is not dead.

Vocabulary

__araucania__ *(n.)*   flower native to Central America
betrayed *(adj.)*   deceived
__centaur__ *(n.)*   mythical creature said to be half man and half horse
(referring here to the Spanish conquerors mounted on horseback)
__Chac__ *(prop. n.)*   Mayan raingod, portrayed with a long nose resembling a
rainspout
__Chacmol__ *(n.)*   Mayan stone altar in the form of a reclining man holding
a bowl to receive the hearts of human sacrifices
__crater__ *(n.)*   bowl-shaped area around the opening of a volcano
__Cuscatlecan__ *(adj.) (Mayan)*   belonging to Cuscatlan, "Land of the
Jewel," capital and territory of the Pipil native tribe, a group culturally
like the Aztecs
flank *(n.)*   side
foliage *(n.)*   leaves

*Denotes low-frequency word.

*guerrillero (n.) (Spanish)   fighter

*Izalco (prop. n.) (Mayan)   "Lighthouse of the Pacific"; a 6,183-foot-high volcano in El Salvador that has been active intermittently since the eighteenth century

*Jacintos, Pascuas, and Mulatas (prop. n.) (Spanish)   here, the names of flowers as well as children

mansion (n.)   large, impressive house

meander (v.)   to wander without direction

orphan (n.)   child whose parents have died

peer (v.)   to look curiously at something

*railing (n.)   fence consisting of posts with a bar across the top

sack (v.)   to strip of valuables; to loot

screech (n.)   high, shrill piercing cry (as a symbol, the Mayan screeching bird is associated with the end of the universe)

*Siete de Junio (Seventh of June)   Salvadoran song popular during the 1917 volcanic eruption of Izalco

swell (v.)   to expand; to get bigger

thrive (v.)   to grow very well

*Tlaloc (prop. n.)   Mayan god of rain and sacrifice whose written symbol, or glyph, is a sign of war and bloodletting

*yanqui (n.) (Spanish)   North American person

Activities

1. With your small group or class, read the poem "Flowers from the Volcano" aloud. What evidence of oral tradition do you see in the poem?

2. Make notes in your journal about the way Alegría uses the image of flowers in the poem. What do they symbolize? How do the rich respond to them? What do you think the poem's title means? Discuss your ideas with your class.

3. Read the poem again, making notes in your journal about the way Alegría uses myth to compare the past and the present. What does she imply will happen in the future? Discuss your ideas with your group.

4. What is the purpose of Alegría's poem "Flowers from the Volcano"? What feelings does she want her audience to experience? What does she expect her audience to do? Support your point of view with specific lines from the poem.

5. Write an essay based on your notes and discussion on Claribel Alegría's use of myth in "Flowers from the Volcano."

6. Write an essay arguing for or against poetry with a political message.

*Denotes low-frequency word.

For Further Reading

Flakoll, Darwin, and Claribel Alegría, eds. *New Voices of Hispanic America: An Anthology.* Boston: Beacon, 1962.

McClintock, Michael. *The American Connection: State Terror and Popular Resistance in El Salvador.* London: Zed, 1985.

Rojas, Mario A. "Some Central American Writers of Liberation," In *Culture, Human Rights and Peace in Central America.* Ed. George F. McLean et al. Lanham: UP of America, 1989.

Santos, Rosario, ed. *And We Sold the Rain: Contemporary Fiction from Central America.* New York: Four Walls Eight Windows, 1988.

Schele, Linda, and David Freidel. *A Forest of Kings: The Untold Story of the Ancient Maya.* New York: Morrow, 1990.

Additional Reading

Sacred Hymn of Sacrifice to Tlaloc[†]

Anonymous (fifteenth century)
Oral Tradition and Poetry: Sacred Text

Background

Two sixteenth-century Spanish priests observed and recorded in great detail the cultures of the indigenous Aztecs and Mayans they encountered in Mesoamerica. One, Fray Bernardino de Sahagún, arrived in Mexico in 1529 and wrote a multivolume work entitled *General History of the Things of New Spain*, which included native hymns and prayers. Another priest, Fray Diego de Durán, detailed the oral tradition as well as the written codices, or painted books, that preserved Aztec and Mayan traditions. Fray Diego describes the dramatic religious ceremony of the sacrifice of a seven-year-old girl to Tlaloc to ensure the fertility of the maize crop:

> The feast of [Tlaloc] took place on the twenty-ninth of April and was so solemn and important that every king and lord, the old and the young, all came with their offerings from every part of the land. . . . It was devoted to petitioning a good year for the maize which was already sprouting. . . . The priests took out the child who . . . was all dressed in blue, which represented the great lake and all the fountains and small rivers, with a band of reddish leather around her head and fastened to it a tuft of blue

feather. . . . Facing the idol . . . they brought a drum and all
sat down without dancing, with the girl in front, and they sang
many and varied songs. (Quoted in Leon-Portilla, 99–100)

Sacred Hymn of Sacrifice to Tlaloc
Anonymous

CHORUS: In Mexico we beg a loan from the god.   1
   There are the banners of paper
   and at the four corners
   men are standing.

PRIEST OF TLALOC: Now, Tlaloc, it is time for you to weep!   5
   Alas, I [the child] was created
   and for my god
   festal bundles of blood-stained ears of corn
   I carry now
   to the divine hearth.   10
   You are my chief, Prince and Magician,
   and though in truth
   it is you who produces our sustenance,
   although you are the first,
   we only cause you shame.   15

TLALOC (A MASKED PRIEST): If anyone
   has caused me shame,
   it is because he did not know me well;
   [he did not know my power];
   you are my fathers, my priests,   20
   Serpents and Tigers.

CHORUS [speaking in the name of the child victim]:
   I will go away forever,
   it is time for crying.
   Send me to the Place of Mystery,   25
   under your command.
   I have already told
   the Prince of the Sad Omen,
   I will go away forever,
   it is time for crying.   30
   In four years
   comes the arising among us,
   many people

without knowing it;
in the place of the fleshless,   35
the house of quetzal feathers,
is the transformation.
It is the act of the Propagator of Men.

PRIEST OF TLALOC: Go to all parts
spread out . . .   40
in the region of mist.
With [clouds] of mist
our word is carried to the house of Tlaloc.

Fray Diego continues his account of the sacrificial ritual:

> After this hymn, dances and other songs were offered to the rain
> god. The priests then took the child victim in a boat to the center
> of the lake where they sacrificed her, letting her blood and a num-
> ber of jewels fall into the water. The ritual drama with songs,
> dances and costumes, asking Tlaloc for life-giving rain, had been
> acted out. (Leon-Portilla, 100–03)

Activities

1. Choose one or two symbols in this religious ritual and explain their
   meaning and significance in an essay.
2. Reread the poem "Flowers from the Volcano." What does the poet
   mean when she states that "Tlaloc is not dead"?
3. Compare the child in the religious ritual to the children in the poem
   "Flowers from the Volcano."

For Further Reading

Leon-Portilla, Miguel. *Pre-Columbian Literatures of Mexico.* Trans. Grace
    Lobanov and Miguel Leon-Portilla. Norman: U of Oklahoma P, 1986.
Morley, Sylvanus G., and George W. Brainerd. *The Ancient Maya.* Rev.
    Robert J. Sharer. 4th ed. Stanford: Stanford UP, 1983.

CHAPTER **26**

From *Praisesong for the Widow*

Paule Marshall (b. 1929)
Fiction: Novel

Background

The earliest West Indian literary sources originate in Africa and are part of oral tradition. However, much of the eighteenth- and nineteenth-century West Indian literature is based on European models. For example, among the early written works are slave narratives similar to the European picaresque novels. Such narratives recount the life of an African taken from home by force, sold into slavery, and shipped to the Caribbean or to North America.

The contemporary period, which includes the work of Paule Marshall, has included a focus on the quest for identity through a journey to the white Western world (England or the United States) and then to Africa before a return home, approximating the experience of the Middle Passage. Like the ancient epic hero, the protagonist gains wisdom and pride to be shared with others.

Although Paule Marshall was born and educated in Brooklyn, New York, her parents are from Barbados, a small island in the West Indies in the Caribbean. Marshall has lived in Barbados while working on her writing and, therefore, exhibits a strong West Indian influence in her work. In her rich descriptive passages, Marshall evokes the tropical landscape of the Caribbean. Furthermore, her dialogues reflect West Indian

201

idioms and dialect, and she uses the rhythms of Afro-Caribbean music to evoke a closeness with mother earth.

Marshall's first novel, *Brown Girl, Brownstones* (1959), is the story of a Barbadian immigrant girl whose parents struggle to preserve their ethnic heritage in the assimilation process. Her 1983 novel, *Praisesong for the Widow*, describes the journey of an unhappy, assimilated African-American woman to discover her ethnic roots. An affluent, middle-aged widow, Avey Johnson takes a vacation cruise to the Caribbean. She unexpectedly relives the terrible Middle Passage her ancestors experienced when they were brought across the Atlantic Ocean to the New World as slaves to work on sugar plantations. An appreciation of her rich African heritage brings new meaning to Avey's life.

Throughout her work, Marshall contrasts the potential destructive power of Western technology with Afro-Caribbean harmony with the natural world. The reader is made aware of the tremendous human and ecological cost of materialism and "progress." Without seeming to preach, Marshall clearly indicates that the American dream of relentlessly pursuing materialism may result in the sacrifice of moral or ethical principles. She reminds us that the traditions of the past still have a place in the contemporary world.

Pre-Reading Activities

1. What do you think are some of the reasons people leave their country for a new one? Is the departure always voluntary? How would someone's reasons for being in a new land affect their feelings about their old and new countries?

2. In your study group, discuss what you feel might be some of the reasons people would want to know about their ethnic heritage.

3. What does it mean to be a tourist? What is the difference between visiting a place as a tourist and returning to a place associated with one's ancestors?

Key Terms

assimilation	feminist movement
Barbados/Barbadian/Bajan	Harlem Renaissance
Caribbean	materialism
civil rights movement	Middle Passage
ecological harmony	slave narrative
ethnic heritage	West Indies/West Indian

Figure 28 • Cruise ship in port *(Fritz Menle/Photo Researchers)*

From *Praisesong for the Widow*
Paule Marshall

With a strength born of the decision that had just come to her   1
in the middle of the night, Avey Johnson forced the suitcase shut on
the clothes piled inside and slid the lock into place. Taking care not to
make a sound, she then eased the heavy bag off the couch onto the
floor and, straining under her breath, her tall figure bent almost in
two, **hauled** it over the thick carpeting to the door on the other side
of the cabin. . . .

From the moment she had awakened in a panic less than an   2
hour ago and come to the reckless decision, her mind had left to go
and stand down at the embarkation door near the waterline five
decks below. While she swiftly **criss-crossed** the room on her bare
feet, **spiriting** her belongings out of the closet and drawers, her
mind had leaped ahead to the time, later that morning, when the
ship would have arrived at the next **port of call**. . . . [A]long with
her fellow passengers going ashore for the day, she would step from

the **liner** onto the waiting **launch**. For the last time. And without so much as a backward glance.

Avey Johnson's two traveling companions, with whom she   3
shared the large deluxe cabin, were asleep in the bedroom on the other side of a divider with narrow shelflike openings on top and a long chest of drawers below, facing what was called the living area. Not to risk waking them, she had left off the lamps in the living area, where she always volunteered to sleep each cruise because it was more private. . . .

Slipping back over to the couch, her feet struck a chair. Quickly   4
she **stifled** her outcry, shook off the pain and kept going. When was the last time she had gone barefoot around the house? . . . Halsey Street? Had it been that long ago?

Back then the young woman whose headstrong ways and high   5
feelings Avey Johnson had long put behind her, whom she found an embarrassment to even think of now with her 1940s **upsweeps** and pompadours and **vampish** high-heeled shoes, used to kick off her shoes the moment she came in from work. . . . The 78 [records] on the turntable in the living room: Coleman Hawkins, Lester Young, The Count, The Duke. Music to usher Jay in the door. Freed of the high-heels her body always felt restored to its proper **axis**. . . . And the floor **reverberating** with "Cottontail" and "Lester Leaps In" would be like a rich nurturing ground from which she had sprung and to which she could always turn for sustenance. . . .

She was down to the last of the six suitcases.   6

"But why six, Mother? Why would anyone in their right mind   7
need to take this much stuff just to go away for a couple of weeks?"—Marion, Avey Johnson's youngest, the morning she had come to drive her mother to the pier before her first cruise three years ago. Entering the house, Marion had stopped short at sight of the half-dozen bags neatly lined up in the downstairs hall, had stood staring at them for the longest time, trying to contain her exasperation but failing. When she finally looked up it had been all she could do, from her expression, not to reach out and grab her mother by the shoulders and shake her the way she might have one of her pupils in the small community school she helped run in a church in Brooklyn. To shake sense into her. Around the face which **bore** [her father] Jay's clear imprint, her hair had stood **massed** like a raincloud about to **make good its threat**. And the noisy necklace of **cowrie shells** and **amber** she had brought back from Togo her last visit had sounded her angry despair with its rattle each time she breathed.

"Why go on some meaningless cruise with a bunch of white   8 folks anyway, I keep asking you? What's that supposed to be about? Couldn't you think of something better to do on your vacation? And since when have you started letting Thomasina Moore decide how you should spend it? You don't even like the woman. . . ."

. . . [W]hatever doubts [Marion] had managed to **sow** in Avey   9
Johnson's mind vanished the moment she saw the ***Bianca*** *Pride* that first time in her **berth** at West Fortieth Street and the river, with the flags and pennants flying from all her stations, her high bow **canted** toward the sun. All that dazzling white steel! Her **hull** appeared to sweep clear across to New Jersey. . . . Her group had stood awestruck and **reverent** before the [ship's] **console** with its array of keyboards, switches and closed circuit television screens. . . .

The marathon packing was done. On an armchair near the   10
window lay the clothes she had hastily set aside to wear. The suit-cases, all six of them along with the shoe **caddy** and hat box, stood assembled near the door, ready for the steward. Giving the **apprehensive** glance over her shoulder, she immediately headed toward them, not even allowing herself a moment to rest her back or wipe the perspiration from her face—or to consider, quietly and rationally, which was normally her way, what she was about to do.

Outside the glow of the deck lights was slowly being absorbed   11
by a pearl-gray light that was both filtering down from the clearing sky and curling up like mist from the sea. And the sea itself had become a wide, silvertoned sheet of **plate metal**, which was already, out near the horizon, reflecting the subtle mauve and rose and pale yellows of the day.

Amid the **burgeoning** color stood the liner—huge, sleek, im-   12
perial, a **glacial** presence in the warm waters of the Caribbean. The long night run completed, it had come to rest and drop anchor a short time ago in the same smooth and soundless manner with which it had moved over the sea.

From its decks could be made out the faint, almost **insubstan-**   13
tial form of an island across the silvery **moat** of the harbor. The next port of call.

Avey Johnson had finished in good time.   14

Vocabulary

amber *(n.)*   hard yellow or brown fossil material that can be polished and is used chiefly in making jewelry
apprehensive *(adj.)*   anticipating with anxiety, dread, or fear
axis *(n.)*   line of orientation

bear (bore, borne) *(v.)*   to carry
***berth** *(n.)*   place for a ship at a dock
***bianca** *(adj.) (Italian)*   white
***burgeoning** *(adj.)*   growing and expanding rapidly
***caddy** *(n.)*   container for holding objects when not in use
***canted** *(adj.)*   inclined; tilted
console *(n.)*   panel; cabinet
***cowrie shell** *(n.)*   glossy, often brightly colored shell found in warm
    seas, formerly used as a form of money in Africa
criss-cross *(v.)*   to move back and forth across
glacial *(adj.)*   like a glacier (a large mass of ice)
haul *(v.)*   to pull
***hull** *(n.)*   body of a ship
insubstantial *(adj.)*   lacking substance, firmness, or solidity
launch *(n.)*   boat that takes people to and from a ship
liner *(n.)*   passenger ship
make good its threat *(v. phrase)*   to carry out something negative that
    was impending
massed *(adj.)*   collected; formed
***moat** *(n.)*   channel of water, usually around a castle
***plate metal** *(n.)*   smooth, flat, thin piece of metal
port of call *(n.)*   harbor town where cruise ships stop
reverberating *(adj.)*   echoing
reverent *(adj.)*   worshipful
sow *(v.)*   to introduce; to implant
spiriting *(adj.)*   carrying out secretly
stifle *(v.)*   to hold back
***upsweep** *(n.)*   1940s hairstyle with the hair combed up and piled on top
    of the head
***vampish** *(adj.)*   seductive

Activities

1. Notice that the author moves between the recent past (as in the first
   three paragraphs) and the more distant past (paragraphs 5 and 7–9).
   As you read, try to figure out the relationship between events in the
   distant past and in the recent past.

2. What is Avey Johnson's daughter Marion like? What specific details
   does Marshall use to describe her? How do we know Marion is proud
   of her African heritage?

3. What do you think Marion's view is of her mother's taking a cruise to
   the Caribbean? What is Avey Johnson's view of her cruise? What values are important to her when she takes her first cruise?

*Denotes low-frequency word.

4. Marshall uses the cruise ship as a symbol of mainstream white American culture. In your journal, analyze the presentation of the inside and outside of the cruise ship. What are the specific details and images that Marshall provides? What do you think she is saying about American culture?

5. Contrast the image of the cruise ship with the ships that brought most Africans through the Middle Passage to America. Why is it ironic that Avey Johnson takes her vacations on a cruise ship?

6. In your journal, make notes about the details Marshall gives to describe Afro-Caribbean culture. How does Afro-Caribbean culture contrast in the story with white American values?

7. Inferring from the selection, write an essay on why you think Avey Johnson has decided to abandon the Caribbean cruise.

8. Write an essay arguing for or against the importance of learning about one's ethnic heritage.

For Further Reading

Cartey, Wilfred. *Whispers from the Caribbean: I Going Away, I Going Home.* Los Angeles: U of California P, 1991.

Lewis, Gordon K. *Main Currents in Caribbean Thought.* Baltimore: Johns Hopkins UP, 1983.

Glossary of Literary Terms

action or **plot**   The events that happen in a narrative or play.

antagonist   A character who opposes the main character.

ballad   A narrative poem in quatrains (groups of four lnes), with the second and fourth lines rhyming.

character   A person appearing in a work of literature; also, the personality of an individual.

chorus   A group of actors in a Greek tragedy who represent the community; they comment on the action and advise the characters.

comedy   A play with a happy ending; something funny.

epic   A long narrative poem focusing on a central character; sometimes called a **heroic poem**.

epithet   A standard word or phrase describing a god or person, such as "godlike Odysseus."

framed story   A story within a story, usually told by one of the characters.

genre   A literary form, such as the novel or poem.

Gothic tale   A literary form popular at the end of the eighteenth and beginning of the nineteenth century. It is characterized by use of the supernatural, images of dark and mysterious castles, ghosts, and other terrifying phenomena.

lyric   A short poem of strong feeling or emotion, originally sung to the accompaniment of the lyre (a stringed musical instrument).

Magical Realism   A Latin American literary movement begun in the 1960s that stressed an imaginative reality.

metaphor   A kind of figurative language that compares one person or object to another, as in the phrase "the arrows of snow."

meter   A recurring, rhythmic beat in a poetic line.

metonymy   A kind of figurative language in which the name of one thing is applied to the whole thing with which it is associated, as in "The stormgray sea yields to his prows."

Naturalism   A nineteenth-century literary movement, especially in France, that stressed the objective role of the novelist. Emile Zola compared the novelist to the experimental scientist and stressed determinism based on heredity and environment.

ode   Originally a Greek form, a lyric poem that praises a person or an object, such as "Ode to Joy."

pathetic fallacy   A literary device in which nature reflects the poet's feelings.

protagonist   The main character of a piece of fiction.

pseudonym   A false literary or pen name.

Realism   A nineteenth-century movement that stressed truthful representation of the world in literature. Details of everyday life were important in Realist works.

Romanticism   An artistic movement that began in Germany at the end of the eighteenth century and spread to the rest of Europe and America in the nineteenth century. The Romantics stressed the artist's sensations and impressions.

scene   A brief portion of a play; occurs in a single place.

setting   The location of the action of a play or piece of fiction.

Shakespearean sonnet   A 14-line poem consisting of three quatrains and a couplet, with a rhyme scheme of *abab cdcd efef gg*.

simile   A comparison using *like* or *as*.

sonnet   A 14-line lyric poem. The first three stanzas state a problem that is resolved in the final stanza.

tragedy   A drama in which the main character suffers a decline or, in modern plays, dies.

Appendix: Genre Descriptions

Drama: Comedy
(Chapter 13)

Drama is the oldest and most popular literary form. Its origins are rooted in ritual dance and song, with certain members of a group acting out roles while others form the audience. The interaction between the actors and the audience is necessary to the play. Generally, if the drama turns out well, it is called a comedy. The main character undergoes some minor difficulties that are resolved during the play. Chekhov's comedies resemble the *comedy of manners*, in which the behavior and relationships of ladies and gentlemen are gently ridiculed.

Drama: Tragedy
(Chapter 4, 8)

Serious drama that ends in death or suffering for the main character (protagonist) is called a tragedy. Tragedy is performed throughout the world, but in the West it has been shaped by the ancient Greeks. In his *Poetics*, Aristotle (383–322 B.C.E.) analyzes the tragedy as "an imitation of an action"—that is, role-playing—to show the decline of a noble character. The suffering of the protagonist and his efforts to avoid his fate bring the audience to a sense of fear and pity. The shared emotional effect of the tragedy and its sad ending brings the audience together as a community.

Shakespeare and other tragedians of the Elizabethan age wrote several types of tragedies, including the *revenge tragedy*, that involved complicated plots, adultery, incest, and multiple murders. Shakespeare's *Romeo and Juliet* is an experimental tragedy that has been criticized for the major role played by chance in the death of the two lovers. However, earlier prose forms—such as the novels of chivalry—had already hinted at the potential tragic consequences of uncontrolled young love.

Fiction: Novel
(Chapter 11, 16, 17, 18, 19, 23, 24, 26)

The art of storytelling can entertain us, let us experience events vicariously, or help us understand ourselves or others. Even though the events of a story may seem real (*Praisesong for the Widow*) or fantastic (the dream in *O Pioneers!*), the author carefully uses language to create a fictional world. The longest fictional form is the novel, which narrates a series of events, called the *plot*, about a number of people, the *characters*. A novel may have several plots or subplots, and many characters. An important quality of fiction is the *tone*, or the way in which the author shows a particular attitude or feeling toward the subject. Tone, especially *irony*, is important in Dickens's fiction. In Dinesen's fiction, a special *atmosphere* and *setting* are also important.

Fiction: Novella
(Chapter 12, 21)

The novella is narrative fiction which is longer than a short story and shorter than a novel. It usually concentrates on fewer matters than a novel and has fewer characters. Most novellas, including *The Turn of the Screw*, have no subplots, but they do possess a complex structure, frequently a framed story or a story within a story. The structure of *Chronicle of a Death Foretold* is very complicated because the author presents the same events several times, but each telling is from the perspective of a different character.

Fiction: Philosophical Novel
(Chapter 20)

A distinctive feature of the modern novel is the use of important intellectual currents as a framework. For example, in the late nineteenth century the world was shaken by the radical view of Karl Marx, put forth in his book *Das Capital* (1867–1884), that history was a struggle between the capitalist middle class and the workers. Marx believed this class conflict would be won by the workers through revolution. Other important intellectual works of the late nineteenth-century were Charles Darwin's *Origin of Species* (1859) and Sigmund Freud's 1899 work *Interpretation of Dreams*. Both helped to undermine the confidence in human beings as rational creatures. Modern Western philosophers such as Nietzsche and Sartre have promoted a view of the universe as indifferent to human suffering. In their view, God does not exist. These intellectual views are reflected in the modern existentialist novel with its underlying sense of disillusion and emptiness.

Fiction: Short Story
(Chapter 5, 6, 14, 15, 22)

In the Western world, the briefest written fictional form is the short story. It has a single plot, few characters, and is told in prose. In Asia, however, the short story combines prose and poetry. The traditional Chinese short story is based on the ancient practice of storytellers entertaining the public at periodic festivals such as the New Year's celebration. Storytellers drew from their oral tradition and frequently included important historical figures and political events in their tales. In both East and West, the short story has a carefully controlled structure, with a beginning, middle, and end. The ending usually brings a climax that shocks or surprises the reader. The master of the short story in the West is the American Edgar Allan Poe (1809–1849).

Nonfiction: Autobiographical Essay
(Chapter 10)

Essay comes from the Old French *essai*, meaning "to try"; it was established by Montaigne in the sixteenth century. It is normally a brief prose composition that makes a point or persuades an audience, usually in an informal manner.

Poetry: Epic or Heroic Poem
(Chapter 1, 3)

Since the time of the ancient Greeks, the epic or heroic poem has formed an important part of the Western literary tradition. The Greeks of the fifth and sixth centuries B.C.E. (Before the Common Era) believed that their culture had in its past a golden age between the Iron and Bronze ages when great heroes fought battles at the cities of Thebes and Troy. Long after that Heroic period, in the eighth century B.C.E., Homer drew on oral tradition to compose his epic poems, The Iliad and The Odyssey. Both his works are traditional epics—that is, they are based on historical figures who represent the ideal of a culture or nation united by language, religion, and customs.

Poetry: Free Verse
(Chapter 25)

Although it is written with the typical short lines of poetry, free verse (unlike most poetry) has no regular meter or beat, and usually no rhyme.

Poetry: Odes and Sonnets
(Chapter 8, 9)

The ode is an ancient poetic form dating back to the Greeks. It is also the most formal and complex lyric form, which is used to praise someone or something in a stately, ceremonial way. The lyric form is clos-est to poetry's musical origin (the lyre is a musical instrument) and is writ-ten in the first person ("I"). A second poetic form, the sonnet, usually ex-presses personal feelings about love, death, or other emotional issues. The Elizabethan sonnet is a 14-line poem divided into three quatrains (a group of four lines) and a couplet (two lines). Although it may vary, usually the rhyme scheme is *abab cdcd efef gg*.

Poetry: Verse Narrative
(Chapter 7)

Although its main point is to tell a story, verse narrative is written in poetic form. The lines are rhythmic and usually rhyme in pairs (cou-plets). Chaucer introduced into English the *heroic couplet,* with a meter called *iambic pentameter* (five metrical units or *feet,* each having one un-stressed and one stressed syllable).

Prose: Sacred Text
(Chapter 2, 25)

The best-known sacred texts are associated with world religions: the Jewish Torah, the Christian New Testament, the Moslem Koran. Others have only recently been recorded from oral tradition. Each sacred text is an ancient source of wisdom that teaches a world view and a code of moral behavior.

Acknowledgments *(continued from copyright page)*

Marie de France. Excerpt from Chapter IV, "Bisclavret" pp. 68–72 *The Lais of Marie de France* translated by Glyn S. Burgress and Keith Busby (Penguin Classics, 1986), Translation copyright © Glyn S. Burgress and Keith Busby, 1986. Reproduced by permission of Penguin Books Ltd., London, England.

Chaucer, Geoffrey. 257 lines from "The Miller's Tale" (pp 105-122) from *The Canterbury Tales* by Geoffrey Chaucer, translated by Nevill Coghill (Penguin Classics, Revised edition 1977), copyright © 1951 by Nevill Coghill, 1958, 1960, 1975, 1977.

Shakespeare, William. Excerpt from *The Tragedy of Romeo and Juliet.* Evans, G. Blakemore (Editor), *The Riverside Shakespeare.* Copyright © 1974 by Houghton Mifflin Company. Used with permission.

Wharton, Edith. Excerpt from "Roman Fever." Adapted with the permission of Charles Scribner's Sons, an imprint of MacMillan Publishing Company from *Roman Fever and Other Stories* by Edith Wharton. Copyright 1934 by Liberty Magazine, renewed © 1962 by William R. Tyler.

Kafka, Franz. Excerpt from "The Metamorphosis." From *The Metamorphosis* by Franz Kafka, trans. by Willa and Edwin Muir. Copyright 1946, 1948 by Schocken Books Inc. Reprinted by permission of Schocken Books, published by Pantheon Books, a division of Random House, Inc. Reprinted by permission of Martin Secker and Warburg Limited.

Cather, Willa. Excerpt from *O Pioneers.* Reprinted by permission of Virago Press.

She, Lao. Excerpt from "Rickshaw." From *Rickshaw* (the novel *Lo-T'o Hsiang Tsu*) by Lao She translated by Jean M. James. Reprinted by permission of the University of Hawaii Press. Copyright © 1979 by the Univeristy of Hawaii Press. Published originally in the serial form in the periodical *Yu-chou-feng* September 1936 to May 1937.

Achebe, Chinua. Excerpt from *Things Fall Apart.* Reprinted by permission of William Heinemann Limited.

Dinesen, Isak. Excerpt from *Out of Africa.* From *Out of Africa* by Isak Dinesen. Copyright 1937 by Random House, Inc. and renewed 1965 by Rungstediundfonden. Reprinted by permission of Random House, Inc. Copyright 1937, 1938 by Random House, Inc. Copyright renewed by Rungstedlung Foundation.

Abe, Kobo. Excerpt from *Woman in the Dunes.* From *The Woman in the Dunes* by Kobo Abe, trans., E. Dale Saunders. Copyright © 1964 Alfred A. Knopf, Inc. Reprinted by permission of Alfred A. Knopf, Inc. and Martin Secker and Warburg Limited.

García Márquez, Gabriel. Excerpt from *Chronicle of a Death Foretold.* From *Chronicle of a Death Foretold* by Gabriel García Márquez, trans., G. Rabassa. Translation copyright © 1982 by Alfred A. Knopf, Inc. Reprinted by permission of Alfred A. Knopf, Inc. and Random Century Group. Published in the British Commonwealth by Jonathan Cape.

Munro, Alice. Excerpt from "Boys and Girls." Reprinted from Alice Munro, "Boys and Girls" in *Dance of the Happy Shades, 1968.* Reprinted by permission of McGraw-Hill Ryerson Limited. Excerpted from "Boys and Girls," story included in the collection *Dance of the Happy Shades* by Alice Munro, copyright © 1968 by Alice Munro. Reprinted by permission of the Virginia Barber Literary Agency, Inc.

Desai, Anita. Excerpt from *Fire on the Mountain* by Anita Desai. Copyright © 1977 by Anita Desai. Reprinted by permission of Harper Collins Publishers Inc. and Rogers, Coleridge & White Ltd.

Mahfouz, Naguib. Excerpt from *The Thief and the Dogs.* From *The Thief and the Dogs* by Naguib Mahfouz, translated by Trevor Le Gassich. Translation copyright © 1984 by The American University in Cairo Press. Used by permission of Doubleday, a division of Bantam Doubleday Dell Publishing Group, Inc.

Alegría, Claribel. "Flowers from the Volcano." Reprinted from *Flowers from the Volcano,* by Claribel Alegría, translated by Carolyn Forché, by permission of the University of Pittsburgh Press. © 1982 by Claribel Alegría and Carolyn Forché

Leon-Portilla, Miguel. Excerpt from *Pre-Columbian Literature of Mexico.* From *Pre-Columbian Literature of Mexico* by Miguel Leon-Portilla. Copyright 1969 by the University of Oklahoma Press.

Marshall, Paule. Excerpt from *Praisesong for the Widow.* Reprinted by permission of The Putnam Publishing Group from *Praisesong for the Widow* by Paule Marshall. Copyright © 1983 by Paule Marshall. This excerpt was reprinted with the permission of Paule Marshall.

Index

About the Authors

Carole M. Shaffer-Koros is professor and chair of the Department of English/ESL at Kean College of New Jersey and a former director of the ESL program there. She has taught a broad range of literature and language courses as well as developmental English, ESL, and Spanish. She was recently elected vice-president of the International Edith Wharton Society.

Jessie M. Reppy is an associate professor of ESL at Kean College of New Jersey and is a former director of the ESL program there. She has been an ESL teacher and administrator—both in the U.S. and overseas—for 25 years. Throughout her career she has been active in state and national professional associations, including TESOL, New Jersey State TESOL-BE, and New York State TESOL, and has served on the boards of the two state affiliates.

Explorations in World Literature grew out of a New Jersey Humanities grant awarded to both instructors in 1988.

DATE	AFRICA	AMERICAS
3200 B.C.E.		
2000 B.C.E.		
1000 B.C.E.		
900 B.C.E.		
700 B.C.E.		
500 B.C.E.		
400 B.C.E.		
100 B.C.E.		
0		
800 C.E.		
1000		
1100		
1200		
1300		
1400		
1500		
1600		
1700		
1800		
1900		

Instructor's Manual to Accompany

Explorations in World Literature

Readings to Enhance Academic Skills

Carole M. Shaffer-Koros
Jessie M. Reppy

Instructor's Manual
to Accompany

EXPLORATIONS

IN

WORLD LITERATURE

Readings to Enhance Academic Skills

CAROLE M. SHAFFER-KOROS

and

JESSIE M. REPPY

Manufactured in the United States of America.
8 7 6 5 4
f e d c b a

For information, write:
St. Martin's Press, Inc.
175 Fifth Avenue
New York, NY 10010

ISBN: 0-312-09225-3

CONTENTS

PREFACE
Suggestions for Using *Explorations in World Literature*

CLASS ORGANIZATION: STUDY GROUPS

It is recommended that students be organized into study groups of three or four individuals for each literary work. Groups work best with a mix of students of varying linguistic and national backgrounds and academic skills. As the term progresses, students in the groups can be rotated. Study groups can discuss pre-reading questions, compare notes after mini-lectures, and work on activities at the end of each chapter.

PRE-READING ACTIVITIES

New material must be set into a schema, or framework, of prior knowledge of the students. The following are recommended:

1. Geographical orientation

Using the world map in the text, a large wall map, and/or smaller local maps, give geographical orientation about the author and the work. Ask if students have knowledge of the culture, country, or work under discussion. In an ESL class, encourage contributions of student informants without embarrassing them. Knowledgeable students may serve as valuable resources.

2. Historical orientation

A time-line, or chronology, is included in the text. Have the students locate the author and the work in the appropriate place on the time-line.

3. Pre-reading questions

Study groups can be used for discussion of the pre-reading questions in each chapter. These questions focus the attention of the students on the selection and probe their existing knowledge. There are no "correct" answers to these questions, and not all students may be able to contribute to discussion. Still, the peer interaction of a study group is very valuable here. After a period of time for study group discussion, the class can be brought together to share the ideas discussed.

4. Key terms

Key terms from the mini-lecture and introductory material to each chapter are in the text. As these terms are important for understanding the cultural background of the literary selections, it is recommended that students learn the definition and significance of these terms. To establish familiarity with the list at the first presentation, the instructor may wish to read the terms aloud and have the students repeat them.

5. Mini-lecture

A suggested text of a mini-lecture for each chapter is provided in the manual. Students should be instructed to take notes on the lecture. The text may be adapted in any way that the instructor wishes. For example, it could be lengthened, shortened, or divided into parts. It is recommended that the lecture be delivered at a reasonable pace and that key terms be emphasized as they appear in the lecture. Repetition and restatement may be necessary. Generally students find the mini-lectures a bit difficult at the beginning of the semester, but as the term progresses, they become more skilled in understanding and taking notes.

6. Note-check
At the end of a mini-lecture, students may be asked to do a note-check. Note checks may be handled in various ways. Suggested approaches follow: a. Students compare their notes with other members of their study group and clarify anything not understood well. b. Students exchange notes with other study group members; they check for clarity and accuracy of facts. Groups can be asked to choose the best set of notes and to defend their choice. c. A model set of notes can be shown to the students. These notes may have been taken by an academically strong student, a tutor, or the instructor. After reviewing the model notes, students may modify their own notes.

After the note-check students may be given the opportunity to clarify information in full class discussion. At this point or in a subsequent class, the instructor may wish to have the students reiterate main points in the lecture as review.

READING
1. Reading journal
It is recommended that students be introduced to the triple-entry journal. This journal is used to engage the student more deeply in the reading. Ask the students to fold a sheet of notebook paper into thirds. In the first column, they are to write what they are reacting to from the text: a word, a phrase, a sentence, a concept. The second column is used for comments, questions, observations, reactions, or connections. The final column is left blank for the answers to their questions, which may be learned from peers or further reading, through class discussion, or from the instructor. Sample entries for Chapter 1, "The Huluppu Tree" from *Inanna* follow:

What I Am Reacting To	My Reaction	Answers/Comments
A huluppu tree	What is it?	
	It sounds funny.	
First three lines	Lot of repetition.	Why?
Uruk	What is it?	Seems like a place name.

These entries could be in a student's journal after the reading of the assigned work. As a starting activity, the class could be instructed to divide into study groups and exchange journals. If students know the answer to a question in Column 2, or if they wish to comment on anything in Column 2 on another student's paper, they are instructed to write it down in Column 3. On returning to full class, questions unresolved in study groups can serve as starting points of discussion for the reading. One caveat: Students tend to want to write only vocabulary words in Column 1. They must be encouraged to think more deeply about the reading and make connections, especially after reading more than one work.

2. Vocabulary and literary terms
It should be pointed out to students that there is a list of selected vocabulary from the reading in each chapter. Students are very relieved to see the list. They should be

encouraged, nonetheless, to get the meaning of terms from context whenever possible. Additionally, there is a literary glossary and appendix at the end of the book for reference.

ACTIVITIES
An instructor may choose from a variety of activities at the end of each chapter. These activities include reading, writing, listening, speaking, and critical thinking tasks. The reading journal is used in some of the activities. It is up to the discretion of the instructor to choose the number and type of activities for a particular class.

QUIZZES/EVALUATION
Periodic quizzes in the form of short essay questions are recommended. It is also recommended that mid-term and end of semester evaluations be composed of essay questions and short sentence identification items. A sample quiz on *Inanna* follows:

To the student:
Answer each question with a complete sentence.
 1. Who is Inanna? What did she do with the tree?
 2. What kind of brother is Gilgamesh?
 3. What does the poem tell us about the Sumerian attitude toward women?
 4. In what part of the world was Sumeria located? What is the area called today?

Note: Principal secondary sources for the Instructor's Manual are listed in the For Further Reading section of each chapter in the student text.

CHAPTER 1
From "The Huluppu-Tree" from *Inanna, Queen of Heaven and Earth*

Historico-cultural Background
Sumerian Culture

Expert Sumerologists have noted that Sumeria was the earliest culture to develop in the ancient area called Mesopotamia (Greek for "between rivers"). In that fertile region, the domestication of grains such as wheat, oats, and barley, as well as animals such as goats and sheep, enabled civilization to develop. Urban areas were created and began to expand.

Life in urban areas needed to be regulated in order to run smoothly, and by 3200 B.C.E. (Before the Common Era, a neutral archaeological term), the invention of *cuneiform* writing helped the Sumerians to establish and govern a well-organized bureaucracy. Each city-state was ruled by a priest-king, such as the epic hero Gilgamesh and Dumuzi, husband of Inanna.

Oral Tradition

Cultures without a system of writing cannot depend on written texts to perpetuate their traditions. Such preliterate cultures must pass on information to the younger generation through *oral tradition*. In many cultures, oral tradition is carried on by a special storyteller, or it may be practiced by a group of individuals with exceptional memories. Oral tradition can be recognized by frequent repetitions or refrains used by the storyteller, and by rhythmic or verse form.

When a culture later develops a system of writing and begins to record its cultural traditions, features of oral tradition, such as repetition, frequently are carried over into the written form. Thus we can recognize traces of oral tradition in written texts such as *Inanna* and the Old Testament.

The Epic

The epic is an ancient, largely Western, poetic form derived from oral tradition. Originally sung by a poet, the epic consists of a series of adventures connected by a central, usually male, heroic figure. The hero generally has a miraculous birth and/or death; divine powers aid him in his adventures; he crosses a body of water in his journey or quest for a personal and cultural goal. The object of the hero's quest may be something material--such as valuable wood--or an abstract concept--such as fame or glory.

The Text

Inanna, Queen of Heaven and Earth: Her Stories and Hymns from Sumer is an unusual text in that the "hero" of this earliest of epics is a female. In this cycle, or collection of poems, Inanna evolves from the rather helpless girl shown in our selection to a powerful goddess who later dominates heaven and the earth's cycle of fertility. The selection begins with a summary form of the Sumerian creation story (called *Enuma Elish*), indicating a number of cultural aspects such as polytheism, the systematic division of the universe, assignment of its parts to various gods and goddesses, and the importance of bread. A woman who fears male gods, Inanna rescues the *huluppu* or willow tree and brings it to an Eden-like holy garden. Her ambitions to build a "shining throne" and a "shining bed" symbolize her hopes for political and sexual power;

however, early in her career, she is weak. Without male assistance (from the epic hero Gilgamesh), Inanna is unable to drive from her tree the snake, the monstrous *Anzu*-bird, and the rebellious Lileth (Adam's first wife in the Kabala). When her brother Gilgamesh succeeds, Inanna makes him a *pukku* and a *mikku*, a hoop and stick believed to represent objects of royal power such as a more modern orb and scepter.

MINI-LECTURE on *INANNA*

According to historians and archaeologists of Middle Eastern culture, the rise of Sumerian culture was critical in the development of the modern West. In the prehistorical period, that is, the time before the invention of writing, people in Mesopotamia probably lived in nomadic tribes. They passed important cultural information from one generation to the next through word of mouth, called *oral tradition*. This information included ideas about the creation of the world or stories of the gods. These myths were told by good storytellers or sung by poets with good memories.

The land in Mesopotamia was very fertile, allowing the people to domesticate grains as well as animals. With time, industrial skills such as weaving, leatherworking and carpentry were developed. Using their new technology, the Sumerians built several large urban areas, called city-states. The network of city-states in Sumeria shared two important things: a common polytheistic religion and a written language.

By 3200 B.C.E. (Before the Common Era), the Sumerians had invented a system of writing, called *cuneiform*. It consisted of triangular characters that were pressed into wet clay with a stick. In Mesopotamia, stone, metal, and wood were difficult to find, but clay was everywhere. Clay was the material for making many kinds of objects such as cooking utensils and statues of the gods. Even houses and important religious buildings or temples, called *ziggurats*, were made of clay. The Tower of Babel, mentioned in the Bible, is an example of a *ziggurat*.

A system of writing enabled the Sumerians to establish a well-organized bureaucracy to run their city-states. The Sumerians made other contributions to Western civilization, including military use of the wheeled, horse-drawn chariot; creation of a written code of law; and a system of mathematics based on the number six, still used today in the measurement of the circle (360 degrees), in the division of time (hours and minutes), and in some weights and measures. We continue to study the Sumerians not only because of their important technological inventions, but because of their religious and literary contributions to civilization.

Among the literary texts the Sumerians recorded in clay were *The Epic of Gilgamesh* and stories of the goddess Inanna. Sumerian epics tell us much detail about their human heroes and their polytheistic beliefs. For example, *The Epic of Gilgamesh* contains the story of the gods' destruction of a corrupt world with a great flood. These mythological stories are important because they influenced later cultures, especially the Hebrews in the writing of the Old Testament.

The poem *Inanna* is an example of an epic, a long poem combining fact and fiction, which tells the story of an important hero. In its earliest forms, it derived from oral tradition; the original composer is unknown. The epic consists of a series of adventures connected by a central hero, usually a male. Our poem, however, centers on a female figure, Inanna. The well-known male hero, Gilgamesh, helps in rescuing the *huluppu* tree from her enemies.

The epic hero is helped by the powers of the gods in his (or her) adventures; his journey or quest represents not only a personal goal, but something of great import to the hero's culture. Since the efforts of the epic hero benefit his entire culture, by studying a particular epic, we can learn much about the values of the culture which created it.

"The Huluppu-Tree" begins with a brief summary of the Sumerian creation. Then Inanna cares for her sacred tree, a symbol of life, in a garden that resembles the later garden of Eden in Genesis. Other Sumerian influences on Hebrew culture will be seen in a study of the Old Testament.

CHAPTER 2
Genesis (Chapters 1 and 2) from the Old Testament

Historico-cultural Background

Religious tradition traces the Hebrews to Abraham, who came from the Mesopotamian city of Ur ("Ur of the Chaldeans," Genesis 11.28). Although Abraham's twelve grandsons are identified with twelve Hebrew tribes, recent archaeological evidence suggests that at the end of the thirteenth century B.C.E., the source of Israel's unity and common identity was *not* blood kinship, but rather the belief in one god, Yahweh.

Some archaeologists have explained that certain groups settled into agriculture before others, leading to tension between farming and semi-nomadic herding groups. This tension is seen in the competition between suitors for Inanna (one, a farmer, the other, a herder), and in the conflict between Cain and Abel. Thus, the early Canaanites were an agricultural people who had first settled the eastern Mediterranean shores. Gradually there settled among them formerly nomadic people who gave allegiance to one deity, Yahweh. The polytheistic Canaanites referred to these people as *h'apiru*, foreigners or outlaws. The new settlers were later joined by Hebrew refugees from Egypt (after the Exodus), and together they revolted against the Canaanites, conquered the area, and founded Israel.

Abraham's origin in Mesopotamia was not the only connection between the early Sumerian and the Hebrew cultures. Under Nebuchadnezzar, king of the Babylonian successors to Sumer, Jerusalem was sacked in 598-597 B.C.E., and Jewish captives were deported to Babylon. Again in 587 B.C.E., Babylonians burned Jerusalem and destroyed Solomon's temple, sending more Jews to Babylon. As captives there, the Hebrews came into intimate contact with Babylonian culture, including the religion and oral tradition. By 539 B.C.E., when the Persian king Cyrus the Great captured Babylon and returned the Hebrews to Jerusalem, they carried back with them many stories of the gods and epic heroes.

In the first century B.C.E., when rabbis gathered in Jamnia to organize the Torah, or five books of Moses (the first five books of the Christian OT), they drew from numerous cultural traditions. Scholars of the biblical canon have identified three major sources for the first books of the OT, and refer to them as J (Yahweh), E (Elohim) and P (Priestly). Our text contains passages only from the J and P sources.

Sources of Genesis, Chapters 1 and 2

All of Chapter 1 and up to verse 3, Chapter 2, is from the P (Priestly) source. In this text, the divine being is called "God" in the English translation. The style is very repetitive. There is no great detail given about the creation. It was just *done*. However, the time frame is very specific, with events assigned to each of seven days.

The portion from Chapter 2, verses 4 to 25, is from the J (Yahweh) source. In this text, the divine being is named "Lord God" in English. He is more human; e.g., he breathes. Moreover, there are more details. Compare, for example, the creation of man and woman in Chapters 1 and 2. Note the details given in Chapter 2. The inclusion in the Old Testament of two different creation stories is evidence of material being drawn from two rather different, but nevertheless sacred, sources.

Original Form of the OT

It is important to note that the original language of the *Torah*, or the beginnings of the Old Testament, was Hebrew mixed with some Aramaic. During the first millennium B.C.E., Hebrew was the most important literary language, while Aramaic was the common or vernacular language. At a later period, the Greeks divided the original text into books or verses. However, their divisions did not always fall where appropriate. An example is the division between Genesis, Chapters 1 and 2. The division should fall between Chapter 2, verses 3 and 4, where the first creation story ends and the second one begins, rather than where it is, in the midst of the first story.

MINI-LECTURE on GENESIS

(Review carefully before giving the mini-lecture. You may wish to present this material in more than one class. When discussing the OT sources, refer to the chart in the student text.)

At the time of early Sumerian cities, about 2500 B.C.E. (Before the Common Era), Hebrew civilization consisted of twelve nomadic tribes spread across a large area in the Middle East. Religious tradition traces the origin of the patriarch Abraham to the city of Ur of the Chaldeans, a Sumerian city. Abraham's grandson Jacob (also called Israel) had twelve sons identified with the twelve Hebrew tribes.

Archaeological evidence shows that at the end of the thirteenth century B.C.E., the Jews were united by devotion to one god, Yahweh. They came into the Canaanite area between the eastern Mediterranean Sea and the Jordan River. Because the monotheistic Hebrews did not believe

in the many gods of the Canaanites, the Canaanites called these people "h'apiru" (later, Hebrew), meaning foreigners or outlaws. Eventually the Hebrews conquered the area of Canaan and established Israel.

Ancient Israel reached its highest power under wise King Solomon (961-922 B.C.E.), when the great temple at Jerusalem was built. However, after his death, the nation was divided into two kingdoms, Israel in the north, and Judah in the south. Twice during Israel's history (598-597 and 587 B.C.E.), the Babylonians, successors to the Sumerians, invaded Israel. King Nebuchadnezzar conquered the Hebrews and deported them to Babylon. There the Hebrews came into contact with Sumerian/Babylonian written and oral tradition.

When Jewish rabbis came to write the five books of the Torah, later incorporated into the Old Testament, they drew upon a number of sources, several of which had been influenced by Sumerian tradition. Two very important sources for the OT are called J and P sources. J, the oldest, refers to the one God as Yahweh, translated into English as Lord God. In the text from the J source, the Lord God is described in human terms, with lively, concrete, picturesque images. This source, written in Solomon's time (950 B.C.E.), comes from the area of Judah.

The second source we shall consider is the P, or Priestly, source, dating from 539 B.C.E. In this source, the law is very important, and the language is abstract and repetitive. Originating from Solomon's Temple at Jerusalem, it shows an interest in genealogies and precise dates. Both sources were used to create the Torah.

The original text of the Torah was written in Hebrew on a continuous papyrus scroll. Papyrus was prepared in large quantities in the city of Byblos on the eastern shore of the Mediterranean. Because of its export of papyrus, the Greeks connected the name of Byblos with a book or scroll. Not only did the Greeks give the name Bible to the collection of the Old and New Testaments, they also divided the text into chapters and verses. As we shall see, because the Greeks were not familiar with the J and P sources, some divisions were not correct. Finally, it was the Greeks who named the first book of the Old Testament Genesis because of its opening line, "In the beginning."

CHAPTER 3
From *The Odyssey*

Historico-cultural Background

In spite of the ancient Greek belief in a true Heroic Age, more modern historians felt that the events described in Homer's epics *The Iliad* and *The Odyssey* were nothing but myths. Opinions changed, however, after the German Heinrich Schliemann began in 1870 to excavate the site of Bronze Age Troy. Located near the

Dardanelles, Troy is described by Homer's stock phrases as "well-walled" and "a broad city." The Trojans are "horse tamers."

As for Homer, the prolonged controversy over his identity has involved issues such as when he lived and where he came from, and whether he represents one or more poets; Samuel Butler even believed the poet was a woman. The influence of Homer's work cannot be underestimated. First, it formed the basis for Greek education and culture to the time of the Roman Empire. Second, because of renewed interest in Homer during the Renaissance and in more recent times, his work has had major influence throughout the western world. Indeed, Homer is the standard for epic.

The detailed studies of the two epics by Milman Parry indicate that *The Iliad* seems to be the earlier work as its structures are simpler; *The Odyssey* is a product of a more mature poet. Parry has shown that oral tradition was the source of Homer's poetry. This is evident in such characteristics as formulaic structures that helped the singer to remember as he sang; these include stock epithets ("godlike Odysseus"), repetitions of groups of lines and sometimes of entire stories.

While *The Iliad* recounts the story of Troy and the wrath of the hero Achilles, the action of *The Odyssey* takes place after the fall of Troy to the Greeks and the ten-year struggle of Odysseus to return home to Ithaca. The most powerful enemy of the Trojans was Agamemnon, King of Mycenae, who had secured his power by marrying Clytemnestra, daughter of Tyndareus of Sparta and sister of Helen, "the face that launched a thousand ships." The beautiful Helen married Agamemnon's brother Menelaos, who became King of Lakonia, giving control of southern Greece to the two brothers. The kidnapping of Helen by Paris, Prince of Troy, led to the Greek siege and defeat of Troy.

Unfortunately, during Agamemnon's absence from Mycenae, his wife Clytemnestra plotted with her lover Aigisthos to kill Agamemnon on his return. Later their son Orestes took revenge on his mother and Aigisthos. This story contrasts with that of Odysseus and his twenty-year absence from his home in Ithaca. Unlike Agamemnon, Odysseus is fortunate enough to possess a faithful wife, Penelope, and a loyal son, Telemachus. And except for Poseidon, the gods and goddesses on Mount Olympus want to see him safely home.

MINI-LECTURE on *THE ODYSSEY*
(Refer to the chart of Greek gods and goddesses where appropriate.)

Homer's epic material was drawn from oral tradition which told the details of the Greek war against Troy and the return of the Greek heroes to their homes after many years. Archaeological investigations seem to indicate that Troy fell about 1250 B.C.E during the Bronze Age glory of the city of Mycenae. At that time, southern Greece was dominated by the two sons of Atreus: Agamemnon, king of Mycenae, and his brother Menelaos, husband of Helen and king of Lakonia. After Paris, Prince of Troy, kidnapped Helen and returned with her to Troy, Menelaos and Agamemnon organized the Greek armies to attack and defeat Troy.

Unfortunately, to achieve success, before departing for Troy, Agamemnon had sacrificed their daughter, thus making his wife Clytemnestra very angry. Upon his return home, Clytemnestra and her lover Aigisthos murdered Agamemnon. Later, her son Orestes took revenge on both his mother and Aigisthos. The tragic story of Agamemnon's marriage is told in Book I of *The Odyssey*.

The Odyssey begins with an invocation--an appeal to the muse or goddess of inspiration--for the poet to sing well of the epic hero Odysseus. Techniques that help the singer to remember his lines include the use of formulas--that is, repeated phrases, lines or entire stories; and stock epithets, such as "godlike Odysseus" and "excellent Aigisthos," which show qualities associated with one of the heroes or the gods.

While most of the poem focuses on the adventures of the epic hero Odysseus, the opening book draws on Greek mythology and shows the main gods on Mount Olympus behaving very much like humans. They are jealous, become angry, and enjoy good dinners. It is the anger of Poseidon, god of the sea, that keeps the epic hero on his long sea odyssey to return home to his faithful wife Penelope and loyal son.

Homer's epics are the model for this poetic form in the West. As with all epics, *The Odyssey* has significance on two levels: the personal, that is, the man who struggles long and hard to return to his home and family; and the social, that is, the king who returns to his native land, drives out the younger men of Ithaca who desire his power, and reestablishes his rule in justice and prosperity. For the culture that creates it, the epic defines the personal qualities and behavior of the much-admired hero.

CHAPTER 4
From *Antigone* from *The Theban Plays*

Historico-cultural Background

Tragedy originated in the worship of Dionysus, a Greek nature god associated with wine and spring fertility rites. Female worshippers concluded their orgiastic songs and dances with the ritualistic shedding of blood, usually that of a goat, to guarantee agricultural fertility. Their songs, called dithyrambs, refer to the "double birth" of Dionysus, rescued from his dying mother's womb by his father Zeus, who sewed him into his own leg for a second birth.

By the end of the sixth century B.C.E., worship of Dionysus was civilized and organized into choral groups. The first known individual performer, Thespis, combined choral song with the speech of a masked actor who engaged in dialogue with the chorus. With the great tragedians of the Athenian Golden Age, tragedy evolved further: Aeschylus added a second actor, allowing dramatic conflict; Sophocles added a third actor, permitting further elaboration of individual characters. Both based their plays on ancient myths known to the Greek public. Euripides, the youngest of the three, subjected the received myths to a critical view in his dramas.

Public performance of dramas during the fifth century B.C.E. was no mere entertainment; it was a religious event that all Athenians were expected to attend. Presented in a large open-air amphitheater, male actors performed the roles of humans and gods using few theatrical properties. A mask was worn, along with platform shoes ("larger than life"); individual actors declaimed from the stage (*skene*), while the chorus performed in the orchestra, or open circular area. Scenery was scant; a mechanical device, called the *deus ex machina* (god from the machine), was used to lift an actor playing a god above the stage.

MINI-LECTURE on *ANTIGONE*
(When discussing the characters in *Antigone*, use the genealogical tree of the Royal House of Thebes in the student text.)

The history of Greek tragedy can be traced back to prehistorical ritual song and dance in honor of the ancient god of wine and fertility, called Dionysus or Bacchus. Under the influence of wine, female worshippers of Dionysus carried out wild, bloody sacrifices to ensure fertility of the earth. There is evidence that in the earliest rites the sacrificial victims were men. Later victims were animals, especially goats, giving rise to the name *tragedy* (*tragodoi*), meaning goat song. The religious group songs and dances were taken from rural areas to the city and became more formal. They were now divided into a large group, called the chorus, and an individual actor. The first single performer was Thespis; a form of his name, thespian, is now used to describe all actors.

Near the end of the sixth century B.C.E., Athenians honored Dionysus at annual spring competitions in which prizes were given to the best tragedies and comedies. The Dionysia was an important four-day religious festival when business was suspended, and every Greek, regardless of class or gender, was expected to attend. In open-air theaters that could hold 13,000 spectators, playwrights competed for prizes for the best comedy and tragedy. Those who wrote tragedies based their plays on Greek myths, that is, stories filled with complex meaning that are passed from generation to generation.

The Greek drama reached its height during the fifth century B.C.E. in Periclean Athens. Because of Pericles' military skill, the city-state of Athens dominated Greek culture. A time of relative peace, this unprecedented golden age saw the development of the concept of democracy and the flourishing of the all the arts. During this time, Pericles built the famous Parthenon and other religious buildings on the Acropolis.

Pericles governed his city with a group of ten men selected by the Athenian citizens. Among the ten was the dramatist Sophocles. In 468, Sophocles had come to Athens to successfully compete in the annual dramatic contests. Along with Euripides and Aeschylus, Sophocles is one of the most important figures in the development of the classical Greek tragedy. Author of over 120 plays, Sophocles' innovation in the tragedy was the addition of the third individual actor. The plot, or the series of events, in the tragedy was known to the audience from myths drawn from Greek oral tradition.

The tragic hero always struggles courageously against his fate and suffers the gods' punishment with dignity; therefore, Sophocles' contribution to tragedy was not the invention of stories; his innovation was his creative use of poetic language to tell the story. In addition, Sophocles' dramatic art develops a character by contrasting him or her in a dialogue with another character; we can see this technique in the dialogue between the sisters, Antigone and Ismene.

The plot of the play *Antigone* is based on the Legend of Thebes. Because Cadmus, the legendary founder of the city of Thebes, angered the gods, he and all the descendants of the Royal House of Thebes were cursed with misfortune. His great-grandson Oedipus, for example, was fated to kill his own father and marry his mother Iocaste. Shortly before the action of this play, their sons Polyneices and Eteocles killed one another over the throne of Thebes, leaving their uncle Creon to rule. Creon has given a full military funeral to Eteocles. However, Creon has forbidden the burial of Polyneices because he had attacked his own city. Their sister Antigone defies Creon's law and demands a religious burial for her brother Polyneices. Creon's insistence on not burying him leads to the suicides of Antigone, his son, and his wife, Iocaste, leaving him to suffer alone. He realizes too late that even the king cannot defy the laws of the gods.

According to Aristotle in his *Poetics*, a tragedy shows the decline of a single tragic hero from good fortune to bad. He considers Creon the tragic hero whose tragic flaw or defect causes his downfall. Aristotle also states that women cannot be tragic heroes. Modern audiences, however, frequently are moved by Antigone's concern for her brother and identify her as the tragic hero.

The role of the chorus in the tragedy is to comment, to summarize, and to explain to the audience the meaning of the action. As old men, they represent the collective wisdom of the community. Their good advice is frequently ignored by the tragic hero until it is too late. That is what happens in the tragedy *Antigone*.

CHAPTER 5
From "Red Thread Maiden"

Historico-cultural Background

Although isolated in many ways, China has long played an important role in world history. Physical barriers such as the Gobi Desert to the north, and mountain chains running north to south, tend to isolate parts of China, making central government control difficult. Indeed, historically, only three governments succeeded: the Han (206 B.C.E. - 220 C.E.); the T'ang; and the Ch'ing (1644 - 1911).

As in Mesopotamia, the earliest civilization in China arose between two rivers, the Yellow and the Yangtze, in Shen-si province. In this fertile area, settlements based on rice and millet culture developed and spread along the Kansu corridor to the lower reaches of the Yellow River (Huang Ho). Excavations at the ancient Shang capital at An-yang have brought to light a large group of exquisite bronzes as well as bones and tortoise shells bearing the first evidence of Chinese writing. These pictographs, dating to about the twelfth century B.C.E., were used in divination rituals.

The native Chinese religion, Taoism or Daoism--meaning "the way"--is a mystical, nature-oriented system. Its beliefs were overlaid by the humanistic teachings of Confucius (K'ung Fu-tzu, "K'ung the Master"). Confucianism taught a system of appropriate behavior in a political and social hierarchy.

The third major religious influence of ancient times came with the introduction of Buddhism by Indian monks following the Silk Route in the first century C. E. Based on the teachings of the Indian prince Gautama Shakyamuni, who lived in the sixth and fifth centuries B.C.E., Buddhism appeals to people of all classes. Gautama left his life of luxury to become a wandering monk; at age 35, he attained spiritual enlightenment and became known as Buddha. Unlike Confucianism, Buddhism devalues the present, physical world and seeks peace for the spirit in a state of nothingness.

MINI-LECTURE on "RED THREAD MAIDEN"

China is the largest of all Asian countries and has the greatest population of any country in the world. At present, it consists of 21 provinces, some larger than European countries. The people of China are ethnically and linguistically diverse. Until the twentieth century, only three governments, including the T'ang, were able to control all of China.

The Chinese literary tradition is the oldest continuous written tradition in the world. The earliest literary works in the canon date to the fifth century B.C.E. and are referred to as the Confucian Five Classics. All of these works have been extensively commented upon by the followers of Confucius. The Five Classics includes *The Book of Songs*, a collection of poems which at an early time became models for every scholar. Indeed, the writing of poetry was considered necessary for any learned man and formed part of the civil service examinations. Prose literary forms such as short stories, plays, and novels were developed many centuries later.

Historically, China has a distinct religious and ethical system. The native Daoism or Taoism is based on mystical beliefs related to the natural world. Added to this are the teachings of the master Confucius. Confucianism taught a system of appropriate behavior in a political and social hierarchy that viewed the emperor as the Son of Heaven and earthly life as a mirror of the heavenly world. Confucius valued filial piety and piety toward the ancestors. Confucianism could best be summed up as a humanist respect for oneself and others, expressed by self-control, good faith, and charity. This courtesy is very similar to the European ideals in the age of chivalry.

The third religious element added in ancient times is Buddhism. Brought from India in the first century, Buddhism taught that the attractions of the physical world must be resisted and strong emotions overcome; Chinese converts retreated from the world to isolated monasteries. Buddha also believed that the deeds of the past, karma, affect repeated rebirths, or reincarnations, in the cycle of existence in which a being suffers pain for past sins. Endless suffering ends when one has achieved moral perfection and realized a state of nirvana. In the story, Red Thread has been reincarnated to pay for the sins of her previous life.

After 624, the T'ang dynasty pacified and unified an empire that lasted for three hundred years. The Chinese even conquered the eastern Turks and spread their kingdom westward. Trade grew with the West, with Central Asia, and with India. Along with ancient Buddhist shrines, temples were built by many other non-Chinese religions.

During the reign of young Emperor Kao Tsung, real power passed into the hands of Empress Wu, the only independent woman sovereign in Chinese history. Through court intrigue, and contrary to Buddhist principles, Wu rose from a low-ranking position to be a dominant, ruthless empress. In 657, she moved the royal court to a second capital at Lo-yang. She undermined the power of the nobles by allowing civil servants to enter court administration through examination alone, rather than through social rank. By 705, the T'ang family rule was reestablished as the Second Imperial Period, and prosperity followed.

A second major disturbance occurred in 755 with the rebellion of An Lu-Shan, a non-Chinese general who gained military control over three northeast commands. With 160,000 troops under his command, the armed confrontation nearly destroyed the T'ang dynasty. After An Lu-Shan and his subordinates were suppressed in 763, the northeast provinces continued under the control of non-Chinese semi-independent rule. This rebellion was followed by a wave of others, the subject of our story.

"Red Thread Maiden" is told in the style of the T'ang period: It Is simple and direct, with the main interest in the plot. A female storyteller such as Yuan Chiao would have told her story, sung, and accompanied herself on a musical instrument to entertain her audience. Her gestures and facial expression would have been important in conveying theemotions of the characters to the listeners. Invoking the humanist code of ethics of Confucianism and the principle of reincarnation, Yuan Chiao tells the story of the peaceful resolution to political rebellion against the T'ang.

CHAPTER 6
"Bisclavret" from *The Lais of Marie de France*
Historico-cultural Background

By the end of the eleventh century, Europe was divided into roughly two areas, one dominated by speakers of Germanic dialects and the other dominated by speakers of various vernacular forms of Latin, the Romance languages. In 1066, the Norman conquest brought England into the French-speaking world as well. French reformers spurred the Crusades to Jerusalem, the new schools of learning, and the growth of academic centers. These were built in expanding urban areas, that developed around cathedrals such as Canterbury in England, and Chartres and Orleans in France. The forerunners of modern universities, these centers promoted the study of arts and sciences.

The late twelfth century marks a period of political turmoil when Europe struggled with the Byzantine world for dominance over the Mediterranean Sea. Europe felt unified by Latin Christian principles, but close contacts with the Moslem world left cultural effects, especially in lyric poetry.

Marie de France

The woman known as Marie de France was probably a native-born French woman ("de France" means from France) residing in England at a time when the English aristocracy was French-speaking. In an age when few women were educated, her knowledge seems to indicate that she was an aristocrat.

There are a number of theories about her exact identity, but none has been thoroughly proven. She is known chiefly through her work composed from 1160 to 1215: *Fables*, a collection of animal fables translated from English into French; *Saint Patrick's Purgatory,* a moralizing poem based on a Latin tract; and the *Lais*. In all three works she tells us that she is "Marie," and, in the *Fables*, that she is from France.

Marie de France also tells us that she wrote *The Lais* for a "noble king" and *The Fables* for a "Count William." The king was probably Henry II of England, but the identity of Count William is not certain. We do know that Marie associated with the aristocracy and that she was writing for that audience.

The Lais

The lais of Marie de France are written in Old French in octosyllabic couplets. (The story in the text is a prose rendition.) Old French was the language spoken from the ninth century until Modern French evolved in the sixteenth century. After the Norman conquest, Old French was also the language of the English court.

The style of Marie de France is relatively simple. She uses a fairly small vocabulary and frequent repetition of words. Marie herself tells us that she used Breton lais (lais from Brittany, an area in northwestern France which spoke a Celtic language) as her source material. The Breton lai was traditionally an adventure of ancient origin told in verse and set to music. At the beginning of the lai "Equitan," Marie states that the Bretons composed lais for posterity to keep alive the adventures of heroic nobles. Marie tells us that she is the first to put the lais into rhyme. What she states cannot be verified as there are no extant Breton lais.

Literary Considerations

The lai derives from the love lyric of Provence. Troubadours sang love songs (*cansos*) of "courtly love," based on the values of the aristocrats of court. But as the love lyric moved northward in France, the form became more narrative and focused on the action of the characters. This transitional form, still written in verse, was the lai. In its final form, the romance, the themes of courtly love were submerged in prose narrative filled with the adventures of a noble hero.

In her lais Marie de France emphasizes adventure, creating a narrative poem to be recited rather than sung. The subject matter of the 12 lais is love. The relationship between courtly love and chivalry, the medieval system of knighthood, is explored from many different points of view. For example, "Guigemar" is about a young man who does not know how to love until he meets a woman married to a possessive old man; in "Laustic" the lovers are unable to meet because the woman is married; in "Bisclavret" the supernatural affects the relationship between husband and wife.

A further connection between the lai and later literature appears in Geoffrey Chaucer's *Canterbury Tales.* Written in the fourteenth century, the work contains "The Franklin's Tale," identified by Chaucer as a Breton lai.

The subject of "Bisclavret" was one of fascination for Europeans of the day: the power to transform oneself or another into a wolf by the use of magic. In this story the transformation of the husband into a werewolf puts the wife's love to a severe test which she fails. In fact, her treachery also attempts to destroy the human aspect of her husband. However, in courtly fashion, the husband is not unworthy, and so the wife's behavior must be punished. Indeed, the punishment visited upon the wife's progeny from her second husband exquisitely fits the crime committed.

Two types of loyalty, one of the main values of the chivalric code, are tested in this lay: the loyalty of the wife to the husband and the loyalty of the vassal to his king. Indeed, loyalty triumphs; disloyalty is punished.

MINI-LECTURE on *THE LAIS OF MARIE DE FRANCE*

The Lais of Marie de France were written between 1155 and 1170, a period of vigorous artistic activity in France and her political ally, England. Earlier in the Middle Ages, art and culture had been in the hands of the Catholic Church. Latin was promoted as the written academic and literary language. But by the twelfth century, growing academic centers extended education beyond church control. A new, secular audience wanted literature written in the vernacular, the spoken language of the people. It was here that Marie de France made her contribution. She was the first known woman to write narrative poetry in Old French, the French spoken from the ninth to sixteenth centuries.

The exact identity of Marie de France is not known. She says at the end of one of her works that she is from France, and she probably resided in England. Marie was educated in Latin, French, English and perhaps Celtic, the language of Brittany in northwestern France. She knew of the Greek and Roman classics, the tales of the Celts and King Arthur of England. She was a member of the aristocracy and wrote for that audience. She wrote in Old French, the language of both French and English courts.

Marie de France is known for her lais, twelve short narrative poems written in Old French and read widely, not only in both English and French courts, but also translated into other languages, including German and Italian. She tells us that her poems are based on Breton lais (lais from Brittany). The Breton lai was traditionally an adventure of ancient times told in verse and set to music. The subject matter of the twelve lais is courtly love.

Courtly love is found in the love lyrics from Provence, an area in southern France. In the Provençal love lyric, the courtly relationship depended on an idealized lady worshipped from a distance, the total devotion of the lover, and the ennobling power of the ideal love which the lover tried to achieve. In the lais, themes of courtly love were made more narrative than they were in the lyric. From many different points of view, the lais explore the relationship between courtly love and chivalry, the medieval system of knighthood. Chivalry valued Christian principles for knights and ladies such as loyalty, truthfulness, courtesy, piety, respect of women, purity, and bravery.

"Bisclavret" deals with chivalry, love, and the supernatural, the power to transform oneself into a wolf, to become a werewolf. In her lai, Marie de France skillfully combines folklore and courtly literature.

CHAPTER 7
From "The Miller's Tale" from *The Canterbury Tales*

Historico-cultural Background

On a small Celtic site on the English River Stour, the Romans built an important fort called Durovernum Canticorum and occupied the site for 400 years. On this site the first cathedral in the land was established by Ethelred, King of Kent, who had been converted in 597 by Christian missionaries. The fort was then renamed in Anglo-Saxon Cantwaraburh, or "stronghold of men of Kent." It later became the administrative seat of the Archbishop of Canterbury as well as Ethelred's base for extending his power across southern England.

The peaceful coexistence of political and religious power in Canterbury ended in the twelfth century with the conflict between King Henry II and Thomas à Becket, named by the king as Chancellor of England and Archbishop of Canterbury. Defending the legal rights of the church against the crown, Becket was viewed by King Henry as a traitor. On December 29, 1170, while Henry was in France, four of his knights murdered Thomas à Becket in the cathedral.

Within several years of his death, Becket's tomb became the object of reverence for religious pilgrims from all walks of English life. By the 1530s, the Reformation was underway, and Protestant King Henry VIII removed the treasury of Canterbury and burned St. Thomas's remains. Nevertheless, Henry VIII's actions did not eliminate religious fervor, and even today pilgrims continue to visit St. Thomas's shrine at Canterbury Cathedral.

Geoffrey Chaucer

The son of a London wine merchant, Chaucer was sent at an early age to be educated in the household of the Countess of Ulster. Chaucer's courtly education included the study of Latin language and literature and French, the language of the English nobility after 1066. He was versed in French literature in the form of romances and *lais* of chivalry as well as the popular fabliaux. In 1373, Chaucer was sent as the king's ambassador to Italy, where he became acquainted with Boccaccio's *Decameron*, a framed story of aristocratic refugees from a plague raging in Florence.

Among Chaucer's most powerful memories was the Black Death or bubonic plague which came to England in 1348 and decimated the population. In 1359, at age sixteen, he was sent to France to fight in the Hundred Years' War. Furthermore, in June 1381, he witnessed first-hand the Peasants' Revolt, the invasion of London by an army of peasants and artisans from Kent protesting the horrible conditions under which they worked and lived. In an age of poverty, pestilence and war, Christians clung desperately to their religious beliefs which promised a better life in the next world. It seems natural, therefore, that Chaucer would set his most famous work, *The Canterbury Tales*, in a frame of upper-middle class Canterbury pilgrims who are glad to be alive and seek the blessing of St. Thomas à Becket to ensure their longevity.

Since in the fourteenth century literacy was uncommon, Chaucer was close to oral tradition. He enters the narrative of *The Tales* as the story-telling "I" in two ways: he is the world traveler and sophisticate with a strong sense of irony who parodies the very literary traditions on which he draws--for example, Absalon as the parodic courtly lover; Chaucer also is the simple fellow who speaks directly to the characters, as in "Now, show your paces, Nicholas you spark!" In "The Miller's Tale" Chaucer comments ironically on his contemporary society; for example, he describes the "lecherous" and faithless Alison as "...a lollypop / For any nobleman to take to bed / Or some good man of yeoman stock to wed."

MINI-LECTURE on *THE CANTERBURY TALES*

During the later European Middle Ages, access to educational opportunities was given to sons of middle-class families. Young men such as Geoffrey Chaucer could receive a fine classical education. Chaucer's formal education and his experiences served as important sources for his writing. First, since French was the language of the English court, Chaucer's studies included French literature in the form of romances and lais, and also popular fabliaux, stories that frequently mixed sexuality and religion. Second, Chaucer read Greek and Latin classics, and third, he was very familiar with biblical literature from both Old and New Testaments. Last, his literary formation was influenced by a journey to Italy in 1373. There he became acquainted with Boccaccio's *Decameron*, a collection of one hundred tales told by ten nobles over a ten-day stay in the country in order to avoid an epidemic of plague in the city of Florence. All four sources can be seen in "The Miller's Tale."

Influenced by Boccaccio, Chaucer's original plan for *The Canterbury Tales* seems to have been for each of the 29 pilgrims and the Host to tell two tales on the way to Canterbury and two on the return. He admits in the poem that the plan was too ambitious and was not completed. The "frame" for the story is a medieval pilgrimage to seek a blessing at the tomb of the martyr St. Thomas à Becket, buried at Canterbury Cathedral. Murdered by King Henry II in 1170, Thomas à Becket was seen as protector of the Catholic faith against ruthless kings.

Pilgrimages were an important institution in the Middle Ages; they were taken not only for religious reasons but were a kind of travel vacation. The way to Canterbury Cathedral was not especially interesting, so pilgrims entertained themselves by singing, gambling, drinking and telling stories. In his Prologue, Chaucer has the pilgrims gather at the Tabard Inn in London and agree to the storytelling plan. The good-humored Miller leads them out of the city playing his rude bag-pipe.

The first tale is one of courtly love told by the Knight. His tale is followed immediately by that of the Miller, who parodies or makes fun of the Knight's courtly conventions. Writing in Middle English, Chaucer uses comedy or humor to balance the difficult life led by average citizens in an age of plague, war and poverty. The bawdy or obscene tale affirms life. Even slapstick, as seen in the scene of branding Nicholas, has its place. Furthermore, Chaucer's tales are a satire of his contemporary society.

Chaucer literally paints a picture of his medieval characters by describing in fine detail their clothing and behavior. His realism is balanced in "The Miller's Tale" by wonderful blending of literary sources: the Greek and Latin classics, seen in this tale in the reference to Cato, Roman author of a book on moral principles; the biblical, here in the Old Testament figure of Absalon and references to Noah's Flood; the French fabliaux, or bawdy stories; and the framed narrative of Boccaccio's *Decameron*.

CHAPTER 8
From *Romeo and Juliet*

Historico-cultural Background
In 1558, six years before Shakespeare was born, Queen Elizabeth I (1533-1603) ascended the throne of England. Daughter of Henry VIII and Anne Boleyn, Elizabeth I reigned during the English Renaissance, a period of the rebirth of intense study of the Greek, Roman, and biblical past. The Elizabethan era also saw great social and political activity and many changes in England.

Elizabeth I was a strong monarch who expanded royal power and encouraged England to become a great maritime power. To protect English interests, Elizabeth surrounded herself with intelligent, ambitious men, regardless of their social background. She was a skilled politician who encouraged the spread of the state-supported Anglican church and expanded the power of England in America. During her reign, the English felt a new national strength and importance. English replaced Latin as the language of academic and literary works. The stage was set in Elizabethan England for William Shakespeare to make his great contributions to her language and literature.

William Shakespeare

William Shakespeare was born in 1564 in the village of Stratford-on-Avon, Warwickshire. His formal education ended with grammar school, but he studied Latin and Greek literature and history. The English language was not taught as a subject in schools, but his innate gift allowed Shakespeare to use the language with extraordinary perfection. Judging from his writing, he possessed a broad general knowledge and a deep understanding of human nature.

In 1585, Shakespeare left Stratford for London. By 1592, he had a growing reputation as an actor and a playwright, and he soon became an owner of the Globe and Blackfriars theaters. He was so successful that in 1597 he was able to return to Stratford to purchase a large home. In his retirement years, he devoted himself completely to writing.

Shakespeare's plays were written primarily for performance rather than publication, and as there were no copyright laws in those days, actors and other parties made changes in the text to suit their needs. Only about half of his plays were printed individually in his lifetime.

Luckily, in 1623, two of his colleagues collected his plays into a book called *First Folio* and classified the works into tragedies, histories, and comedies. Ben Jonson, one of Shakespeare's fellow actors, wrote in the *First Folio*, "He was not of an age, but for all time!"

Drama in Elizabethan England

William Shakespeare was a man of the theater who was fortunate to have lived at a time when drama in England flourished. During the first two decades of the reign of Elizabeth I, professional acting companies were officially sanctioned in London. As well, drama was performed in academic institutions, private halls, and inn yards.

Under Puritan influence, the English thought it immoral for women to be on the stage. The limited number of female roles were generally played by boys, and in a number of plays the "women" disguised themselves as boys.

MINI-LECTURE on *ROMEO AND JULIET*

William Shakespeare was born in 1564, six years after Elizabeth I (1533-1603) ascended to the throne of England. He spent most of his life under her reign in Elizabethan England. During this period, English society was in a state of change. Under the strong reign of Elizabeth I, England became a maritime power--that is, a country that controlled the seas--and expanded her empire to America.

Shakespeare was born in Stratford-on-Avon, about 100 miles north of London. In his twenties, he went to London, where his reputation as an actor and a playwright grew, and he became an owner of two theaters. Shakespeare wrote at least 37 plays, 154 sonnets, and some longer poems. Most of his plays were written for public theaters such as the Globe, where he worked with his acting company, Lord Chamberlain's Men, later known as the King's Men. Shakespeare had the ideal conditions for a playwright: a resident company in its own facility.

The conditions in the public theaters influenced the plays that Shakespeare wrote. As there was no lighting, plays were performed in the day without interruption. Continuous action was used to keep the attention of the audience. The stage was an uncurtained platform extending into the audience. Toward the rear of the stage was a balcony from which characters could look down on the action. There were tiers of seats for wealthy patrons; ordinary people sat or stood in the pit, the area below the stage. The audience freely let the playwright know how they felt about the play. Perhaps the great range of people in his audience inspired Shakespeare to include such a variety of characters in his plays.

Shakespeare was so successful as a playwright, actor, and theater owner that he was able to return to Stratford-on-Avon where he purchased a large house. He devoted his retirement years completely to writing.

Shakespeare's direct source for *Romeo and Juliet* appears to have been a 1562 poem in English, "The Tragical History of Romeus and Juliet" by Arthur Brooke. Shakespeare adapts Brooke freely, and his skill as a dramatist makes *Romeo and Juliet* one of the greatest love tragedies of all time.

The sonnet prologue to the play presents the blood feud, or conflict, between the two families, the Montagues and the Capulets. The argument is so deep that neither family would have chosen a mate from the other. The tragic fate of the lovers is told in the prologue and seems to be written in the stars.

The balcony scene is the most famous portion of *Romeo and Juliet*. Juliet, heiress of the Capulets, had met Romeo at a Capulet family banquet. Romeo, heir of the Montagues, had attended uninvited and disguised. A passion captures them both. That night, on her balcony overlooking the garden, Juliet speaks of her secret to the moon and stars. Risking his life, Romeo has entered the Capulet garden. After meeting and declaring their love like true courtly lovers, they decide to act, and they are married the next morning. At the conclusion of the play, because of Fate, Romeo and Juliet are dead by their own hands. Juliet's father extends his hand to Romeo's father. Montague says that he will build a gold statue of Juliet. After great tragic loss, a kind of equilibrium is restored.

CHAPTER 9
Romantic Poetry

MINI-LECTURE on SCHILLER AND WORDSWORTH

In Europe during the eighteenth century (the 1700s), scientific investigation and rational thinking had been emphasized. Perhaps in reaction to the "cold" reason of that period, called the Enlightenment, at the end of the 1700s, poets and other artists began to focus on human emotion and feeling. The new movement, called Romanticism, valued intense feelings or passions, qualities that were especially important in Germany in the poetry of Friedrich Schiller, and in England in the lyrics of William Wordsworth.

Responding to the limitations on political rights set by powerful kings, both Schiller and Wordsworth sang of individualism, freedom, and brotherhood among human beings. The Romantic poets explored nature and felt an identity with her. In fact, Wordsworth often uses pathetic fallacy, a literary device that shows the poet's human emotions being reflected and felt in nature. For example, if the poet feels a violent passion, nature will mirror those feelings, perhaps with a storm, strong winds, lightning, and thunder.

The common literary form of the Romantics is the lyric poem. It usually concerns the poet's very personal feelings about a topic such as death, love, loneliness, or loss of freedom. By writing about these topics, poets were responding to historical events in Europe and in the Americas. The American Revolution in 1776 and the fall of the French Bastille in 1789 were the beginnings of a period during which many monarchies fell. For a time Europe moved toward democracy, and the cry "Liberty, Fraternity and Equality" became the motto of the Romantics.

The democratic ideals of the Romantics were popularized through poetry and music, giving the musical composer and the poet a special position in their nation. According to Wordsworth's Preface to the Lyrical Ballads, published in 1800, the poet is "endowed with more lively sensibility, more enthusiasm and tenderness"; he is a person "who has knowledge of human nature, and a more comprehensive soul, than are supposed to be common among mankind."

The work of the poet was often taken up by a composer and translated into music. For example, Schiller's Romantic call for universal brotherhood in his "Ode to Joy" inspired Ludwig van Beethoven to set the poem to music in the *Symphony Number 9, Opus 125*.

Schiller personifies joy, that is, he gives human qualities to a non-human object, shown in English by capitalizing the word *Joy*. Ironically, the call for universal brotherhood did not extend beyond national borders. As a result, the nineteenth century saw a rise of nationalism that led directly to international wars.

CHAPTER 10
"Ain't I a Woman?"

MINI-LECTURE on "AIN'T I A WOMAN?"

A slave is a person who is owned by another and who may have no freedoms or rights; slavery, or the holding of slaves, has been practiced at various times throughout the world. European development of the Americas was largely based on involuntary labor, especially slaves brought from the west coast of Africa. The English, for example, sailed from London carrying rum, guns, and cotton goods to the African coast. They traded their products for African slaves, and sailed across the Atlantic to the American coast or the West Indies. Selling the blacks who survived the horrible "middle passage," the English returned to London with molasses, cotton, and other products.

Following the example of the British, the United States prohibited the slave trade after 1807. However, the exploitation of black labor continued, especially in the southern portion of the country, where the economy was built upon cotton, tobacco, and sugar plantations. The struggle over slave-holding was brought to a head after the 1860 election of Abraham Lincoln to the presidency.

The conflicting lifestyles and the issue of slavery severely strained the unity of the United States, and from 1861 to 1865, the nation suffered civil war. The Union, made up of the northern states, was led by Lincoln against the southern states, the Confederacy, headed by Jefferson Davis.

People who opposed slavery and wanted to eliminate it were called abolitionists. Among others, Frederick Douglass, a free black, and the writer Harriet Beecher Stowe (*Uncle's Tom's Cabin,* 1852) tried to show the evils of slavery. The abolitionists established the Underground Railroad, a cooperative arrangement which enabled fugitive or runaway slaves to escape into the safety of Canada or free states. The emancipation, or freeing of slaves, took place during the Civil War. In 1863, President Lincoln issued a formal document, the Emanicipation Proclamation, giving freedom to all slaves in the Confederacy.

Sojourner Truth had been a slave for 40 years before she secured her freedom in 1827. She acquired a deep knowledge of the Bible, and having experienced religious visions, became a traveling preacher. As a result of her work with the abolitionists, Truth published her autobiography, *The Narrative of Sojourner Truth.* Modeled on the traditional slave narrative, several of which had been written by women, Truth told the story of her life as a slave in the north. Unable to read or write, she dictated the details of her narrative.

The abolition of slavery was not the only social issue to which Truth gave her energies. In the 1850s, she became involved with feminist issues and the women's rights movement. At that time, a woman could not vote or hold public office. If she married, her property was controlled by her husband. Sojourner Truth began attending meetings on women's suffrage, that is, the right to vote. Truth gave her speech, "Ain't I a Woman?" at one of these suffrage meetings. A magnetic personality who electrified her listeners, Sojourner Truth was one of America's first African-American woman activists.

CHAPTER 11
From *Oliver Twist*

Historico-cultural Background

Romanticism was a dominant artistic movement during much of the nineteenth century. But its idealization of nature and human virtues was in direct conflict with the harsh realities of everyday European life. The Industrial Revolution, particularly in England, not only destroyed much of the country's natural beauty, but it brought masses of rural folk to the cities for a better life. What they found was misery and poverty. Writers, especially novelists, responded by focusing on the common person and the details of his or her actual situation. This almost photographic detailing of ordinary life was called Realism.

Charles Dickens's youth also saw the defeat of Napoleon by the British and the settlement of hostilities between the United States and Britain. Both events cost England and her people dearly.

MINI-LECTURE on *OLIVER TWIST*

Charles Dickens always identified his literary imagination as memory, especially the memory of childhood events. He seems to have had an extraordinary memory for people, events, places, and conversation. Many of his comically drawn characters and depressing interior scenes come from his difficult childhood years.

When he was 10 years old, his father, John Dickens, was arrested and sent to debtors' prison for not paying his bills. This brought great shame to the family. His mother and siblings went to live with his father in prison while he went to work in a factory putting labels on bottles. He lived in a boarding house with other unwanted children. The finances of his family eventually improved, and Dickens returned to school. But this experience had a very great effect on Dickens and can be seen in his repeated portrayal in his writing of irresponsible father figures named John.

In 1832, Dickens became a journalist, earning the reputation of being a very fast and accurate reporter. Also he began to write short descriptions of London life, or sketches, which were published in a monthly magazine. He signed the sketches "Boz," a pseudonym or pen name that he chose to write under. These were later published in book form as *Sketches by Boz, Illustrative of Everyday Life and Everyday People.* Much of the material in these sketches found its way into his later novels.

In 1837, Victoria began her sixty-four-year reign as Queen of England. Dickens was 25 years old and on his way to literary fame with the publication of *Oliver Twist* and another novel, *Pickwick Papers.* Dickens first signed his own name to the novel *Oliver Twist*, which, like many very long novels in Victorian England, was originally published in magazine installments.

Oliver Twist is said to be the first novel in the English language to take a child as its central character. In the novel, Dickens draws heavily on autobiographical details, particularly the time of his family's financial difficulty. He also uses the old but still popular form, the picaresque, or rogue novel. The picaresque shows a fictional, poor anti-hero struggling to survive from birth to maturity. Along the way he ironically observes the behavior of every class and type in his society.

Oliver Twist, a typical rogue, is a London boy born in a workhouse or poorhouse, where his mother had been taken after being found in the street. After giving birth, she dies, leaving Oliver Twist in the hands of cruel authority figures. Readers of the novel viewed it as an attack on the New Poor Law of 1834, which tried to break up poor families in the workhouse so they would not apply for welfare aid. Dickens shows the corruption and dysfunction of society at large and within English families.

Through his literary realism, Dickens publicized the social and moral evils of his time and their effects on the poor. These evils were in part caused by the costs of wars and the expanding British Empire and by the Industrial Revolution that was sweeping Europe. The replacement of hand tools by machines and the development of industrial production resulted in social and economic changes that were not always good, especially for the poor. Charles Dickens was not only an outstanding leader of the nineteenth-century literary world, he was as well a speaker for the conscience of his age.

CHAPTER 12
From *The Turn of the Screw*

Literary Considerations

Henry James was part of a generation of Americans who still felt very close ties to England and the European continent. In his youth, he came under the influence of the strict religious tradition of New England Calvinism and of the literary tradition of Hawthorne and Poe. He later acknowledged the importance of European writers such as Balzac and George Eliot (Maryann Evans) in his formation.

The end of the nineteenth century saw profound changes marking the transition from the Victorian to the modern novel. The former convention of the omniscient narrator had become a problem under the influence of the work of William James, Henri Bergson, and Sigmund Freud on modern consciousness. The difficulty of human communication had to be recognized by creators of fiction. Unlike the traditional English novel which dealt with public affairs, the modern novel focuses on an internal reality and an exploration of individual psychology. Furthermore, time appears in a continuous flow, and the reader is made aware of a multiplicity of consciousness.

Henry James is an important figure in the creation of the modern novel; not only was he an imaginative creator of fiction who achieved fame on both sides of the Atlantic, but he was a radical innovator in the art of fiction. An unusually well-read individual, James wrote ten volumes of critical essays on most of the outstanding nineteenth-century authors of the United States, England, and the European continent. Even his fiction varies widely in its settings, ranging from Italy, England, and France to America; his achievements in the international novel are impressive.

The Gothic Novel

The Gothic form appeared at the end of the eighteenth century; it tried to arouse the reader's emotional response to the plight of a victim, and it explored the human relationship to evil. The characteristics of the Gothic novel were highly conventionalized, with reduplicated mysterious settings, characters struggling between good and evil, complex plots and images. Probably the best known contemporary writer of Gothic novels is Stephen King.

MINI-LECTURE on THE TURN OF THE SCREW

As a young man, Henry James was a serious reader who absorbed the best of both American and European writers. He admired the dark, Puritan-influenced works of the New England author, Nathaniel Hawthorne, about whom he later wrote a biography. He enjoyed the Gothic tales of Edgar Allan Poe, as well as the realism of the English writers Charles Dickens and George Eliot (Maryann Evans).

James's youth was full of terrible world events, including several European revolutions and the American Civil War (1861- 1865), which drew two of Henry's anti-slavery brothers to the battlefield. In 1857-1858, a general economic crisis threatened the security of his family. These unsettling events and his father's desire to give a good education to his four sons kept the James family moving between the United States and Europe. Perhaps this lack of a clear national identity aroused Henry James's interest in writing later about Americans living with difficulty in European exile, as in his novel *Daisy Miller.*

Gothic fiction had long explored the struggle of the human spirit with good versus evil. However, after the 1895 publication of Sigmund Freud's work, *Studies on Hysteria,* authors took a new interest in the psychological analysis of fictional characters. In *The Turn of the Screw,* for example, James uses the old Gothic literary conventions of frightening events and the "good" governess protecting the children from her double, the "evil" ghost. Every level of the complex plot and the framed story, or story within a story, has an ambiguous meaning.

Freudian critics suggest that the governess, who tells her story through indirect narration, is a case study of hysteria, an expression of nineteenth-century sexual repression. Neither her motives nor the truth of her story are made perfectly clear; only the reader can decide what the story means.

CHAPTER 13
From *Uncle Vanya*

Historico-cultural Background

Anton Pavlovich Chekhov was an infant when the Great Reforms of the Russian Czar Alexander II were instituted. Nonetheless, these reforms had great impact on his life. Chekhov came from a family of former serfs, and it was the reform of Alexander II that had provided for the emancipation of all serfs. Among other reforms was the institution of a system of administrative units, called *zemstvos*, that provided social services to the people. These services included free medical, dental, and surgical care for the villages. Chekhov's experiences as a physician in the system provided material for his writing.

In 1881, Alexander II was assassinated, and Alexander III ascended the throne, and with him, a wave of repression swept the country. Chekhov frequently describes the 1880s small provincial towns whose intelligentsia seem defeated by their environment and unable to do anything constructive. Hopes were raised briefly in 1884, when Alexander III died. However, Czar Nicholas II, the last Russian czar, continued the reign of terror begun under his predecessor. In the last years of Chekhov's life, Russia was on the eve of its great upheaval, the Revolution of 1917.

Literary Considerations

Chekhov was influenced by a range of literary figures including the French authors Zola, de Maupassant, and Flaubert. As well, he read and was influenced by the naturalist Charles Darwin. Chekhov most admired Leo Tolstoy and considered him as his teacher. A number of his stories show Tolstoyan influence. Tolstoy preached non-resistance, belief in a god of abstract goodness rather than a personal deity, the necessity of man to avoid greed and hate, and the evil of holding property. However, as years passed, Chekhov became irritated by Tolstoy's pronouncements, saying that Tolstoy's morality ceased to move him.

It was Charles Darwin, the naturalist, who developed in Chekhov the ability to distinguish the animal in man. He prepared Chekhov for the literary theories of Emile Zola, Gustave Flaubert, and Guy de Maupassant, who embraced a kind of Realism called Naturalism. In particular, de Maupassant helped Chekhov to master the short story, whose brevity had the ability to shock the reader.

In the 1890s Chekhov was accused by critics of being socially apathetic and indifferent in his writing. In fact, Chekhov did not wish to be involved with party programs, political conflicts, and ideologies. His independence makes it difficult to fit him into the nineteenth-century system of labeling and classifying writers. However, at the time of his death at the age of 44, Chekhov was celebrated as a master artist by the Russian literary public. He became internationally well-known after World War I when his works were translated into many languages.

Chekhov the Dramatist

Before Chekhov, theater in Russia was regarded as pompous, dishonest, and corrupt. Performers habitually overacted. As a counteractive, an innovative theater, the Moscow Art Theater, was founded by a group that included Konstantin Stanislavsky. The founders dedicated their theater to the art of truth; they believed in Realism and Naturalism built on solidity and seriousness. It was here that most of Chekhov's plays were produced.

On stage, Chekhov was distinctive in drawing on his encyclopedic knowledge of Russian life. *Uncle Vanya* was premiered in 1899 by the Moscow Art Theater. Though it was only a moderate success, the founders begged Chekhov to write plays expressly for the Moscow Art Theater, which he subsequently did.

Uncle Vanya resulted from the rewrite of an earlier play, *The Wood Demon.* The setting is a country estate. Alexander Serebrakoff, a retired professor, and his young wife Helena have returned to the estate from their life in the city. Sonia, the professor's daughter from his first marriage, and her uncle, Uncle Vanya, the professor's brother-in-law, have been running the estate for the professor. Michael Astroff is a visiting physician.

The play consists of the reflections of the characters. There is no climax or moment of recognition. At one point, the professor says that he cannot bear life on the estate and so has decided to sell it. He disregards the fact that Uncle Vanya and Sonia have devoted their lives to caring for the estate, sending the profits to the professor. At the end of the play, the professor and his wife have decided to return to the city. Uncle Vanya tells him that funds will be remitted as before and that everything will be the same.

At the conclusion of the play, a circle is closed. There is a return to life as it was on the estate before Serebrakoff's arrival. Yet disturbing events of the play ensure that things will never be exactly as they had been before.

MINI-LECTURE on *UNCLE VANYA*

In 1860, Anton Chekhov was born into a family of emancipated serfs in southern Russia. Serfs were workers whose labor tied them to the land on which they lived. Under the government of the Russian king, called the czar, life was difficult for the masses of poor. The czar generally governed in a repressive and dictatorial manner, making great demands on the serfs. But despite a difficult childhood, Chekhov finished secondary school and went to the university in Moscow. After his father suffered bankruptcy, he worked to support his family.

In his 20s Chekhov began writing stories, authoring more than 50 in his lifetime. From 1881 until his death, Chekhov lived under several repressive czars. During this period aristocratic landowning systems were breaking down, but no great progress was being made by reformers.

Outside of its few larger cities, Russia was quite backward compared to Europe. Life in these Russian provincial areas is the major topic of Chekhov's writing.

Chekhov acknowledged the influence of a number of literary figures. First, Chekhov admired Leo Tolstoy, a well-known Russian writer. Although born to the ruling class, Tolstoy had a "mystical" conversion and subsequently adopted the ways and dress of the peasants from whom he thought society could learn. As the years passed, however, Chekhov became irritated by Tolstoy's views. In one of his stories, Chekhov speaks to Tolstoy, saying that hiding oneself on an estate is not life and that man needs the entire globe to develop his free spirit.

Furthermore, Chekhov was influenced by three French writers, Emile Zola, Gustave Flaubert, and Guy de Maupassant, all of whom believed in a kind of Realism called Naturalism. Naturalists believed that writers should apply scientific thought, objectivity, and precision in the observation and treatment of life. They should not idealize, impose value judgments, or avoid the repulsive. Chekhov followed these principles in his writing, but with the compassion and humanity of a physician.

Chekhov used his observations of Russian life to stage plays in a simple, direct technique. For example, he rediscovered the dramatic potential of silence in drama. In fact, Chekhov hated overexplanation. His "indirect method" brought about a revolution in Russian theater. Chekhov's fresh and original presentations were in direct opposition to the existing theater, which was exaggerated in style and filled with overacting. His plays were performed by the Moscow Art Theater, a new theater devoted to what was considered truth in art.

Whether in the short story or drama, Chekhov describes contemporary Russian life, revealing the secret motives of his characters in his distinctive style.

CHAPTER 14
From "Roman Fever"

Literary Considerations

Edith Wharton is frequently classed as a novelist of manners, that is, an author preoccupied with critiquing the social behavior of the bourgeoisie or the upper class. But careful examination of her work reveals her concern with serious issues such as politics, history, philosophy, and morality. Although she was born during the American Civil War, no direct mention of it occurs in Wharton's work. As a resident of France in her adult years, however, the destructive force of war forms an important part of works such as *A Son at the Front*. In her Pulitzer Prize-winning novel, *The Age of Innocence* (now a successful film), Wharton examines closely the weakening of the moral fabric of New York society in the 1870s. It is in this framework of serious preoccupations that one needs to read "Roman Fever."

MINI-LECTURE on "ROMAN FEVER"

Because of her Gothic novel, *Ethan Frome,* Edith Wharton has been identified with women regionalist writers. On the other hand, her use of international themes, that is, Americans taking the Grand Tour of Europe or living abroad, has caused some critics to group her with Henry James. Indeed, many have called her "a disciple of Henry James." She is known widely as a novelist of manners for her concern with the social behavior of old-money families and the nouveaux riches replacing them in New York City. Only recently have critics viewed Wharton as a writer with serious concerns such as history, politics, and philosophy. All of these appear in the short story, "Roman Fever."

Wharton sets up her story as a kind of dramatic dialogue between the two characters, Mrs. Slade and Mrs. Ansley. Indeed, they are sitting on a kind of stage-like balcony overlooking the ruins of the Palatine Hill, the Colosseum, and the Forum. While all are the remains of the glory of ancient Rome, the Colosseum, in particular, is associated with the bloody sacrifice of innocent Christians in the final days of a corrupt Roman Empire.

Wharton also calls up the return of the Roman past by having the two innocent daughters of these women flying off to Tarquinia with air force pilots. Tarquinia is an ancient Etruscan site named for Tarquin, the last king and non-Roman ruler of the growing empire. Tarquin's reign came to a violent end with his rape of the Roman matron, Lucretia. Tarquin's subjects rebelled and founded the Roman Republic.

The Etruscans established the use of the *fasces*, or bundle of sticks with an axe, which signified authority. It was this ancient symbol of power which Benito Mussolini chose in the 1920s as the emblem of his political party, the Fascists. Mussolini viewed himself as the Nietzschean "superman," beyond good and evil, who would lead Italy to renewed glory of the Roman past. By her references to Roman fever, Tarquin, and the name "Barbara," Wharton ironically suggests that the 1920s and 30s are not to be a return to past glory for Italy but a sinking into horror and barbarism.

CHAPTER 15
From "The Metamorphosis"

MINI-LECTURE on "THE METAMORPHOSIS"

Franz Kafka was born in 1883 in Prague, then a large provincial capital in the Austro-Hungarian Empire, and now the capital of Czechoslovakia. The Kafkas were German-speaking Jews, a marginal, minority group living in a predominantly Slavic (Czech) and anti-Semitic environment. Although not a religious Jew, Franz Kafka turned to the humanism of Jewish culture, especially in the Yiddish theater. He was later considered a master writer among the Prague Circle, a group of German Jews living in Prague until World War II. Prague Jews, including Kafka's family, were murdered by the Nazis during the Holocaust in the 1940s.

In his numerous, detailed diaries, Kafka expressed his admiration for various writers. He admired the Romanticism and the importance of love in Goethe, creator of *Faust* and *The Sorrows of Young Werther.* He also closely identified with the father-son conflict in Ben Franklin's *Autobiography.* But probably the greatest influence was Charles Dickens;indeed, Kafka was reading Dickens's biography and his novel *David Copperfield* while writing "The Metamorphosis." Kafka was impressed with Dickens's distorted perspective presenting a grotesque picture of the world. The bitter irony, the dark and gloomy interiors, and the dysfunctional family and society Dickens describes are from the view of the unloved child. This is the view Kafka gives us in "The Metamorphosis."

In reality, Franz Kafka also identified with Dickens's poor relationship with his dominating father. As an only son, Franz was expected by his father to join the family business. Although Franz earned a law degree from the German University in Prague and worked in the insurance business for a time, writing remained his life's passion. Franz believed his father did not value his writing nor understand his son. Despite the constant stress, Franz remained living in his parents' home for many years. Kafka's mother was unable to mediate between father and son; the closest family relationship Kafka had was with a favorite sister.

Like most of his stories, "The Metamorphosis" is highly autobiographical. The similarities between the Kafka family members and the characters in the story are evident. Even the name of Gregor Samsa is a cryptogram (rearranged letters) of Kafka's name. Nevertheless, from the beginning of the story, Kafka uses an objective, distanced tone to present his central character as having been changed into a gigantic insect. The insect, a kind of repulsive vermin, is a metaphor, that is, figurative language that makes an indirect comparison. As an insect, Samsa experiences the kind of alienation and loneliness that Kafka had experienced in his own life.

Although Kafka knew the psychoanalytic work of Sigmund Freud, especially regarding the unconscious competition between father and son, Kafka refused to acknowledge this possible interpretation of his work. He frequently commented as a critic on his writing as did his best friend and literary executor, Max Brod. After Kafka's early death from tuberculosis, Brod published Kafka's works, widely and persuaded critics that their significance lay in their philosophical analysis of modern life. Certainly, the Existentialist writers of the 1950s, who saw little meaning in life, acknowledged Franz Kafka as their forerunner.

CHAPTER 16
From *O Pioneers!*

By the time Willela Cather was born in Virginia in 1873, the passionate feelings of the American Civil War (1861-65) were largely spent. Still, the young child heard many stories of the involvement in the war of members of her family on both sides. She also liked to associate with many of the local colorful countryside figures, whose names and personalities she kept in her memory until they reappeared in her fiction.

After her family's move to the Great Divide in Nebraska, she drew from the magic of the land and the mixed ethnic groups struggling to make a living in the new land as a source for her writing. She was later attracted to the world of music, especially Wagnerian opera, and French culture. Her love for Franco-American history is evident in *Death Comes for the Archbishop* (1927), a work about the encounter of cultures in the American Southwest, and *Shadows on the Rock* (1931), a novel about the early days of Quebec.

Throughout her adult life, Cather alternated hectic days of travel and attendance at cultural events with quiet periods spent with her companion Edith Lewis in Maine and New Hampshire. They lie buried side by side in the sleepy hamlet of Jaffrey, New Hampshire.

MINI-LECTURE on *O PIONEERS!*

At the end of the nineteenth century, the United States experienced a major movement toward the frontier in the American West. Willa Cather's family was caught up in the excitement. In 1883, the family moved to the American Midwest prairie, settling in Red Cloud, Nebraska. They joined many other Americans and immigrants from eastern and northern Europe. The Cather family constructed a modest sod home in the flat, treeless prairie between the Republican River and the Little Blue, a place called locally "the Divide." The Great Divide and this part of the American Midwest were so different from what Cather had known in the East, that the landscape seemed to possess a mystical and romantic spirit of its own.

The combination of a mixed immigrant population and the magical power of the land were to become important themes in Willa Cather's fiction. As she grew up she observed the personal dramas of many of those struggling to survive in a difficult environment; these ethnically diverse people became the basis for characters and plots in her saga of the Midwest.

As a young person, Cather read widely and began writing, first as a journalist, and later as an author of fiction. She was also eccentric in her behavior, calling herself "William" and dressing like a boy. Although she was attracted to science and medicine, in 1906 she began a literary career by buying pieces of fiction and writing music and drama reviews. Her own first serious fiction was published in parts in *McClure's Magazine*.

In 1912, Cather worked on several subplots which were later brought together in *O Pioneers!* The main character, Alexandra Bergson, is a strong woman who is one of Cather's most remarkable heroines. The story itself is full of the mystical spirit of the Nebraska prairie, and in a Romantic sense, the land mirrors the emotional life of the important characters.

In her novel, Cather also uses symbolic figures such as the unnamed Corn God, a personification of the land's fertility. Perhaps Cather was influenced in creating the Corn God by the 1890 book on universal mythology, *The Golden Bough,* written by James Frazer. Besides myth, *O Pioneers!* bears the influence of the Bible, Greek and Latin classics, and the Romantic pastoral tradition.

Well-known for her other novels, such as *My Antonia* and *Death Comes for the Archbishop*, Cather was deeply affected by the tragedy of World War I. Her war novel, *One of Ours*, evokes both her childhood in Nebraska and her love for France and earned her the 1923 Pulitzer Prize for fiction.

CHAPTER 17
From *Rickshaw*

Historico-cultural Background

It is impossible to summarize the complicated history and culture of a nation as enormous and ancient as China. The end of the nineteenth century saw an increase in industrialization and modern technology in China, as well as conflict with Western imperial powers. Under pressure from the attempted Russian Revolution in 1905 and reforms elsewhere in Asia, the 250-year-old Qing dynasty collapsed in the winter of 1911-1912. Sun Yat-Sen assumed office as "provisional president" of the Chinese Republic. By February, 1912, Emperor Puyi had abdicated the throne.

The following period saw the collapse of the first republic with rising political insecurity and violence. By the 1920s, an alliance was formed between Communists and Nationalists in an effort to save China from complete chaos, but in 1927 the Nationalists under Chiang Kai-shek drove the Communists away from the urban areas. While the Nationalists tried to deal with Japanese occupation of Manchuria, the Communists, led by Mao Zedong, built up their influence in vast rural districts.

In 1937, a full-scale war with Japan broke out, and once again Nationalists and Communists united against a common foe. But by 1941, the two parties were engaged in a civil war. At war's end in 1948, the Communists captured Chiang's power base in Manchuria; his power was eroded further by the loss of support of the majority of China's intellectuals. In 1949, Chiang and his forces retreated to Taiwan, and Mao declared the formation of the new People's Republic of China.

Lao She and *Rickshaw*

In the midst of large-scale political turmoil, millions of Chinese struggled in miserable poverty. Since conditions for the masses had not improved under the imperial rule of the Manchus (an ethnic minority), Han intellectuals began a vigorous anti-Manchu campaign that branded the Manchu as "barbarians" and called for revolution. Political chaos touched Lao She, member of a Manchu family, when his father was killed in the Boxer Rebellion of 1900. The continuing turmoil in Peking (Beijing) during Lao She's youth had a tremendous impact on his future writings.

As a struggling poor Manchu, Lao She realized that he could only succeed through hard work. Idealistic, he gave up the opportunity to obtain work in a corrupt bureaucracy and chose to teach in the provinces. In 1924, he went to London, where he taught Mandarin and Classical Chinese for five years. During this period, Lao She became familiar with Charles Dickens's novels about the life of London's downtrodden poor; he later became a Christian.

The 1920s saw a major movement in China to create a new modern literature emphasizing humanism and realism. Part of the movement was to use the vernacular, or language of the people, especially that of Beijing (formerly Peking). These elements characterize the novel excerpted here, *Rickshaw* (sometimes entitled *Camel Hsiang Tzu*). Lao She's eighth novel, *Rickshaw* shows for the first time the author's belief that socialism may be a remedy for the plight of China's masses. The struggle of the poor rickshaw-puller Hsiang Tzu to survive in a morally corrupt world reflects Lao She's personal observations of ordinary Chinese in the difficult 1920s and 1930s; the novel also reflects Lao She's sense of dilemma that concern for the material welfare of the masses calls for social reform while the loss of Confucian principles leads away from a humane and moral society.

During World War II, Lao She became more politically active, urging social reform. He wrote five plays during this period, criticizing corrupt officials and an immoral system that forced women into prostitution. After the war, under the Communist regime, he continued to write but rejected class struggle as a theme for his work. In 1966, Lao She was visited by a foreign couple and was quoted as saying, "I can understand why Mao Zedong wishes to destroy the old bourgeois concepts of life, but I cannot write about this struggle because I am not a Marxist, and, therefore, I cannot feel and think as a Peking student in May 1966 who sees the situation in a Marxist way" (quoted in Vohra 164). Shortly afterward, Lao She was visited by the Red Guards of the Great Cultural Revolution; apparently humiliated, perhaps beaten up, Lao She drowned himself the following day.

MINI-LECTURE on *RICKSHAW*
The literary work of Lao She, author of *Rickshaw*, is closely connected to political events in modern Chinese history. Lao She was born in 1899 in Peking, now Beijing, capital of the present People's Republic of China. After his father, a palace guard, was killed in a political uprising in 1900, he and his mother suffered serious financial problems. Their life was especially difficult as they were Manchus, an ethnic minority in China. Lao She nevertheless finished secondary school and later graduated from Peking Normal School, a teachers' college. He became a teacher of the Chinese language, first in China and then in 1924, in London, where he taught at the School of Oriental and African Studies.

During his six years in England, Lao She began to write novels, in part because he was so lonely and nostalgic for China. During that period, he was greatly influenced by the novels of Charles Dickens, who had described the miserable lives of the urban poor of London. Lao She returned to China and later went to the United States for three years. Again returning to China, he was an active and respected writer who held a number of important cultural posts.

In 1917, when Lao She was only eighteen, Puyi, the last emperor of China, was deposed, and through the following years, the nation suffered invasion by the Japanese and civil war. The novel *Rickshaw* takes place in 1934 when the Japanese were in Manchuria, part of northern China, and it ends shortly before the outbreak of war between the two nations.

During the conflict between China and Japan, civil war began between two Chinese political factions, the Communists and the Nationalists. After victory by the Communists, Mao Zedong founded the People's Republic of China on the mainland in 1949. The Nationalists were forced from the mainland and set up another government, the Republic of China, on the island of Taiwan, under Chiang Kai-shek.

Lao She could be called a socialist rather than a Communist; his novels reflect serious concern for the great number of urban poor in China who suffer largely because of the corruption of political officials. Even after the establishment of Communism, Lao She continued to write works that were critical of the political system. The author's intellectual honesty proved very dangerous, for after the violent actions of the Cultural Revolution had begun in 1966, Lao She was politically persecuted by the Red Guards because he was not a Marxist and because of his continuing contacts with the West. After a particularly humiliating experience, he committed suicide.

The novel *Rickshaw* is one of eight novels written by Lao She, who also composed plays and short stories. *Rickshaw* is important because it was the first Chinese work to have a main character from the poor, uneducated class. In fact, the novel is the first important study of a laborer in twentieth-century Chinese literature. Like the poor workers in Charles Dickens's novels, the main character, Hsiang Tzu, is a laborer, a rickshaw-puller in Peking (now Beijing). Part of the major nineteenth and early twentieth-century literary movement called Realism, Lao She writes in the language of the streets, using the colorful Beijing dialect rather than classical Chinese. With realistic, detailed description, the author tells the reader of Hsiang Tzu's aspirations, his struggles, and his tragic defeat.

CHAPTER 18
From *Things Fall Apart*

Historico-cultural Background

Africa is an enormous and culturally diverse continent whose modern history has been turbulent. It should be recognized by non-African readers that while Achebe and Nigeria are important, they represent only part of the diverse African experience. Furthermore, a common reaction to the word "Africa" may conjure up significantly negative images such as "the dark continent" or "primitive," expressions of centuries of Western colonial thought. Such images continue to be perpetuated today in media such as television and film. Therefore, it is necessary to clearly indicate in discussions about Africa its rich geographical, linguistic, and cultural differences. Incursions of Asians, Arabs, and Europeans occurred centuries before the mid-nineteenth century period of European imperialism, leaving a long history of major religions such as Islam and Christianity as well as other cultural influences.

African Literary Tradition

Africa's literary history is an ancient one, dating to 5000 years ago in the Nile valley and later in the kingdoms in West Africa. Ancient Egyptian literature was principally recorded in hieroglyphics, while until modern times, south of the Sahara, oral tradition was the major literary mode. Beginning about 1930, African literatures fused the popular oral literary sources and the written tradition of Egypt and of Western colonial powers, especially Great Britain and France.

In sub-Saharan Africa, the oral tradition is centered around the figure of the *griot*, or traditional storyteller. The *griot* possesses an astounding repertoire of folktales embodying the village cultural values as well as the genealogical history of village families. It was such a figure that African-American writer Alex Haley, author of *Roots*, consulted in Gambia in his search for his ancestor Kunta Kinte.

A second important feature of African oral tradition is the popular use of proverbs. While proverbs such as "A new broom sweeps clean" are also used in the West, their frequency in conversation is a dominant feature of African speech, especially among the Ibo. Many African authors, including Chinua Achebe, include this realistic detail in their works.

While Nigeria could point to an earlier written tradition in fiteenth-century Arabic poetry, by the twentieth century, English prose had become important. The first Nigerian writer to become internationally famous was Amos Tutuola, whose *Palm-Wine Drinkard* [sic] was popular in the English-speaking world. Nobel Prize winner Wole Soyinka has dominated in the field of drama, while the novel has been largely the domain of Ibo writers, led by Chinua Achebe. Achebe's earlier novels, including *Things Fall Apart*, focus on the collapse of traditional African groups under the force of colonialism; later works center on the complex problems of westernized Africans in postcolonial societies.

Literary Considerations: *Things Fall Apart*

Literary critics place Achebe's first novel in a group of works concerned with African nationalist movements. Using Realist techniques, Achebe's work to a certain extent idealizes and romanticizes the world of the precolonial Ibo. The title of the novel is taken from William Butler Yeats's poem, "The Second Coming." According to Yeats, civilizations rise and fall, to be succeeded by the next civilization. ("Things fall apart; the centre cannot hold; / Mere anarchy is loosed upon the world, / The blood-dimmed tide is loosed, and everywhere / The ceremony of innocence is drowned. . . .")

The first part of the novel describes the protagonist Okonkwo and every major aspect of his Ibo life, including religion, funeral customs, and arranged marriages. Several Ibo practices, such as the killing of twins, are described as well. The unacceptability of such practices to some Ibos make these easy targets for Christian conversion by invading British missionaries. The latter part of the novel shows the gradual conquest of the area by the British military, civil, educational, and legal authorities. Not only is the traditional way of life changed forever, but the personal effect is seen through the downfall of the tragic hero Okonkwo.

Chinua Achebe has taken seriously the responsibility to educate fellow Africans about the richness of their native culture. He states that the theme of African writers "is that African people did not hear of culture for the first time from Europeans; that their societies were not mindless but frequently had a philosophy of great depth and value and beauty; that they had poetry and, above all, they had dignity" (*African Writers on African Writing* 8).

Achebe's literary career is typical of many African writers today in his struggle with the problem of composing in the language of a former colonial power rather than using native African languages, which would, of course, limit their audience. They must also balance the combination of native African forms with European literary forms. In our excerpt from *Things Fall Apart*, the reader finds African oral tradition in both the mother's and the father's story. As a whole, the novel is much like a classical Greek tragedy, with the hero's "tragic flaw," his temper, driving him inexorably to his downfall.

MINI-LECTURE on *THINGS FALL APART*

Africa is a very large and diverse continent whose modern history has brought about many major changes. Africa's geography ranges from major deserts such as the Sahara to rain forests and savannah or grasslands. The ethnic groups of the continent are quite diverse: hundreds of languages are spoken; local animistic beliefs which give powers to the natural world coexist with the world's major religions of Islam and Christianity; areas such as Egypt have controlled ancient royal kingdoms, while other places have been part of small political units such as a village.

Studying a single African literary work does not mean learning everything about the entire continent. However, reading a novel such as *Things Fall Apart* can help us to understand the impact of nineteenth century invasions of a colonial power.

Chinua Achebe was born in southeastern Nigeria, West Africa to an Ibo (Igbo) family. He completed secondary school in Umuofia, a town which appears in his novels, and received a university degree in Nigeria. He has an international reputation as a writer and critic.

Things Fall Apart, first published in England in 1958, is a classic of modern African writing. Achebe chose to write in English to gain a larger audience, and, as a result, the novel is one of the most widely read works by an African. To better understand the novel, which takes place around 1900, it is necessary to know something about the history of colonialism on the African continent.

By comparing maps of Africa before 1885 with modern maps, one can see what major changes happened on the continent. Before 1885, there were few clear political divisions; areas were loosely divided by language, religion and/or ethnicity. However, based on agreements at the 1885 Berlin Conference, which excluded Africans, European colonial powers went to Africa and claimed parts of the continent. These European powers included Spain, Germany, France, Portugal, Italy, Great Britain, and Belgium. Over time, they drew boundaries of new countries to suit their own purposes. European imperialism was motivated by Africa's rich natural resources such as minerals and food products, as well as the desire to expand their national boundaries.

In Africa, the colonizers encountered a variety of ethnic groups, including the Ibo, living in well-developed societies. However, the colonizers ignored non-European ways and regarded the native residents as "children" or "savages." Moreover, when the Europeans made their political divisions, they did not pay attention to historical relationships among African peoples. Incompatible ethnic cultures were grouped in the same country, and compatible groups were separated to suit European purposes. Such was the case in Nigeria when it was colonized by the British.

The Ibo live in Nigeria with two other main groups, the Hausa and the Yoruba. Historically, there has been conflict with these groups because of social, economic, political, and religious differences. After Nigeria's independence from Britain in 1960, dissent was intensified when large oil deposits were discovered in southeastern Nigeria. In 1965, the Ibo attempted to withdraw from Nigeria and form a separate nation, called Biafra. A civil conflict, the Biafran War (1965-67), resulted. During this war, Chinua Achebe became a diplomat for the Ibo people and gained an international reputation. The Ibo secession attempt, however, was not successful, and the southeastern part of the country (Biafra) is still part of the Nigerian nation today.

The encounter between the English and the Ibo people in the process of colonization is the subject of Achebe's novel *Things Fall Apart*. The novel is autobiographical, that is, Achebe drew from his own family's history for the book. He describes what life was like for his grandfather's generation in precolonial Ibo society and what happened after the British arrived. The story is a most tragic one.

CHAPTER 19
From *Out of Africa*

Historico-cultural Background

Things Fall Apart (Chapter 18) presents an African's view of the conflict of traditional African society with European colonizers. In *Out of Africa*, the point of view is that of a colonist, Isak Dinesen (nee Karen Dinesen), a Danish settler in Kenya, British East Africa.

At the Berlin Conference (1884-1885), the African continent was divided up by European powers without consultation with Africans. In 1890, with the signing of the Anglo-German Treaty, Germany recognized British claims to a number of areas including Kenya, East Africa. Europeans were encouraged to emigrate to the newly acquired colonies. After her marriage in 1912, Karen Dinesen decided to purchase land and emigrate to Kenya. Her intended husband, Bror, who was Swedish, preceded her to Kenya and purchased the 6,000 acre Swedo-African Coffee Company. They were married upon her arrival in Nairobi.

Dinesen, one of five children, was born to a wealthy Danish family. Her father was a soldier, writer, hunter, traveler, and politician. As her father's favorite child, she was greatly affected by his suicide when she was nine years old. Karen was schooled mainly at home but did attend art school for a period. Like most women of her class, she was not prepared to earn a living. However, she began writing as a girl, and as a young woman, she traveled in Europe and the British Isles.

Although her full name was Baroness Karen Dinesen von Blixen-Finecke, she used a number of pseudonyms, including Isak Dinesen. "Isak," an Old Testament male name, means "one who laughs." She was also known as "Tanne" and by English speakers as "Tania." Karen Blixen is the name on her tombstone.

Literary Considerations

Dinesen returned from Africa to her family home in Denmark bankrupt and in psychological and physical stress. Suffering from syphilis contracted from her former husband, Dinesen began to write *Out of Africa*. She later composed a collection called *Seven Gothic Tales* and *Shadows on the Grass*. From a distance, Dinesen recollected Africa as a lost Eden; like Wordsworth, but in prose, she romanticizes the pastoral life. Dinesen joins two other white women colonialists who wrote their memoirs of Africa: Beryl Markham in *Straight on Till Morning* (1942) and Elspeth Huxley in *The Flame Trees of Thika* (1957). Though their experiences differed, all three were writing for the white middle and upper classes of Europe, Britain, and America. Each recollects Africa in a nostalgic mood. In the 1980s, interest in each of these colonial writers was revived by film recreations of their literary work on Africa.

MINI-LECTURE on *OUT OF AFRICA*

With the signing of the Anglo-German Treaty in 1890, Germany recognized British claims to a number of areas in Africa including Kenya, East Africa. Colonization was to provide Europeans with raw materials for their factories and markets for their products.

In 1912, Isak Dinesen and her husband Baron Bror von Blixen-Finecke joined the European emigration to Kenya. They purchased 6,000 acres of land on which to grow coffee for the international market. However, conditions for growing coffee on their farm were not suitable. As a result, l7 years later the coffee plantation had failed and the marriage had ended in divorce.

While in Kenya, Dinesen had an affair with an aristocratic young Englishman, Denys Finch-Hatton, later killed in a plane crash. They spent many hours together reading, reciting poetry, and telling stories. As well, she spent time storytelling with the native farm workers, members of the Kikuyu ethnic group. During these years Dinesen created the earliest versions of some of her African stories.

Out of Africa is a prose pastoral, a piece of literature which portrays life in the countryside in a romantic, idealized manner. Separated from Africa by time, space, and experience, Dinesen recalls Africa in a romantic way. The fact that there are no dates for specific events contributes to the nostalgia.

The book consists of five parts, opening with a description of the African countryside. In the description, Dinesen uses a number of similes, that is, a figure of speech comparing two things using the word "like." For example she writes, "In the middle of the day the air was alive over the land, like a flame burning. . . ." She also writes of the Kikuyu people who lived and worked on her farm. She also writes about the Muslim Somalians employed in her house.

Dinesen contrasts Nairobi, today the capital of Kenya, as "our town," meaning the town of the Europeans, with the "Swaheli town," the town of the native peoples. Swaheli (or Swahili) was also the language used by native peoples of east central Africa for trading and general communication. The last part of the book, "Farewell to the Farm," tells of a number of catastrophes which end with Dinesen's departure from Kenya.

With *Out of Africa,* Dinesen made her name as a modern classical writer. However, her view is that of the colonialist and the autobiography is part of colonial literature. Africans are called "my Kikuyu," "my squatters," "my boys." They function in a feudal way, that is, they live and work on land which she owns and must work for her a certain number of days each year. Dinesen cares for them in a paternal way: She doctors them, builds a school for the children, and before leaving Kenya, secures their land claims. Dinesen joins other colonial writers who wrote of an Africa to which they could never return and which they remembered as a lost paradise.

CHAPTER 20
From *The Woman in the Dunes*

Literary Considerations

Although much of modern Japanese literature has been classified with the "I" novel, that is a story told in a confessional manner through the consciousness of a single narrator, many writers are difficult to label. Certainly, the departure from Realism and the focusing on the bizarre and the absurd in literature are understandable after the devastating effects of the atomic bombs on Japan.

Contemporary writers include Yukio Mishima, author of a tetralogy, *The Sea of Fertility*, and a three-time nominee for the Nobel Prize. His failed passion for a return to traditional Japanese nationalism led to his committing ritual suicide in 1970. An entire generation of post-World War II writers, led by Kenzaburo Oe, has felt sympathy for Western Existentialists such as Jean-Paul Sartre. The immediate and long-range destruction caused by the atomic bomb has, in fact, rendered modern life as godless, grotesque, and meaningless.

MINI-LECTURE on *THE WOMAN IN THE DUNES*

Throughout its long history, Japanese culture has absorbed and changed various foreign influences. For example, after the Chinese brought their religion and system of writing to Japan, the Japanese adapted them to their own taste. Kobo Abe represents this Japanese adaptability in literary form. Particularly after the horror and tragedy of the dropping of two atomic bombs on Japan in August 1945, Abe and other contemporary Japanese authors have concerned themselves with the human search for identity and meaning in a world that appears absurd and alienating.

Growing up in Manchuria, away from Japanese culture, Kobo Abe felt a deep sense of personal alienation. His isolation is echoed in the philosophical Western writers that attracted him. His poems, plays, and novels show the cross-cultural influence of Existential philosophy, which questions the existence of God and the meaning of life. Drawing on earlier philosophical writers such as the Russian Fyodor Dostoevsky (1821-1881) and German-Czech Franz Kafka, the Existentialist movement was especially strong in France in the 1950s. The philosopher Jean-Paul Sartre systematized much of Existentialist thought in works such as *Being and Nothingness*. The absurdity of modern life can be seen in Sartre's novels, for example, *Nausea* (1937), as well as those of the French-Algerian Albert Camus.

Like Gregor Samsa, Kafka's protagonist in "The Metamorphosis," a number of Abe's characters undergo a bizarre metamorphosis from human form to a common object such as a box or a stick. This dehumanization seems to reflect Abe's belief in the twentieth-century isolation of the individual not only from God but from other human beings. Communication becomes impossible.

In the strange story of *The Woman in the Dunes*, a young, nameless scientist tries to escape temporarily from his boring and lonely existence as a teacher in Tokyo. The man takes a one-day holiday at the beach in order to collect insects. By chance, he misses the last bus returning to the city. Residents of the beach village offer him shelter for the night in a small house at the bottom of a hole in the sand dunes. When he tries to leave the next day, however, he discovers that he is trapped in the sand dunes.

Like the beetles he has come to catch, he himself has been caught. He is expected to become the partner of a village woman who spends her life digging out the endlessly blowing sand to protect her entire community. In comparison to his life in the city, the woman's life seems to him to be completely absurd. When his rational efforts to overcome the sand fail, he decides to "go with the flow" of his existence and remain in the sand dunes. Ironically, the sacrifice of reason seems the only possible way to achieve happiness.

CHAPTER 21
From *Chronicle of a Death Foretold*

Historico-cultural Background

For hundreds of years the traditional Eurocentric view of the arrival of Christopher Columbus in the New World had been a extremely positive one. However, by the time of the 1992 celebration of the quincentenary of his landing, the perspective had been broadened to include the views of the original inhabitants whose territory had been invaded by the Europeans. The destructive impact of the Spanish explorers and colonizers had long been appreciated in Latin America, especially in areas where large numbers of indigenous peoples remained. For example, Mexican artists such as José Orozco Clemente (1883-1949) and such novelists as Mariano Azuela (*The Underdogs*) concerned themselves with the conflict between Spanish and indigenous cultures. And in the much later fiction of Colombian Gabriel García Márquez, the question of the Spanish conquest is never satisfactorily resolved.

García Márquez burst onto the international literary scene with the publication of his novel *One Hundred Years of Solitude* (1967). The novel is characterized by fictionalized history and a nonlinear plot, both features of his novella, *Chronicle of a Death Foretold*. The story is a journalistic investigation (a chronicle) of a murder, with various witnesses recounting the same events from their own perspective. The book has a certain filmic "replay" quality like the novels of the French writer Alain Robbe-Grillet or the Japanese film *Rashomon*. It is a kind of detective story, but unlike the traditional form, both the victim and the murderers are known from the beginning. García Márquez has publicly acknowledged his debt for nonlinear structure and the combination of history and fantasy to several writers including the American writer William Faulkner (1897-1962), especially in his novels *As I Lay Dying* and *The Sound and the Fury*.

MINI-LECTURE on *CHRONICLE OF A DEATH FORETOLD*

Gabriel García Márquez is part of a generation of extraordinary authors in the Latin American literary "boom" of the 1960s. By 1981, the year he published his novella, *Chronicle of a Death Foretold*, he was already an internationally known novelist. In this novella, as in much of his fiction, he skillfully combines journalistic technique (chronicle or history writing) with the fantastic. This technique is called "Magical Realism," a style which grew out of the work of Modernist writers such as James Joyce and William Faulkner.

The story is based on the real murder of a young man in Sucre, a small town in Colombia, for a supposed breaking of the primitive code of honor. All the real individuals were known to each other and to García Márquez or members of his family. In the novella, the author-narrator has returned 27 years after the murder to record the testimony of witnesses to the crime. Each repeats the same events from his or her own perspective. Echoing the group voice of the Greek chorus, each witness claims his own innocence of the crime; yet each had prior knowledge that the murder was about to be committed but made no effort to prevent it. The ritual murder of Santiago is truly a cooperative effort, a kind of Dionysian blood sacrifice. The collective will of the community has permitted an innocent man to be killed because they believe he defied the cult of virginity. His innocence is made clear by his name "Santiago," an allusion to the saint that Spanish Christians had called upon to defend themselves in their battles against the Moors. Besides being Semitic like Christ himself, his family name, "Nasar," alludes to Christ, the Nazarene.

The name of every character in the novella bears some significance in the New Testament story of Christ and his giving over by Pontius Pilot to the Roman mob as a sacrifice. But the human sacrifice here is to a barbaric code of honor that requires death as the penalty for loss of female virginity. Through exaggeration and irony, García Márquez points up the unfair treatment of women and the useless attempt to deny the human body.

García Márquez writes against the macho code of honor which regards the virginity of daughters and wives as sacred. The code of honor, brought to Latin America from Spain, is a major theme of Spanish drama during the Golden Age (fifteenth and sixteenth centuries). García Márquez powerfully attacks this code as primitive and unchristian. He shows the community, and principally the Church--the bishop is expected the day of the murder--as having responsibility for upholding double standards of sexual behavior that lead to senseless violence.

CHAPTER 22
From "Boys and Girls"

Literary Considerations

Until recently, Canadian literature has not received the attention it so richly deserves. Among the older generation of master storytellers, the British-born comic essayist Stephen Leacock (1869-1944) is best known for his satire of a small Ontario town in *Sunshine Sketches of a Little Town* (1912). More recent successful authors have been Margaret Laurence (1926-1980), known mostly for her novels such as *The Stone Angel*, and the currently popular Margaret Atwood (b. 1939), author of *The Handmaid's Tale*, a feminist's nightmare vision of the future. In the 1970s, Atwood and Alice Munro gained recognition in North America for their feminist view of contemporary life and the continuing struggle of women for equality.

MINI-LECTURE on "BOYS AND GIRLS"

The intimate details of small-town and rural life in provincial southwestern Ontario are incorporated into Alice Munro's growing body of fiction. To date, Munro has been almost exclusively a writer of short stories; in 1990, she published *Friend of My Youth*, her seventh collection of stories.

Taken together, Munro's short stories form a composite picture of every stage in the life of a female growing up in twentieth-century North America. In the postmodern period, many writers use unusual and difficult styles in their fiction; Munro, however, continues to write in the Realist tradition. The writer Cynthia Ozick has called Munro, "our Chekhov."

Munro's stories are usually narrated by a young female character whose eye carefully and objectively observes fine details such as colors and textures. In spite of their apparent matter-of-factness, her short stories frequently end with a sudden, unexpected or ironic twist.

While the author has not publicly discussed many details of her writing, it seems clear that much of her fiction is autobiographical. For example, an important recurring literary theme in her work is the problematic mother figure. The troubled mother in her stories also bears close resemblance to the suffering mother in much of Southern American fiction, as for example, the work of Faulkner or Flannery O'Connor. Munro has admitted her obsession with the mother-daughter relationship, perhaps caused by the difficulty in watching her own mother suffer a prolonged, and eventually fatal illness.

Whatever the autobiographical reality may be, however, Munro has carefully crafted her ideas into flawless, fictional form. In "Boys and Girls," Munro paints a detailed portrait of the importance of traditional gender roles in a young girl's struggle for equality in a sexist, male-dominated world. No matter how closely she identifies with her father and his values, with the approach of adolescence, her gender and anatomy cannot be denied. Ultimately, she is relegated to what she regards as the dullness and powerlessness of the female role. The feminist theme of being "merely a girl" in the short story "Boys and Girls" was to become the major focus of Munro's 1971 collection, *Lives of Girls and Women.*

CHAPTER 23
From *Fire on the Mountain*

Literary Considerations

Earlier Anglo-Indian fiction was best known for the contributions of British writers such as E. M. Forster (*A Passage to India*) and male Indian authors, especially R. K. Narayan. The tradition of Indian women writers is a fairly young one, distinguished by the feminist novels of Bharati Mukherjee and Santha Rama Rau. It is to this generation of women writers that Anita Desai belongs. The work of these authors is quite distinct, but it is concerned with gender roles in Indian society, particularly the role of women in the patriarchal, traditional system.

Unlike the male authors in the Anglo-Indian tradition who frequently look at larger social problems from an external point of view, Anita Desai concentrates on the narrow scope of an individual human psyche. She has expressed admiration for a variety of writers including the Modernist D. H. Lawrence, Dostoevsky, and Kawabata; she extols what she calls "the fine feminine sensibilities" of Marcel Proust and Henry James. The prose style of all of her models is characterized by poetic imagery, a refined sensitivity, and emotional detail.

MINI-LECTURE on *FIRE ON THE MOUNTAIN*

Indian literary tradition is a complex and ancient one. A collection of Sanskrit hymns, the *Rig-Veda*, comes from oral tradition dating to about 1500 B.C.E. These sacred texts were not written down until the fourteenth century. Poetry, particularly epic, was the most important literary form for centuries.

In modern times, especially during the domination by the British Empire (the British Raj, 1774-1947), Western literary influences have been strongly felt. Even after Indian independence in 1947, prose, especially in novel form, has been important. While the present older generation of Anglo-Indian writers is dominated by men, including R. K. Narayan, beginning in the 1960s, a woman's tradition took root, especially in the novel.

Indian women in this younger group of writers have skillfully incorporated modern psychology, feminist, and social concerns into their fiction. In contrast to the male writers who critique Indian society as a whole and from an external point of view, the women novelists limit their scope to the mind and spirit of a single individual. That individual is usually a woman struggling to fulfill herself in traditional, patriarchal society.

Anita Desai's first successful novel, *Cry, the Peacock* (1963), established her reputation as an internationally known Anglo-Indian writer. The daughter of a Bengali father and a German mother, she chooses to write in a third language, English. Like other women in her generation, Anita Desai's novels reflect the influence of Realism, but like Henry James, they focus on the state of mind of the protagonist. They explore the individual's psychology in a profound, subjective way.

Anita Desai's prose has a definite lyric quality; with poetic images she evokes feelings and moods, relating these to the natural world. For example, deep in thought, Nanda Kaul is called back to reality by the call of the cuckoo in her garden. Furthermore, Desai explores her individual's psyche with fine, descriptive detail; in reality, it is the pattern of images, moods, and feelings that are important in her fiction. Plot is almost incidental.

In *Fire on the Mountain*, Desai explores the psychological state of the bitter loneliness of an aging, Indian widow, Nanda Kaul. Throughout the novel, she is compared to her visiting great-granddaughter, Raka. As a Hindu, Nanda Kaul's *dharma*, or destiny, was to spend her prime years as a householder, caring for her husband and children. As an elderly woman, her natural feeling should be one of Buddhist detachment from life and peaceful preparation for death.

Unfortunately, Nanda Kaul spent her long life of duty meeting those family obligations without any sense of satisfaction. Although her husband is now dead, she still feels jealous of his love affair with a British school teacher. Self-alienated, she is resentful and lives as a recluse at Carignano by bitter choice and without peace of mind. She is constantly reminded of her painful years as wife and mother by an elderly friend.

In contrast to Nanda Kaul, her great-granddaughter Raka is a kind of natural recluse; she enjoys solitude and feels herself in harmony with nature. Like her great-grandmother, Raka's family associations have not been good ones; both she and her mother have been abused by her father. She, too, has come to the country house at Carignano to be alone. Unlike Nanda Kaul, however, the young Raka does not passively accept her *dharma*. Desai brings the novel to a dramatic, feminist close: it is Raka who sets the mountain forest on fire and tries to destroy a world where women are forced into unnatural roles.

CHAPTER 24
From *The Thief and the Dogs*

Historico-cultural Background

Because of its location on the Nile River, the Red Sea, and the Mediterranean Sea, Egypt (now the Arab Republic of Egypt) historically has been a crossroads of

African, Mediterranean, and European cultures. The building of the Suez Canal in 1869 further increased this role.

Since the Arab invasion in 639 C. E., Arabic replaced the original Coptic language. Today, over 90 percent of Egypt's people are Sunni Muslims, pious observers of daily public prayer, study of the Koran, and of fasting during the month of Ramadan. This religious milieu forms part of the background of *The Thief and the Dogs.*

Beginning with Napoleon (1798), Egypt was separated from the Ottoman Empire to the east and entered the sphere of French influence. The French were succeeded by the British, who maintained a strong control from 1882 until 1922. The constitutional monarchy which followed was then overthrown in the 1952 revolution led by Colonel Gamel Abdel Nassar. The military regime severely limited the influence of the intelligentsia; writers such as Naguib Mahfouz found themselves turning to new literary forms to express their reactions to the turmoil of the times.

MINI-LECTURE on *THE THIEF AND THE DOGS*

The Arab world has had a complicated relationship with the West since the rise of Islam in the 7th century. Centuries ago, the Arabs transmitted much of the learning of the ancient world to Europe; later they engaged in a struggle for control of the Mediterranean Sea and the Holy Land. By the nineteenth century, the West colonized much of their territory in search of markets and, later, petroleum. Differences were exaggerated by the end of World War II and the division of Palestine.

Until the 1950s, the strongest Western influence in the Arabic literary world was French. Based on French models, the first Egyptian novel appeared in 1910. After the 1950s, translations of the British poet T. S. Eliot's *The Wasteland* and the American Ezra Pound's *Cantos* brought fresh ideas to young Arabic writers.

The 1950s saw numerous translations of the works of Existentialist writers Jean-Paul Sartre and Albert Camus. In the three literary capitals of Arabic culture, Baghdad, Cairo, and Beirut, new techniques and themes appeared: the struggle for political independence, social justice, and the search for the meaning of human existence.

Foremost among the early Egyptian novelists is Naguib Mahfouz, who at first wrote historical novels. His later novels, especially the 1956-1957 *Cairo Trilogy*, explore social and political themes. The 1952 revolution inspired other Arab writers to look in Marxist terms at class conflict and at the corruption of secular Arabic governments.

Mahfouz's 1962 novel, *The Thief and the Dogs*, blends Symbolism and Realism, modern existentialism with traditional religious mysticism. Said, the thief of the title, has recently gotten out of a Cairo prison and seeks to murder the man who sent him there. At one point, he tries to recover the lost innocence of his youth. He returns to the house of the sheikh where he and his father had prayed and studied the teachings of Islam. Understanding and communication are impossible between him and the mystic. As Mahfouz reveals in a free-flowing stream-of-consciousness, Said is completely alienated from his religion, from his society, and from himself. Pursued like an animal by police dogs, he can only find refuge in death.

CHAPTER 25
From *Flowers from the Volcano*

Historico-cultural Background

Before the arrival of Columbus in 1492, three major civilizations flourished in the Americas: the Aztecs, located in Mexico, the Incas, located in the South American Andes, and the Mayas, situated in the Yucatan peninsula and in Central America. By 1502, when Christopher Columbus experienced his first contact with the Mayas, many major Mayan centers had declined and were abandoned to the jungle. Until recently much of what was known about the Mayas had been taken from Spanish sources, especially the 1566 narratives of Fray Diego de Landa, a colonial Catholic bishop who destroyed every Mayan written record he could find. A number of scrolls survived, however, and with the present continuing translation of the Mayan glyphs written on them and stone remains, knowledge about their civilization is expanding. Archaeological data, especially that gathered at Tikal, Guatemala, by the University of Pennsylvania, has added to our understanding of Mayan social, political, and economic organization.

Precolumbian Mesoamerica, the area extending from northern Mexico into Central America as far as Costa Rica, was for several thousand years the site of important cultural developments. Mayan history can be traced to about 6000 B.C.E., when small villages grew along the Pacific and Caribbean coastal areas; between 250-900 C.E., the Classic period, there emerged in Mesoamerica several politically complex and well-developed civilizations, including the Mayas. In the final period, the Postclassic (900-1500), the Toltecs, Aztecs, and Incas achieved their highest point of development.

During the Classic period, powerful city-states such as Tikal emerged which were ruled by hereditary priest-kings. The elite dominated a large class of farmers, craftspeople, and other laborers. As with the Sumerians, certain precolumbian city-states dominated others, forming kingdoms held together by such cultural traditions as polytheistic religion that included bloodletting and human sacrifice, a 260-day calendar; the cultivation of maize and cacao; the use of hieroglyphic writing; and cities built around pyramids and central plazas.

Predominantly an agricultural society, the polytheistic Mayans held particularly dear Chac or Tlaloc, god of rain and storms. To guarantee continuing fertility of the land, periodic human sacrifices of young girls were made to Tlaloc. In later times, human sacrifices, especially of defeated warriors, were carried out on stone reclining figures called chacmols. "Smoking" hearts were offered to Tlaloc. Needless to say, Spanish conquerors, hoping to make Christian converts for their kings, found these blood-thirsty gods and their cult barbaric and engaged in an intense campaign to destroy the indigenous culture.

In modern-day Central America, Creole descendants of the Spanish dominate political and economic arenas. On the other hand, Mayans and other indigenous peoples remain marginalized. Beginning in the 1960s, in an effort to reform Central American conditions, a number of social revolutionary movements were organized. Following the successful Communist coup in Cuba in 1959, Marxist agitators began activities in several Central and South American countries. As a counter-movement, from the 1960s on through the 1980s, those governments carried out a pattern of terror, with "Death Squad" assassinations, routine "disappearances" and murders of political prisoners, and mass executions in rural areas, all justified as a means of maintaining order and halting subversive activities.

With large numbers of bodies being dumped in rivers and lakes, sometimes causing their waters to run red, and with corpses appearing on the slopes on Central American volcanos, the natural environment of the area came to be identified with the violence. According to Michael McClintock, "A new human dimension has been added to Central America's exotic geography: an association in the popular imagination of the mountains, the volcanos, the lakes and the rivers with the history of repression and resistance" (viii).

Popular resistance to government terror has taken the form of guerilla ("little war") warfare. Except for the Sandinista victory in Nicaragua, which toppled the four-decade-old regime of the Somoza family, to date no other Marxist government has appeared in Central America.

Recent Central American Literature

Political events of recent decades in Central America have had a profound effect on journalists, poets, and novelists of the area. A generation of writers has committed itself to give voice to the poor and oppressed of their nations. Rarely translated into English, and hence relatively unknown in the United States, many live in political exile. Among these is Claribel Alegría, born in Nicaragua in 1924 and raised in El Salvador. A mestizo, Alegría traces her heritage to Spanish and native Pipil roots. Alegría has published fourteen books of poetry, four volumes of short stories and novellas and other works. With her North American husband, Darwin Flakoll, she has also published the testimonies of Central American women who have been tortured as political prisoners or killed in the struggle for liberation. Her volume of poems, *Flowers from the Volcano*, has been translated by the American poet Carolyn Forché. Alegría and her husband presently live in Managua, Nicaragua and Mallorca, Spain.

Literary Considerations

It is clear from Claribel Alegría's work that she is very familiar with the bloody history of warfare among the ancient Mayas, the tragedy of the destruction of precolumbian Mayan civilization, and the present struggle among the oppressed in Central America. She envisions the repetition of bloodshed as a returning cycle of violence that will continue even into the future when the children of the descendents of the Mayas will take revenge on the descendents of the Spanish. The exotic Central American landscape of varied topography, tropical forests, and mountains, erupting volcanos and frequent earthquakes, is identified in her poetry with the violence of human sacrifice, whether that carried out by the ancient Mayas or the present repressive governments. Alegría's Marxist views are apparent in her portrayal of the privileged class isolating itself behind high walls from the poor masses.

MINI-LECTURE on "FLOWERS FROM THE VOLCANO"

Before the arrival of Christopher Columbus in 1492, several major civilizations had developed in the Americas: In South America, the Spanish encountered the Incas; in Mesoamerica, the area extending from northern Mexico to Costa Rica in Central America, were the Aztecs and the Mayas. Mesoamerica consists of coastal plains, foothills, and highlands, each of which gave rise to Mayan centers. A nearly continuous line of volcanos runs east to west throughout the entire region causing frequent earthquakes and volcanic eruptions. Izalco, the most recently formed volcano, has erupted almost continuously since its appearance in El Salvador in 1770. In spite of its violence, the mountains have provided rich soil for Mayan agriculture, obsidian, or volcanic glass, for sharp cutting tools, and special rocks for grinding stones used to prepare maize.

In precolumbian Mesoamerica during the Classic period, from 250 to 900 C.E., important Mayan sites such as Tikal, Guatemala, grew into powerful city-states, sometimes extending their power to a kingdom which included weaker areas. Each kingdom was ruled by a hereditary priest-king who shared his power with an aristocratic elite dominating a large group of farmers, craftspeople, and laborers. An agricultural-based society whose main crops were corn and chocolate, the polytheistic Mayans considered their most important deity to be Chac or Tlaloc, god of rain and storms. To ensure continuing fertility of the fields, human sacrifices were made to Tlaloc; in earlier times a young girl was sacrificed in the sacred cenote or open well. Later, the "smoking" hearts of defeated warriors were offered on the stone reclining figures called chacmols. The glyph, or written symbol, for Tlaloc came to be associated with war and blood-sacrifice and was worn on the shield of the king and other great warriors in battle. Tlaloc can be recognized by the circles around his eyes and the long ribbons representing blood coming from his mouth.

After the arrival of Columbus, the Spanish conquerors gained control of Mayan areas and carried out an intense campaign to destroy Mayan religion with its human sacrifice. For example, under the direction of Fray Diego de Landa, Bishop of Yucatan, they burned Mayan written records and destroyed as many cultural objects as possible. Although Spanish language and religion (Roman Catholicism) have been imposed on the Mayans, today they are mostly marginalized in Central America.

The 1960s to 1980s saw a great deal of social revolutionary activity, largely Marxist, to liberate the poor and oppressed of Latin America. In Central America, a generation of journalists, poets, and novelists frequently influenced by Marxism began to give voice to the oppressed; often they have been forced into exile because of their ideas. To this group of writers belongs Claribel Alegría, a native of Nicaragua who was raised in El Salvador. A mestizo of mixed Spanish and native Indian heritage, Alegría received her college education in the United States. Because of her open expression of Marxist views, the poet has lived many years in exile. Along with her husband, North American Dalton Flakoll, Claribel Alegría has published the testimonies of women who were tortured as political prisoners in El Salvador; she has also published fourteen volumes of poems and four books of short stories and novellas.

Alegría's dominant theme is the suffering of the masses of powerless poor, mostly Indian, population of Central America. Her own mixed heritage has made her sensitive to their suffering. Familiar with the bloody history of the Americas, with its destructive warfare and human sacrifice, Alegría identifies this violence with the violence of the natural landscape of Mesoamerica.

As a poet, Alegría incorporates indigenous mythology and Central American history into her work. As in the Mayan idea of history, Alegría sees time as a never-ending cycle in which the past becomes the present as well as the future. Although she lives in exile from El Salvador, Claribel Alegría continues to write and to edit and translate the work of politically active fellow Central American authors who offer some hope for the future of their countries.

CHAPTER 26
From *Praisesong for the Widow*

Historico-cultural Background

In the centuries after Columbus's encounter with the new world, a number of European nations began to develop colonies in the Americas. Europeans increasingly demanded American products, especially sugar and cotton. However, the native populations which might have served as a labor source for the large sugarcane plantations had been decimated in massacres or by imported diseases such as smallpox. More labor was needed, and therefore Europeans turned to West Africa as a source of slaves.

Hundreds of thousands of Africans were brought against their will to the Caribbean, crossing the Atlantic in cargo ships under inhumane conditions ("the Middle Passage"). The Caribbean became the central point of several trade triangles between the Old and the New Worlds, with slaves going from Africa and finished products from Europe to the Caribbean and thence to the American continent. Sugar, cotton, and rum were shipped back to Europe.

Later laborers brought to the Caribbean were East Indians, Chinese, Portuguese, and Lebanese, all adding to the diverse cultural mixture. Although British territories were emancipated in 1834 and Cuba in 1886, most people continued to work for sugarcane plantations and to live in poor rural areas. On every Caribbean island, the combination of native, African and European elements resulted in a variety of Creole languages and lifestyles, but the African element was most significant. For example, the

West Indian family pattern most closely resembles the polygyny (a series of wives) common in West Africa, with women as the stable center of household life. Furthermore, extended families frequently live in multiple dwellings around a central court, with family members dividing the labor along traditional African lines. Caribbean syncretism, or combining of aspects of various cultures, is also seen in the simultaneous adherence to traditional African religious practices along with Christian beliefs. Thus, an Anglican minister may consult with a voodoo practitioner, or *obeah*.

The rich heritage of the Caribbean crossroads is seen in the unique dance and music produced by the area. Frequently associated with pre-Lenten carnival celebrations, dances such as Trinidad's calypso and Cuba's rhumba are known internationally. Steel-drum instruments made from old oil drums are found throughout the islands and symbolize the Caribbean drive to create an aesthetic object from a foreign form.

West Indian Literature

Like its African origins, the earliest West Indian literary sources are oral tradition. However, much of the eighteenth and nineteenth-century West Indian literature is based on European models. For example, among the early written works are slave narratives, similar to the European picaresque novels. Such narratives recount the life of an African taken from home by force, sold into slavery, and shipped to the Caribbean or to North America. Slave narratives, such as *The Travels of Olaudah Equiano* (1789), are recorded after the protagonist has freed himself through hard work and self-education. Their descriptions of the horrors of forced labor aided in the abolition of slavery in the New World.

In the late nineteenth century, West Indian literature was characterized by its incorporation of folklore and the use of local vernacular. Claude McKay, the first major poet of the area, began to publish his distinctive work in 1912. In the 1920s the literary efforts in the Caribbean were enriched by the innovation and creative energy generated in the Harlem Renaissance. The Caribbean literature produced during the 1930s and 1940s reflected the rising wave of nationalism and desire for self-determination.

The contemporary period, which includes Paule Marshall, has focused on the quest for identity through a journey to the white Western world (England or the United States), to Africa and a return home, repeating the experience of the Middle Passage. As with the ancient epic hero, the protagonist gains wisdom and pride to be shared with others.

MINI-LECTURE on *PRAISESONG FOR THE WIDOW*

Like a number of contemporary writers, Paule (pronounced Paul) Marshall has focused on the theme of the individual's search for identity. For the African-American writer, this search has been a three-sided journey which repeats the historical triangle of slave and sugar trade between the Old World, the Caribbean, and the American continent.

In Marshall's work, the quest for identity is shown in the development of black female characters who discover and accept their connections to the ethnic heritage of the Caribbean and Africa. Her work shows the influence of two important socio-political movements in the

United States in the 1960s: the civil rights movement and the feminist movement.

Although Paule Marshall was born and educated in Brooklyn, New York, her parents are from Barbados, a small island in the West Indies in the Caribbean. Marshall presently resides in Barbados while writing and, therefore, she exhibits strong West Indian influence in her work. In her rich, descriptive passages, Marshall evokes the tropical landscape of the Caribbean tropics. Furthermore, her dialogues reflect West Indian idioms and dialect, and she uses the rhythms of Afro-Caribbean music to evoke a closeness with Mother Earth.

Marshall's first novel, *Brown Girl, Brownstones* (1959), is the story of a Barbadian immigrant girl whose parents struggle between preserving their ethnic heritage and assimilation. Her 1983 novel, *Praisesong for the Widow*, describes the journey of an unhappy, assimilated African-American woman to discover her ethnic roots. An affluent, middle-aged widow, Avey Johnson makes a vacation cruise to the Caribbean. She unexpectedly relives the terrible "Middle Passage" her ancestors experienced when they were brought across the Atlantic Ocean to the New World as slaves to work on sugar plantations. An appreciation of her rich African heritage brings new meaning to Avey's life.

Throughout her work, Marshall contrasts the potential destructive power of Western technology with the Afro-Caribbean harmony with the natural world. The reader is made aware of the tremendous human and ecological cost of materialism and "progress." Without seeming to preach, Marshall clearly indicates that the American dream of relentlessly pursuing materialism may result in the sacrifice of moral or ethical principles. She reminds us that the traditions of the past still have a place in the contemporary world.

DATE DUE		